School
Refusal
Behavior in Youth

School Refusal Behavior in Youth

A Functional Approach to Assessment and Treatment

Christopher A. Kearney

American Psychological Association • Washington, DC

Published by
American Psychological Association
750 First Street, NE
Washington, DC 20002

Copies may be ordered from
APA Order Department
P.O. Box 92984
Washington, DC 20090-2984

In the U.K., Europe, Africa, and the Middle
East, copies may be ordered from
American Psychological Association
3 Henrietta Street
Covent Garden, London
WC2E 8LU England

Typeset in Goudy by World Composition Services, Inc., Sterling, VA

Printer: Edwards Brothers, Ann Arbor, MI
Dust jacket designer: Naylor Design, Washington, DC
Technical/Production Editor: Amy J. Clarke

The opinions and statements published are the responsibility of the author, and such opinions and statements do not necessarily represent the policies of the American Psychological Association.

Library of Congress Cataloging-in-Publication Data
Kearney, Christopher A.
   School refusal behavior in youth : a functional approach to assessment and
   treatment / by Christopher A. Kearney.—1st ed.
      p. cm.—
   Includes bibliographical references and index.
   ISBN 1-55798-699-1 (cb : acid-free paper)
   1. School phobia.   I.Title.
   RJ506.S33 K42 2001
   618.92'89—dc21
                                        00-044174

British Library Cataloguing-in-Publication Data
A CIP record is available from the British Library.

Printed in the United States of America
First Edition

To Kimberlie

and an appleseed

CONTENTS

PREFACE

School Refusal Behavior in Youth: A Functional Approach to Assessment and Treatment represents my ongoing process to better understand and address youth with school refusal behavior. School refusal behavior has long been a nebulous and enigmatic problem for parents and professionals, one that has eluded accurate description and classification. This book, and the functional model described within, is an attempt to help define, organize, assess, and treat one of the most amorphous populations in clinical child psychology. I hope that the book will serve as a state-of-the-art guide and catalyst to move the field beyond antiquated concepts and toward a consensus for addressing this difficult problem.

The development of my knowledge in this area began during my graduate school tenure at the Center for Stress and Anxiety Disorders at the State University of New York at Albany. Working in the center's child and adolescent anxiety section, I became inundated with children who refused to go to school or otherwise had trouble attending classes during the day. As I took on more and more of these cases, I was astounded by the lack of uniformity in symptoms, severity, and attendance records. Many of these children, for example, had various clinical and subclinical anxiety problems, but many more had little or no anxiety at all. As such, I was perhaps the only person in the center's anxiety disorders section who saw clients with no anxiety. In addition, I was getting my first lesson in the quagmire that is school refusal behavior: Heterogeneity is the primary constant.

Following my initial reaction, I thought that focusing on this diverse and interesting population for my dissertation would be highly rewarding and feasible. After all, I had already treated several cases, and many more were asking to be seen. In addition, on the basis of an initial and cursory analysis of the area, I thought that a literature review on this topic would not be all that difficult. When I made this comment to one of my professors, he chuckled and indicated that I would soon find a different truth. He was right, and I learned my second lesson in this area: There are articles and opinions on school refusal behavior everywhere. Years later, I still struggle to review all the material on this topic.

While addressing the many different cases that arrived at the center, I became dissatisfied with several traditional concepts that were described in the literature for this population. Was it school phobia? Most of these kids were not saying they were scared of anything in particular. Was it truancy? The literature said this refers to kids whose parents are unaware of their absence. That did not help me clinically and obviously did not apply to youth whose parents brought them in for treatment. Was it separation anxiety? So many of these kids were unafraid to leave their parents on the weekends, and parents kept complaining of their children's attention-seeking misbehaviors. As I struggled to conceptualize this population, I felt strongly that a fresher approach to school refusal behavior was necessary to cover all of those who missed school.

In developing this alternative view, I reverted to my behavioral roots and looked simply at why these children were refusing to go to school. Yes, some were clearly anxious and refused school to get away from aversive situations there. However, others were not anxious and clearly manipulated their parents to stay home from school. In addition, many of my clients had no psychopathology at all and said that they left school simply because it was more fun to be out of school. From these patterns of basic observations, which I still find consistently today, the functional model of school refusal behavior described in this book was born.

My intention in this book is to provide overviews of (a) the historical literature on school refusal behavior and (b) a functional approach to classify, assess, and treat youth with school refusal behavior. In chapter 1, a brief history is presented of compulsory education and the birth of the school refusal behavior field of study. Chapter 2 summarizes the characteristics of this population, including a discussion of prevalence and distal factors most relevant to youth who leave school. Chapter 3 describes and critiques classification strategies for youth with school refusal behavior, and chapter 4 introduces the functional model in greater depth. Chapter 5 reviews assessment methods that are most pertinent to this population, in general, and most pertinent to a functional assessment approach, in particular. Chapters 6–9 summarize treatment strategies for school refusal behavior, with an emphasis on functionally based treatment packages and extended case examples. Chapter 10 covers overall prevention and individual relapse prevention strategies for school refusal behavior.

This book is intended for various audiences who work with children who refuse school. Indeed, a primary hope of mine is that the book will serve as a clarifying resource for those who address this population and who wish to better understand these youth. The book is oriented primarily to psychologists and those with a working knowledge of therapy and general psychological principles. However, these chapters are meant to be valuable as well for educators, health professionals, parents, and others who confront this population. In addition, the book has a largely cognitive–behavioral–family-systems flavor, so those most familiar with these theoretical perspectives will feel most comfortable during the reading. This flavor does not assume, however, that alternative methods of assessment and treatment are ineffective for this population. A final caveat is that this book cannot possibly cover all of the nuances of education and school refusal behavior that are present in different countries; the reader is referred, however, to Chiland and Young's (1990) book for a fuller explication of cross-cultural school refusal behavior.

ACKNOWLEDGEMENTS

As with any project like this one, an author must take sole credit for its shortcomings but not its assets. In particular, I thank the American Psychological Association and Peggy Schlegel for the opportunity to write this book, Linda McCarter and Amy Clarke for their editing, and two reviewers for their constructive feedback and suggestions. My thanks also go, as always, to my parents and siblings as well as my mentors at the State University of New York at Binghamton, the State University of New York at Albany, and the University of Mississippi Medical Center. Special thanks go to Wendy Silverman, Mark Durand, David Barlow, and Ronald Drabman for their invaluable guidance and support. In addition, I thank Anne Marie Albano for her efforts to help me improve on treatment strategies for youth with school refusal behavior, Cheryl Tillotson for her enormous data management work, and Chuck Rasmussen for maintaining a wonderful work environment at the University of Nevada, Las Vegas. All I thank as well for their friendship. Finally, very special thanks go to my wife Kimberlie who, as a schoolteacher, helps keep me informed about children and what it is like to have a real job. In particular, I thank her for the balance she brings to my life and for all of her emotional support and love. She is my best friend.

I

EVALUATION

1

WHAT IS SCHOOL REFUSAL BEHAVIOR?

Trevor is a 6-year-old boy who cries every morning before school, clings to the staircase banister, and begs his mother not to send him to school because, as he says, "I don't like it there."

* * *

Casey is a 9-year-old girl who sometimes runs out of her classroom and down the street toward her house for little apparent reason.

* * *

Justin is a 12-year-old boy who just started 7th grade and, feeling overwhelmed, slips out of school an hour or two early with friends almost every day.

* * *

Ashley is a 15-year-old girl who is so terrified of tests and gym class that she does all she can to avoid school on certain days when these events occur.

Raising a child is a difficult task, one made harder when a parent's basic expectations about that child's behavior are suddenly violated. Parents generally assume, for example, that children will engage in certain fundamental behaviors, such as eating dinner, sleeping at night, playing with friends, and going to school. When a child unexpectedly ends one of these behaviors, parents usually find themselves amid a highly unpleasant and disruptive life experience.

Of these disruptions, a child's refusal to go to school may be among the most exasperating. Imagine the drain on a family when a child constantly refuses to get out of bed in the morning, locks himself or herself in the bathroom to avoid school, runs away from school at midmorning, or skips classes after lunch. The child may be severely anxious; parents may miss work; frequent or pressuring calls from the school may ensue; legal and academic problems may loom; social embarrassment may develop; siblings may become upset or miss school themselves; and family members as a whole may be confused, conflicted, and anguished over how to respond to

3

the school refusal situation. Appreciating this anguish is a key element in fully understanding this population.

In this chapter, definitions of the basic concepts that surround this phenomenon are initially described. These concepts include school absenteeism, school dropout, school withdrawal, school resistance, and school refusal behavior. In addition, a brief history of compulsory education and the early study of school absenteeism is provided. Thereafter, a history of absenteeism within clinical child psychology is explored with a description of the terms most commonly used to describe this problem. A glossary of definitions for these terms and others is presented at the end of the book. A brief re-examination of historical themes and the current status of research in this area is then provided.

SCHOOL ABSENTEEISM

School absenteeism essentially refers to any absence from school for any legal or illegal reason. Most cases of school absenteeism are temporary in nature, and Hersov (1985) estimated that 80% of school absenteeism may be due to legal or legitimate reasons. However, this estimate likely differs greatly across time, geographical locations, student populations, and other variables. Legitimate reasons for missing school include, among others, illness, religious holidays, the need to attend a family funeral, hazardous weather conditions, and exemptions for college attendance or specific kinds of work.

With respect to illness, a common type related to school absenteeism is asthma. M. G. Fowler, Davenport, and Garg (1992) found that children with asthma missed over three times as many days of school (7.6 days) in a 12-month period compared with children without asthma (2.5 days). This was particularly true for children in poor or fair health (17.4 days absent) compared with those in good or excellent health (6.7 days absent). Asthma by itself thus triggers many school absences, although some cases may also involve attention seeking, malingering, or other misbehaviors to avoid school (Creer, Renne, & Chai, 1982).

School absenteeism has been conceptualized as a syndrome in its own right, one that involves absenteeism as the primary component, a symptom of one or more other major syndromes (e.g., depression), or some combination of these. Much debate remains about the correct conceptualization of school absenteeism. For the purposes of this book, however, school absenteeism and school refusal behavior (discussed below) are discussed within the context of a primary problem for youth and their families.

SCHOOL DROPOUT

Most instances of school absenteeism are temporary in nature, but permanent withdrawal from school prior to high school graduation may occur for any reason and refers to *school dropout*. School dropout frequently occurs as a result of an adolescent's decision to leave school. However, school dropout could follow as well from other factors that are beyond a child's control (see chapter 2). For example, an adolescent may adaptively flee home, and therefore school, to avoid abuse. In addition, a child's family could become homeless and travel among different locations without formalizing school arrangements.

According to the U.S. National Center for Education Statistics, the event dropout rate, or the percentage of students who drop out of school on an annual basis, is 5% for people ages 15–24 years (for current figures over time, go to http://www.nces.ed.gov). The status dropout rate, however—the cumulative percentage of all people who have dropped out of school—currently stands at 11.1%, or 3.61 million, for 16- to 24-year-olds. This rate has declined slightly over time (M = 0.13% per year for the past 25 years), perhaps because of the prolific growth of alternative high school and graduation programs. Status dropout rates in the United States differ across:

- male (11.4%) and female students (10.9%)
- White Americans (7.3%), African Americans (13.0%), and Hispanics (29.4%)
- low- (22.1%), middle- (10.8%), and high-income (2.6%) families
- northeastern (8.3%), midwestern (7.7%), southern (13.0%), and western (13.9%) areas of the country.

Many factors influence or predict school dropout, including community, school, parent–family, social, personal, academic success, and other variables (Kearney & Hugelshofer, 2000). Although it is beyond the scope of this book to fully cover school dropout, these variables and preventive strategies for school absenteeism and dropout are discussed at greater length in chapter 10.

SCHOOL WITHDRAWAL

Some cases of absenteeism or dropout may also be due to *school withdrawal* (Kahn & Nursten, 1962), when a parent actively encourages a child's nonattendance or deliberately keeps the child home from school. In this book, a specific concentration is made on a child's refusal to attend school, but clinicians and educators should be wary of the possibility that one or both parents (or even other family members or people) are responsible for the child's ostensible misbehavior regarding school attendance.

Sometimes school withdrawal is due to maltreatment (see chapter 2), but the phenomenon is often due to less sinister reasons as well. The following represent common or purported reasons for school withdrawal, but any deliberate attempt by parents to subvert a child's school attendance would characterize this process:

- to secure economic support, such as requiring an adolescent to work to help pay family bills
- to sit with younger children or elderly adults or to comfort parents during a crisis (Taylor & Adelman, 1990)
- to protect the child from kidnapping by an estranged spouse
- fear of other harm or violence directed to the child at school
- friction with teachers or other school officials
- to pursue home schooling (in cases of school withdrawal, unnecessarily)
- to maintain the child's status as a "safety person" in cases of parental panic attacks, agoraphobia, or other disorder
- parent-based separation anxiety
- to punish the child for some perceived or actual infraction
- to extend the length of the problem to impart blame on the child (e.g., for the benefit of a therapist); this may follow or parallel extensive conflict with the child about his or her school attendance or parental acquiescence
- to sabotage treatment efforts to reintegrate the child into school.

SCHOOL RESISTANCE

School resistance involves various student behaviors that occur in reaction to perceived injustices or excessive demands at school (Field & Olafson, 1998). Such behaviors range from subtle (e.g., murmuring, note passing) to more disruptive (e.g., noncompliance) ones. In addition, resistance may come in the form of absenteeism. The phenomenon of school resistance highlights the need for clinicians and educators to attend to actual school-based threats or stressors that reframe absenteeism as an understandable reaction.

REFUSAL TO GO TO SCHOOL

As mentioned, a specific concentration is made in this book on instances of school absenteeism that are due to a child's deliberate and illicit refusal to go to school. In trying to understand child-based refusal to go to school, psychologists and educators have variously labeled the problem over time. The most common definitional terms include "truancy," "psychoneurotic truancy," "school refusal," and "school phobia." Related constructs include separation anxiety and separation anxiety disorder, specific phobia of school, and conduct disorder. This plethora of labels accurately conveys the fact that a child's refusal to attend school has traditionally been a substantial area of research in clinical child psychology and education. However, this splintering of terminology has also led to considerable disarray about how to address this population.

To address this problem in this book and elsewhere, I refer to the more inclusive term of *school refusal behavior*. School refusal behavior may be generally defined as a child-motivated refusal to attend school, difficulties remaining in classes for an entire day, or both (Kearney & Silverman, 1996). As discussed in this book, the breadth of this definition incorporates aspects of the constructs just mentioned. Specifically, school refusal behavior refers to youth ages 5–17 years who exhibit one or a combination of the following characteristics:

- are completely absent from school
- attend but then leave school at some time during the day (e.g., skip classes)
- attend school following severe misbehaviors in the morning (e.g., tantrums, clinging, aggression, running away, refusal to move, dawdling)
- attend school under great duress that may precipitate pleas for future nonattendance to parents or others.

The inclusiveness of the term *school refusal behavior* is thus partially based on a continuum of actual attendance (see Figure 1.1). Some children, for example, are continuously absent from school for weeks, months, or even years. Other children miss certain periods of the school year (e.g., 2 weeks after a holiday break) that threatens their academic status and creates other family problems. Still other children miss only part of school

X - - - - - - -X - - - - - - -X - - - - - - X- - - - - - X - - - - - X - - - - - -X

| School attendance under duress and pleas for non-attendance | Repeated misbehaviors in the morning to avoid school | Repeated tardiness in the morning followed by attendance | Periodic absences or skipping of classes | Repeated absences or skipping of classes mixed with attendance | Complete absence from school during a certain period of the school year | Complete absence from school for an extended period of time |

Figure 1.1. Continuum of school refusal behavior based on attendance.

by secretively skipping certain classes or by entering school later than they should (i.e., tardiness). In addition, some children in this population attend school most of the time but do so in conjunction with severe acting-out behaviors in the morning or severe anxiety during the school day. The term *school refusal behavior* includes children who "successfully" miss school time as well as children whose behavior is geared toward missing school time but who have not yet reached that goal.

This continuum foreshadows material in chapter 2 regarding the varied and heterogeneous nature of school refusal behavior. Despite this array of behavior, however, a common thread is a desire to eliminate school attendance to some degree from one's daily life routine. As connoted earlier, school refusal behavior thus represents a problem in achieving or maintaining age-appropriate functioning or coping adaptively with school-related stressors.

HISTORICAL ROOTS OF COMPULSORY EDUCATION

All the world's a stage,
And all the men and women merely players:
They have their exits and entrances;
And one man in his time plays many parts,
His acts being seven stages. At first the infant, . . .
And then the whining schoolboy, with his satchel,
And shining morning face, creeping like [a] snail
Unwillingly to school. (William Shakespeare, *As You Like It*)

* * *

Monday morning found Tom Sawyer miserable. Monday morning always found him so—because it began another week's slow suffering at school. He generally began that day with wishing he had had no intervening holiday, it made the going into captivity and fetters again so much more odious. (Mark Twain, *The Adventures of Tom Sawyer*)

* * *

Tom did play hooky, and he had a very good time. (Mark Twain, *The Adventures of Tom Sawyer*)

As is apparent from these quotes, the phenomenon of school refusal behavior has been alluded to for quite some time. In fact, early references to absenteeism in popular literature sometimes romanticized the phenomenon. This period of romance declined in the 19th century, however, with the advent of industrialization and specific legislative acts in different countries. With respect to the latter, a series of compulsory-education and child labor laws were enacted that essentially moved children from factories, farms, and mines into schools. This movement helped transfigure the phenomenon of school absenteeism as a romantic event into a serious social and behavioral problem in need of study.

For histories of compulsory education in France, Iraq, the Arab states, Pakistan, India, Cambodia, Laos, Vietnam, Indonesia, Thailand, Australia, New Zealand, the Philippines, and Ecuador, the reader is referred to the United Nations Educational, Scientific, and Cultural Organization (UNESCO) series of publications on this topic (see www.unesdoc.unesco.org or; for Australia, e.g., see UNESCO, 1962). For histories of compulsory education in the Netherlands, Italy, Spain, Belgium, Germany, Poland, Canada, and Mexico, the reader is referred to Mangan (1994). Other authors have also discussed compulsory education and methods to control school absenteeism in Denmark and Sweden (Rousmaniere, Dehli, & de Coninck-Smith, 1997) as well as Prussia and Austria (Melton, 1988).

A brief exposition of how compulsory education evolved in the United Kingdom and the United States is presented here for illustrative purposes. Berg, Brown, and Hullin (1988); Galloway (1985); Kotin and Aikman (1980); and Seaborne (1970) have provided cogent summaries of the history of compulsory education in the United Kingdom. According to these authors, compulsory education evolved in the United Kingdom in several stages (see Exhibit 1.1). As with many countries in Western Europe, constant and rapid changes in demographics, political expediencies, and industrialization created needs for social order and a competent work force. These needs were best met, it was believed, by the development of formal schooling (see Gleeson, 1992).

Mulkeen (1994) also provided a cogent summary of compulsory education in the United States, many of whose laws were modeled after those in the United Kingdom. According to Mulkeen, schooling was predominantly home, church, and apprenticeship based prior to the Civil War, as work held a much higher priority than education. Several pressuring factors—namely, industrialization, urbanization, and immigration—then led to a perceived need for increased social order and thus the development of a more formal school system to impart appropriate values. A push was thus made during the 19th and early 20th centuries to improve school attendance and facilities, lengthen the academic year, design graded school systems, develop procedures for supervising teachers, and standardize curricula. By 1900 most states had enacted legislation mandating school attendance, and almost all states had done so by 1918. The advent of child labor laws and vocational educational programs also ensured that youth would be appropriately trained before entering increasingly complex industrial systems. A brief chronology of events (Kotin & Aikman, 1980) regarding compulsory attendance in the United States is in Exhibit 1.2.

EXHIBIT 1.1
Progression of Compulsory Education in the United Kingdom

- *Statute of Artificers in 1563 and Poor Laws of 1601:* Required 7-year period of apprenticeship for unemployed people ages 12–60 years. Required poor people and their children to be trained through apprenticeship.
- *Early 19th century:* London Lead Company establishes schools in northeast England; regular attendance was required to work in the company. Other schools fined those who were absent or produced absentee lists. Free clothing was also distributed at some schools to induce attendance.
- *Gradual adoption of child labor laws:* For example, the Apprentices Act of 1802 and Children and Young Persons Labour Act of 1833 limited time in employment settings and increased time for school. Some laws included clauses mandating school attendance.
- *Elementary Education Act of 1870:* Led to the creation of school boards that were encouraged to make local bylaws to enforce attendance at school for children ages 5–13 years. Exemptions were allowed for children older than age 10 years who needed to work. School attendance committees and officers were established in many areas.
- *Sandon's Act of 1876 and Mundella's Act of 1880:* Created school attendance committees in all areas. Obligated school boards and attendance committees to adopt bylaws mandating attendance for children ages 5–10 years.
- *Elementary Education Act of 1893:* Exemption age from school for work raised initially to 11 years and, in 1899, to 12 years. Fisher's Education Act of 1918 later mandated that all children ages 5–14 years receive compulsory and full-time education.
- *Children Act of 1908 and Children and Young Persons Act of 1933:* Established alternative industrial and reformatory schools for children with delinquency or truancy. Percentage average attendance at primary schools in Sheffield increased substantially from 1873 (65.0%) to 1930 (90.1%; Galloway, 1985).
- *Education Act of 1944:* Compulsory and free education for primary and secondary levels; parents were held legally responsible for a child's nonattendance and could be prosecuted; role of attendance officers expanded to general welfare concerns regarding the child. The permissible age to leave school is set at 15 years and eventually (1972–1973) to 16 years.

THE EARLIEST ARTICLES ON SCHOOL ABSENTEEISM AND TRUANCY

As a result of the drive for a competent and manageable work force by means of formal education, school absenteeism became increasingly viewed as a social problem in need of study and solution. To address absenteeism in the late 19th and early 20th centuries, school administrators relied on specialists from education and the newly forming area of clinical child psychology. Partially as a function of this reliance, the traditional, simple, legal definition of problematic absenteeism (i.e., days missed from school without legal exemption) became woven with attempts to explain the phenomenon psychologically.

Initially during this weaving, the preferred term for children who deliberately missed school remained *truancy*. *Truancy* or *truant* is derived

EXHIBIT 1.2
Progression of Compulsory Education in the United States

- *1642:* Colony of Massachusetts requires all adults with children in their care to educate them in a trade and in reading. This was amended in 1648 to include male children up to age 21 years and female children up to age 18 years. Versions and expansions of this law were adopted throughout New England and elsewhere. Southern colonies adopted laws similar to the English laws of 1563 and 1601.
- *Late 17th century:* Repeal of most compulsory-education laws in New England.
- *Late 18th century:* Enactment of new education laws in Massachusetts and elsewhere after the Revolution. Massachusetts in 1789, for example, required towns of varying sizes to operate grammar or other types of schools.
- *Massachusetts School Attendance Act of 1852:* Required adults with children ages 8–14 years in their care to send them to school for 12 weeks per year.
- *Free public schools:* Funded by taxation, schools were established in Wisconsin (1848), Indiana (1852), Ohio (1853), Illinois (1855), Iowa (1858), New York (1867), Connecticut (1868), Pennsylvania (1868), Michigan (1869), and New Jersey (1871). Adoption of compulsory-education laws for most states by 1900 and in the southern states by 1918. Compulsory school age requirements now range from 16 to 18 years. Legal definitions of truancy in states generally surround any nonattendance outside of recognized exemptions.
- *Child labor laws adopted by 28 states by 1899.* The Fair Labor Standards Act of 1938 represented federal legislation to restrict child labor.
- *Repeal and re-enactment of compulsory-education laws:* This was done in some southern states in the 1950s and 1960s.

from an old French word, *truand*, meaning "beggar," "parasite," "lazy person," "naughty child," or "rogue" (Huguet, 1925/1973). Truancy in early literature essentially referred to an unlawful and willful "absence from school without the knowledge and consent of the parents" (Williams, 1927). This definition of truancy remains popular even today.

In early scientific journals, several key defining features of truancy were reported. In one of the very first articles, for example, Kline (1897) concluded that truancy represented "protests against the narrow and artificial methods of the school room, a rebellion against suppressed activity and a denial of free outdoor life" (p. 417). He stated as well that these children's "homes have a minimal attractiveness and power over their lives" and that the children's "moral sense, self-respect, and ambition are greatly wanting" (p. 418). This helped reinforce earlier notions by laypeople that truancy was simply an aspect of general delinquency and demonstrates that these notions have been formally purported for more than a century. Kline's statements also foreshadow a subtype of children with school refusal behavior who are described later in this book: those refusing school for tangible reinforcement outside of school.

Following Kline (1897), other authors during this early period sought to propose key defining features for truancy. All essentially believed that truancy was a form of delinquency, a separate condition closely related to delinquency, or a precursor to delinquency (e.g., Healy, 1926; cf. Dayton, 1928). Key defining features of truancy included the following, although these are not necessarily supported by empirical evidence today (see chapter 2):

- problematic home and physical conditions, "extreme social suggestibility, extreme love of adventure," poor motivation, and the "influence of bad companions" (Williams, 1927, pp. 284, 285)
- problematic schools, classes, teachers, and grading policies; attractions outside of school, and neglectful parents (Dayton, 1928; Doll, 1921)
- poor school adjustment and lower intelligence (Kirkpatrick & Lodge, 1935; McElwee, 1931; Mercer, 1930).

THE EARLY SPLINTERING OF TRUANCY

The notion of truancy as a constant partner of delinquency began to splinter somewhat with the publication of three seminal articles in 1932, 1939, and 1941. These articles essentially promoted the idea that some children and adolescents with school absenteeism were not necessarily delinquent in nature but instead had some anxiety-related condition (see also Lippman's, 1936, discussion of "neurotic delinquency").

Broadwin and Anxiety-Based Absenteeism

Broadwin (1932) claimed that some cases of absenteeism were related to home-based behavioral symptoms that "represent an act of defiance, an attempt to obtain love, or escapes from real situations to which it is difficult to adjust" (p. 254). It is interesting that these factors generally represent the primary maintaining variables of school refusal behavior described at length in this book. Broadwin further claimed that some absenteeism was caused by a "deep-seated neurosis of the obsessional type" and that its symptomatology resembled "a marked tendency to mixed neuroses or overlapping" (p. 255). In doing so, he accurately portrayed part of this population as anxiety based in nature and the symptoms of school refusal behavior as heterogeneous in nature.

Partridge and Psychoneurotic Truancy–School Refusal

Partridge (1939), like his predecessors, also preferred the term *truancy* to generally describe delinquent and unlawful absences from school. In fact, in delineating five types of truancy, he related four to detached family relationships and antisocial behavior. These included the undisciplined, hysterical, desiderative, and rebellious groups. The key features of each of these groups, respectively, were lack of discipline, running away from difficult situations, desire for something, and oppositional behavior toward domineering parents. Partridge also stated, however, that truancy could represent a symptom of a neurotic or personality disorder as well as a conduct disorder. Partridge's fifth type of truancy was labeled *psychoneurotic* and referred to children who displayed timidity, guilt, anxiety, tantrums, aggression, and desires for attention within an overprotective parent–child relationship. This distinction helped further splinter the study of absenteeism into two camps: (a) a "traditional" camp that viewed the problem as a form of illegal, delinquent behavior (referred to as *truancy*) and (b) a "contemporary" camp that viewed the problem as a more complex neurotic condition (referred to as *psychoneurotic truancy* or *school refusal*).

Johnson et al. and School Phobia

The third article that helped spur an early splintering of truancy was published by A. M. Johnson, Falstein, Szurek, and Svendsen (1941), who stipulated that some children with absenteeism display *school phobia*, a type of psychoneurotic disorder characterized predominantly by overlapping phobic and obsessive tendencies. School phobia in this sense may therefore be thought of as a subset of psychoneurotic truancy–school refusal, the latter of which was thought to contain more general feelings of distress or negative affectivity. Johnson et al. stated more specifically that school phobia consists of three main components proceeding in the following sequence:

1. Acute child anxiety marked by hypochondriacal and compulsive symptoms and caused by organic disease or emotional conflict. There is a resulting wish for dependence. This must occur simultaneously with the next point (No. 2) for school phobia to develop.
2. Increased anxiety in the child's mother due to some life stressor that involves a threat to her security (e.g., marital problems, financial difficulties, illness, etc.).
3. A historically unresolved, overdependent mother–child relationship. As the mother experiences her life stressors, there is a desire to exploit the child's anxiety and wish for dependence for her own comfort. Regression to a period of "mutual satisfaction" then occurs, which is manifested in the child's and mother's desires to maintain school nonattendance. The

symbolic phobic object is the teacher or other school-related item or situation.

Johnson later clarified her description of school phobia, claiming the term was a "misnomer" and that the problem was more accurately a type of separation anxiety present before the advent of school (Estes, Haylett, & Johnson, 1956; A. M. Johnson, 1957). *Separation anxiety* refers to intense distress when anticipating or experiencing separation from a significant other person or people (e.g., parents). Although case studies were used to support her view on school phobia, Johnson (1957) stated that the "etiological factors in this form of behavior have been adequately demonstrated, and require little, if any, further evidence to rest as basic scientific principles" (p. 309). Despite its flaws and this dubious statement, Johnson's psychodynamic interpretation of school refusal behavior has gained broad appeal and made an indelible impression on thinking in this area for decades. The depth of this impression, for example, is evident when one reviews the *Diagnostic and Statistical Manual of Mental Disorders* (4th ed. [DSM–IV]; American Psychiatric Association [APA], 1994) criteria for separation anxiety disorder. This disorder is discussed later in this chapter.

EXPANSION OF THE SCHOOL PHOBIA CONCEPT

School phobia was thus initially seen as a specific, anxiety-based part of psychoneurotic truancy or school refusal, the latter two concepts being marked by more general distress or negative affectivity. Following A. M. Johnson et al. (1941), however, other authors have described comorbid problems that served to broaden the definitional nature of school phobia. These comorbid problems primarily included somatic complaints, depression, and family conflict (Agras, 1959; Campbell, 1955; Suttenfield, 1954; Talbot, 1957), although each author generally supported Johnson et al.'s basic premise of an enmeshed parent–child relationship that triggered absenteeism. As a result of this process, the original concept of school phobia became entangled with the original definitional qualities of broader psychoneurotic truancy or school refusal. This helps to explain why, today, many people use the terms *truancy*, *school refusal*, and *school phobia* interchangeably.

Waldfogel, Coolidge, and Hahn (1957) helped expand the concept of school phobia as well by defining it as "a reluctance to go to school as a result of a morbid dread of some aspect of the school situation" (p. 754). This definition is significant in that it helped trigger the later notion that school phobia was school centered and not completely home or maternally centered. Coolidge, Hahn, and Peck (1957) also hypothesized two subtypes of children with school phobia. The first (the neurotic type) generally represented the original concept of school phobia, whereas the second (the characterological type) generally represented the original concept of general psychoneurotic truancy or school refusal. The neurotic type is characterized by younger children with acute, almost paniclike anxiety symptoms and sudden onset of absenteeism, and the characterological type is characterized by older children with symptoms of depression and paranoia whose onset of absenteeism is more gradual.

It is perhaps not surprising that A. M. Johnson (1957), who proposed the anxiety-based concept of school phobia, criticized the characterological distinction as simply representing children whose symptomatologies are more gradual in onset and longer in duration. Despite this criticism, however, Coolidge et al.'s (1957) distinction was generally well received, albeit with changes. Indeed, the idea that school phobia was triggered by separation anxiety and comprised neurotic–characterological or acute–chronic subtypes became accepted as "working" clinical principles by 1962 (e.g., Berryman, 1959; Chazan, 1962; S. Davidson, 1960; Eisenberg, 1958; Kahn & Nursten, 1962).

From the early 1930s to early 1960s, therefore, the study of school absenteeism generally involved traditional, delinquent truancy and the newer concept of psychoneurotic truancy–school refusal. Within the latter, the subset of school phobia was more specifically defined. As is discussed more in chapter 3, however, considerable overlap among all of these distinctions has created much confusion regarding the classification, assessment, and treatment of this population. In reaction to this, other taxonomies that focused more specifically on overt child and parent behaviors arose in the 1960s and early 1970s.

EXPANDED DICHOTOMIES AND THE ACUTE–CHRONIC DISTINCTION

The evolving study of school absenteeism in the 1960s and early 1970s led to a blend of ideas from past, psychodynamically based approaches and those from the newly ascending behavioral–learning approach (e.g., Garvey & Hegrenes, 1966; Lazarus, Davison, & Polefka, 1965). This blending essentially gave birth to several well-cited, clinically based systems for defining subtypes of school phobia or school refusal (recall that these terms began to be used interchangeably). In this chapter these subtypes are briefly described with respect to their defining features of children who refuse school. A fuller analysis and critique of these subtypes from a taxonomical standpoint is presented in chapter 3.

Kennedy's Approach

Kennedy (1965) reworked Coolidge et al.'s (1957) neurotic–characterological distinction by emphasizing problem duration and overt symptoms. Two specific types were delineated:

- Type 1 school phobia, or the "neurotic crisis," which is characterized by acute onset of the first episode of absenteeism (typically on a Monday following an illness the previous week), low grades, concerns about death, questionable maternal physical health, and good parental relations and adjustment, and
- Type 2 school phobia, or the "way-of-life phobia," which is characterized by insidious onset involving multiple episodes of school refusal, good grades, no concerns about death, irrelevance of maternal physical health, and poor parental relations and adjustment.

Kennedy (1965) also reported that common symptoms across both categories were fears, somatic complaints, separation anxiety, and parent–school official conflict.

Related Approaches

Expansions of Kennedy's approach have been proposed by Sperling (1967); Marine (1968); Berg, Nichols, and Pritchard (1969); and Shapiro and Jegede (1973). Sperling, for example, distinguished between common and induced school refusal. *Common* school refusal is characterized by an unconscious motivation to regain control of the mother in reaction to some precipitating external event (e.g., illness) that threatens such control. *Induced* school refusal is characterized by insidious onset, lack of external precipitating events, and a prolonged, overly dependent parent–child relationship.

Marine (1968) proposed four categories of school refusal, including "simple separation anxiety" when younger children experience initial separation from a parent. This separation was considered painful but fleeting. In addition, Marine characterized mild acute school refusal as similar to Kennedy's Type 1 school phobia and severe chronic school refusal as similar to Kennedy's Type 2 school phobia. Finally, "childhood psychosis with school refusal symptoms" was characterized by a complicated behavioral pattern involving fear, depression, social withdrawal, rituals, somatic complaints, fear of contamination or sexual assault, and regressive behaviors.

Berg et al. (1969) provided a widely cited definition of school phobia based on the following four elements:

1. "severe difficulty attending school," excluding voluntary school absences
2. "severe emotional upset" when attempting school attendance, including fear, anger, somatic complaints, and general "misery" (p. 123)
3. absence of antisocial behavior such as stealing or lying
4. parental knowledge of the child remaining at home during school hours.

Berg et al. (1969) also made a distinction between acute and chronic school phobia. *Acute* school phobia was defined as nonproblematic school attendance for 3 years prior to the current episode of absenteeism, whereas all other cases were defined as *chronic*.

Finally, Shapiro and Jegede (1973) adopted the notion that children with school refusal could be viewed along a behavior continuum that included ego alien and ego syntonic behaviors at the poles of the continuum. Ego alien behaviors were characterized by phobia, anxiety, clinging, and somatic complaints, whereas ego syntonic behaviors were characterized by truancy that is sometimes reinforced by parents in the form of criticism of teachers.

Kearney and Silverman's Approach

Although many of these expanded approaches differed greatly in their terminology, a common theme was to essentially divide children with school phobia–refusal into acute and chronic conditions. To help reconcile past differences with respect to acute and chronic school refusal behavior, Kearney and Silverman (1996) proposed an atheoretical differentiation based simply on length of the problem. This differentiation included self-corrective, acute, and chronic school refusal behavior.

Self-corrective school refusal behavior refers to children whose initial absenteeism remits spontaneously within a 2-week period. Many children in this population, for example, experience fleeting episodes of anxiety about school at the beginning of the academic year or "test" their parents' resolve by occasionally acting out to stay home from school. Oftentimes, the problem dissipates quickly as the child becomes habituated to school or the parents take a firm stand against the misbehavior. Indeed, up to 80% of children have difficulty adjusting to school at some point, but such reluctance is usually managed successfully by parents, teachers, or others without further incident (Watters, 1989). However, school refusal behavior for less than a 2-week period may still be a significant problem for a family and require treatment.

Acute school refusal behavior refers to children whose absenteeism lasts from 2 weeks to 1 calendar year (i.e., 2–52 weeks). *Chronic school refusal behavior* refers to children whose absenteeism lasts longer than 1 calendar

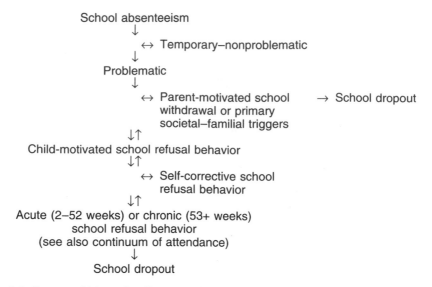

School absenteeism
↓
    ↔ Temporary–nonproblematic
↓
Problematic
↓
    ↔ Parent-motivated school   → School dropout
       withdrawal or primary
       societal–familial triggers
↓↑
Child-motivated school refusal behavior
↓↑
    ↔ Self-corrective school
       refusal behavior
↓↑
Acute (2–52 weeks) or chronic (53+ weeks)
school refusal behavior
(see also continuum of attendance)
↓
School dropout

Figure 1.2. Proposed hierarchy–flow chart for youth with school absenteeism.

year (i.e., 53+ weeks). This necessarily involves school refusal behavior over a 2-year academic period, which is typically a poor prognostic sign for this population (Kearney, 1995). The severity of school refusal behavior may be independent of the length of the problem, however, so refer as well to the continuum of attendance described earlier.

Figure 1.2 outlines a proposed hierarchy of school absenteeism based on the concepts discussed so far in this chapter. It also represents a flow chart that illustrates the potential directions a child could take with respect to school absenteeism. As indicated by some bidirectional arrows, however, some paths are not necessarily binding. For example, a child could experience an episode of temporary–nonproblematic absenteeism that eventually degenerates into a problematic state. A common scenario here is a child who, after a period of actual illness, "plays sick" to extend his or her privileges at home. Another example is an anxious adolescent who experiences intermittent periods of self-corrective school refusal behavior prior to some trauma (e.g., test failure) and subsequent acute or chronic school refusal behavior.

Note that in Figure 1.2 school dropout always follows a unidirectional arrow because of the permanence of the phenomenon. An adolescent, for example, who has been out of school for 2 years and is still considering school dropout would be classified here with chronic school refusal behavior. In addition, this chart assumes that the amelioration of any condition, such as remission of school withdrawal or successful treatment for school refusal behavior, abrogates the need for this chart until the next episode of absenteeism.

EMPIRICAL DISTINCTIONS OF SCHOOL ABSENTEEISM AND SCHOOL REFUSAL BEHAVIORS

The clinically based subtypes of school refusal behavior that were presented in the 1950s, 1960s, and early 1970s generally suffered from a lack of psychometric support. In reaction to this, more empirical or statistical attempts were made to identify the defining features of children who refused school. These attempts generally centered on two strategies: (a) analyses of problematic school refusal behaviors along overcontrolled–undercontrolled or internalizing–externalizing dimensions and (b) analyses of characteristics (e.g., depression) more specific to children who refuse school. These subtypes are briefly outlined here with respect to their proposed defining features of children who refuse school. A fuller analysis and critique of these subtypes from a taxonomical standpoint is presented in chapter 3.

Overcontrolled–Internalizing and Undercontrolled–Externalizing Dimensions

Factor analyses of parent, teacher, and mental health worker reports often result in two broadband factors of problematic behavior: overcontrolled–internalizing and undercontrolled–externalizing (Achenbach & Edelbrock, 1978). Overcontrolled syndromes represent a collection of behaviors including fear, anxiety, and depressive symptoms such as withdrawal. Undercontrolled syndromes represent acting-out behaviors such as aggression, fighting, stealing, and other antisocial or delinquent acts. In Achenbach's Child Behavior Checklist (CBCL), Teacher's Report Form (TRF), and Youth Self-Report (YSR), the items "Fears going to school" (CBCL, TRF) and "I am afraid of going to school" (YSR) are listed on the Other Problems factor. In contrast, the items "Truancy, skips school" (CBCL), "Truancy or unexplained absence" (TRF), and "I cut classes or skip school" are listed on the Delinquent Behavior factor (Achenbach, 1991a, 1991b, 1991c).

With respect to youth with problematic school nonattendance, Young, Brasic, Kisnadwala, and Leven (1990) proposed a similar distinction between "internalizing school refusal disorders" and "externalizing truant disorder" (p. 202):

- *Internalizing school refusal disorders* are marked by "conflict, anxiety, distress about the symptoms, and symptoms of other emotional disorders." These include children with phobia, separation anxiety, depression, and somatic complaints.
- *Externalizing truant disorder* is marked by "impulsive, defiant, manipulative, noncompliant behavior, and other symptoms of a

conduct disorder or delinquency, including nonattendance at school (with) little anxiety" (p. 202).

To foreshadow a point made in chapter 3, it should be noted that many children who refuse school display intermingling symptoms. For example, children with "internalizing school refusal" certainly show nonattendance at school, and children with "externalizing truancy" often evince at least some symptoms of negative affectivity.

Empirical Analyses of Specific School Refusal Behaviors

Attempts have also been made to identify empirically derived categories of school absenteeism from (a) assessments of children with depression and general school refusal behaviors and (b) assessments of school refusal behaviors previously reported in the literature. Three studies are presented here for illustrative purposes. Kolvin, Berney, and Bhate (1984) evaluated children with school phobia with or without depression. Discriminant-function analyses were conducted on participants' background features and symptoms. Several potentially useful dichotomies of school phobia (e.g., acute–chronic, male–female, preadolescent–adolescent, and attends–does not attend school) were assessed, but a significant number of discriminants (five) was found for only a depressed–nondepressed distinction.

Examining a broader set of variables, Berg et al. (1985) conducted a principal-components factor analysis of parent ratings of children with severe school attendance problems. A truancy component accounted for 20% of the variance and included items such as (a) child not with parent or at home and (b) parent does not know whom child is with. A school refusal component accounted for 15% of the variance and included items such as (a) refuses to go to school, (b) stays home, and (c) resists parents' efforts to secure attendance.

Finally, Atkinson, Quarrington, Cyr, and Atkinson (1989) subjected data from the clinical files of children with school refusal (using Berg et al.'s, 1969, criteria for school phobia) to a cluster analysis. Three discernible groups were culled, including (a) separation anxiety and overprotective mothers (similar to A. M. Johnson et al.'s, 1941, description), (b) perfectionism (fear of failure), and (c) extensive school refusal and "psychopathic deviancy." Symptoms of depression and fear were evident also in the first and third clusters. The remainder of the sample (28%) was unclassified.

These attempts to empirically define the nature of school refusal behavior confirmed earlier descriptions regarding the heterogeneity of this population. In fact, much overlap and unexplained variance pervaded these analyses. Still, the identification of key and common characteristics to school refusal behavior, such as depression, was made more precisely. Concurrent with these empirically based attempts at defining school phobia–refusal were attempts to define and classify these conditions by means of diagnosis. A fuller discussion and critique of these classification attempts from a taxonomic standpoint are presented in chapter 3. However, diagnoses most commonly affiliated with school refusal behavior, both symptomatically and historically, are presented next.

DIAGNOSTIC DISTINCTIONS OF SCHOOL ABSENTEEISM AND SCHOOL REFUSAL BEHAVIORS

Diagnostically, little was available prior to 1980 to define school absenteeism or school refusal behavior. Although early editions of the major classification systems for childhood behavior problems were available, including the *DSM*, the *International Classification of Diseases* (*ICD*), and the Group for the Advancement of Psychiatry, little mention was made of youth who refused to go to school.

Such miniscule attention to school absenteeism remains the case in diagnostic systems today, although the third edition of the *DSM* (*DSM–III*; APA, 1980) did spur an increased focus on the problem from a diagnostic perspective. As mentioned, subtypes of school refusal behavior based on diagnosis are presented in greater detail in chapter 3. However, a brief description is made here of the three primary diagnoses from *DSM–IV* (APA, 1994) that are most closely aligned, symptomatically and historically, with school refusal behavior. These categories are analogous to ones in the *ICD–10* (World Health Organization, 1992).

These diagnoses are not the only ones commonly associated or comorbid with school refusal behavior. Other common comorbid diagnoses include, for example, panic disorder and agoraphobia, social anxiety disorder, generalized anxiety disorder, and oppositional defiant disorder, among others. In addition, the description of these diagnoses here does not imply an endorsement of their validity for describing the overall nature of school refusal behavior.

Conduct Disorder

The essential feature of the first diagnosis often associated with school absenteeism, *conduct disorder* (CD), involves "a repetitive and persistent pattern of behavior in which the basic rights of others or major age-appropriate societal norms or rules are violated" (APA, 1994, p. 85). One symptom of CD is "often truant from school, beginning before age 13 years" (p. 90). Other symptoms involve aggression toward people and animals, property destruction, lying and stealing, and serious rule violations. To be diagnosed with CD, a person must exhibit three symptoms that last for at least 12 months (and at least one in the past 6 months) and cause significant impairment in daily functioning. This modern version of CD is thus partially reflective of early work that associated truancy with delinquency.

Separation Anxiety Disorder

The essential feature of the second diagnosis often associated with school absenteeism, *separation anxiety disorder* (SAD), involves "excessive anxiety concerning separation from the home or from those to whom the person is attached" (APA, 1994, p. 110). One symptom of SAD is "persistent reluctance or refusal to go to school or elsewhere because of fear of separation" (p. 113). Other symptoms of SAD generally include (a) worry about harm to major attachment figures or the child on separation; (b) reluctance to be alone or go to sleep alone; (c) nightmares about separation; and (d) physical symptoms, such as headaches or stomachaches, on separation. To be diagnosed with SAD, a person must exhibit at least three of eight symptoms for at least 4 weeks that cause significant distress or impairment in daily functioning. This modern version of SAD is thus partially reflective of early work that associated separation anxiety with psychoneurotic truancy–school refusal.

Specific Phobia

The essential feature of the third diagnosis often associated with school absenteeism, *specific phobia*, involves "marked and persistent fear of clearly discernible, circumscribed objects or situations" (APA, 1994, p. 405). Exposure to such an object or situation (e.g., school) generally involves an immediate anxiety response similar to a panic attack. In children, according to the *DSM–IV*, this may involve "crying, tantrums, freezing, or clinging" (p. 410). The phobic object or situation is also avoided or endured with great dread. To be diagnosed with specific phobia a person must have exhibited the symptoms for at least 6 months and it must cause significant impairment in daily functioning. This modern version of specific phobia of school is thus partially reflective of early work that associated specific fear and anxiety with school phobia.

TERMS OF SCHOOL ABSENTEEISM

Definitions of terms that have been used in this chapter to describe school absence are in the glossary. Note that many laypeople and professionals in education, psychology, social work, medicine, and related fields often use these terms interchangeably (Friesen, 1985; Phelps, Cox, & Bajorek, 1992). However, such practice is invalid and dismissive of the richness and complexity of this population. In addition, the interchangeable use of these terms likely impedes appropriate treatment assignment, and therefore treatment effectiveness, for many youth.

As an example, a common error among professionals is to tell a parent that his or her child has school phobia when, in fact, the child has no intense fear of any school-related object or situation. Indeed, *school phobia* is too frequently used as a catchall term to describe any child who is illicitly missing school. Erroneously believing that a child has such intense fear, however, as implied by the use of the term *school phobia*, could lead parents and professionals to choose an inappropriate treatment and perhaps exacerbate a child's school refusal behavior. Instead, a careful analysis of the context of a child's absenteeism (e.g., is it fear based?, parent based?, recreation based?) is better for deciding on the best treatment for that child. Such consideration of context serves as the basis for the functional model described in chapters 3–10.

REVISITING HISTORICAL THEMES OF SCHOOL ABSENTEEISM AND SCHOOL REFUSAL BEHAVIOR

As one steps back and evaluates the overall historical literature on school absenteeism and school refusal behavior, several major themes are evident and foreshadow later material in this book. First, the study of school absenteeism–refusal behavior has represented a rich and substantial research area in education and clinical child psychology. Indeed, this topic has drawn attention from many professionals in different fields for many years. Part of this immense attention is due to the immediate, crisislike, and pervasive symptomatology often seen in this population. As a result, many people become involved with the problem at its outset, including parents, school officials, psychologists, psychiatrists, social workers, and pediatricians, among others.

Part of the immense attention given school absenteeism–refusal behavior is also due to the highly varied and heterogeneous nature of its symptoms. An enormous amount of research has been conducted to identify the fundamental defining profiles or dichotomies of school absenteeism–refusal behavior. One such dichotomy is the acute–chronic distinction. This distinction, when imbued with symptomatology, does not adequately differentiate children with school refusal behavior. However, when the acute–chronic distinction is based simply on duration of school refusal behavior, as presented in this chapter, clarity and clinical utility are enhanced. Another fundamental profile often formed in the historical literature is anxiety-based versus non-anxiety-based school refusal behavior. At first glance, this distinction seems rather cardinal. However, many youth who refuse school have mixed symptoms that smear any clean dichotomy based on the form of behavior (see chapters 2 and 3).

The heterogeneity of school refusal behavior has produced major disagreement over how to best define, classify, assess, and treat this population. Indeed, this area of study remains in considerable disarray. One of the purposes of this book is to propose a method for systematizing the definition and clinical processes relevant to school refusal behavior. A major premise in doing so is a reliance less on the child's symptoms, or form of school refusal behavior, and more on the child's reasons for refusing school, or function of school refusal behavior.

2

CHARACTERISTICS OF YOUTH WITH SCHOOL REFUSAL BEHAVIOR

Melissa is a 15-year-old girl who has missed the past 2 years of school. She reports little desire to return to regular school, is disengaged from her family, and prefers to spend her daytime with friends. She is worried about her future, however, and is increasingly anxious and depressed.

As mentioned in chapter 1, the characteristic features of youth with school refusal behavior are vast and heterogeneous. In this chapter, the rich symptomatology of school refusal behavior is explored in greater depth. This involves a discussion of prevalence, potential contributing distal factors, and child and family features that comprise school refusal behavior. The chapter concludes with a brief overview of etiological factors relevant to this population.

PREVALENCE OF SCHOOL REFUSAL BEHAVIOR

One of the most difficult tasks when describing children with school refusal behavior is identifying the prevalence of the problem. As discussed in chapter 1, school refusal behavior has been defined as concretely as days missed from school, as amorphously as emotional distress while attending school, and as a mixture of almost all other descriptions in between. As a result, many different prevalence rates have been proposed as well.

To try to pinpoint the prevalence of school refusal behavior, one could evaluate its components individually. Recall that school refusal behavior refers to youth who (a) completely and illicitly miss school, (b) attend but then leave school during the course of the day, (c) attend school (possibly late) only after severe behavior problems in the morning, (d) attend school under great duress that precipitates pleas for future nonattendance, or some combination of these. Identifying the prevalence of these separate components may help clarify the overall frequency of school refusal behavior.

Complete Absenteeism—Days Missed From School

According to the U.S. National Center of Education Statistics (NCES), 5.5% of students are absent from school on a typical school day (go to http://www.nces.ed.gov for periodic updates). This may be a substantial underestimate, however. A brief review of prevalence rates of unexcused absences in different geographical areas of the United States revealed a range of 10%–20% on any given day (Bell, Rosen, & Dynlacht, 1994). In addition, Hibbett and Fogelman (1990) found that 19.4% of 16-year-olds in Great Britain displayed regular unexcused absences, Berg et al. (1993) reported that 13.1% of students at four British high schools missed more than 30% of school days, and absentee rates of 1%–50% have been reported in The Netherlands (Bos, Ruijters, & Visscher, 1990). These rates could include, however, partial absences.

According to the NCES, rates of simple or complete absenteeism differ somewhat across

- inner cities (5.7%), urban fringe–large towns (5.3%), and rural–small towns (5.3%)
- public (5.9%) and private (4.1%) schools
- public elementary (5.2%), middle (6.3%), and high (8.0%) schools
- small (4.9%, 5.4%, 7.8%), medium (5.1%, 6.2%, 7.3%), and large (5.4%, 7.2%, 9.1%) elementary, middle, and high schools, respectively.

Rates of absenteeism for public schools are generally highest among inner-city high schools (9.7%) and lowest among rural elementary schools (4.9%).

Rates of absenteeism are generally greater in schools with larger percentages of minority students and students living in poverty. With respect to schools whose minority-status students represent more than 20% of the total student population, the absentee rate increases across public elementary (5.9%), middle (7.0%), and high (9.6%) schools. Among high-minority-status inner-city schools, these numbers climb to 6.0%, 7.7%, and 10.8%, respectively. In schools where greater than 40% of students are impoverished, the absentee rate increases across elementary (5.8%), middle (7.2%), and high (8.6%) schools. Among impoverished inner-city schools, these numbers climb to 6.3%, 8.6%, and 12.0%, respectively.

With respect to teacher perceptions, a total of 12.9% believe that absenteeism is a serious problem at their school. Dramatic differences in these perceptions occur across

- public (14.4%) and private (2.2%) schools
- public elementary (6.8%), middle (10.9%), and high (29.0%) schools

- inner cities (18.2%), urban fringe–large towns (12.1%), and rural–small towns (9.3%)
- impoverished elementary (11.1%), middle (19.4%), and high (38.8%) schools.

Overall, the rate of simple absenteeism in the United States may be about 5.5% on any given day, although other studies indicate higher frequencies of unexcused absence. This number (5.5%) rises substantially in public schools, inner-city schools, schools with a significant minority population, and schools whose students are largely impoverished. Recall, however, three important points about this overall number. First, not all of these 5.5% of students are necessarily displaying school refusal behavior (although it is possible). If one uses Hersov's (1985) estimate that 80% of school absenteeism is temporary or nonproblematic, than one might conservatively assume that at least 1.1% are completely and illicitly absent from school on any given day. Of course, this adjusted rate would also apply to the other variables listed above (e.g., impoverished inner-city high schools, 2.4%). Second, rates of absenteeism are reportedly as high as 20% in the United States, suggesting that a more liberal, adjusted rate of complete, illicit absenteeism may be 4.0%. Third, this adjusted range (1.1%–4.0%) represents only one of four components (i.e., complete absenteeism) of the definition of school refusal behavior.

Partial Absenteeism—Cutting Classes

The second aspect of school refusal behavior represents youth who attend school only part of the day; in other words, they are skipping, ditching, or cutting certain classes. Complete absenteeism is therefore not present, but the situation is problematic nonetheless. No definitive prevalence data are available for class cutting, although Duckworth and deJung (1989) questioned 5,799 students in six Northwest high schools and found that 22% admittedly cut class at least once per week. A gross estimate of daily class cutting might thus be placed at 4.4% (22% ÷ 5 academic days per week). In addition, according to the NCES, 4.5% of teachers believe cutting class is problematic at their school. This rate differs across

- inner cities (7.6%), urban fringe–large towns (4.2%), and rural–small towns (2.4%)
- public (5.1%) and private (0.7%) schools
- public elementary (0.9%), middle (3.2%), and high (13.1%) schools.

Of course, teacher perceptions are not the same as actual rates of class cutting, but the 4.5% rate is strikingly close to Duckworth and deJung's

(1989) finding. For purposes of estimation here, a 4.4% rate of class cutting is assumed for high school, although the overall rate is perhaps doubled to 8.8% when one adds class cutting in elementary and middle schools.

Partial Absenteeism—Tardiness

Another component of school refusal behavior is tardiness, which may reflect misbehaviors (e.g., tantrums, dawdling) in the morning to refuse school. Like class cutting, no definitive data are available for tardiness. Some schools classify tardiness as a full absence, whereas other schools treat tardiness as a separate phenomenon. If one assumes that tardiness is similar to but separate from class cutting, one could assume a conservative parallel rate of 4.4%.

According to the NCES, 9.5% of teachers believe that tardiness is problematic at their school. This rate differs across

- inner cities (14.8%), urban fringe–large towns (9.4%), and rural–small towns (5.5%)
- public (10.6%) and private (2.5%) schools
- public elementary (5.7%), middle (9.7%), and high (19.4%) schools.

Of course, teacher perceptions of tardiness are not the same as actual rates. However, rates of tardiness are likely higher than class cutting because many teachers and other school officials overlook minor infractions during the chaotic course of the morning. In addition, tardiness rates do not account for youth who misbehave every morning to refuse school but whose parents get them to school on time anyway. For present purposes, a general morning misbehavior–tardiness rate of 4.4%–9.5% is assumed with prejudice.

Duress During School Attendance

The final component of school refusal behavior is severe duress during the school day that precipitates pleas for future nonattendance. Of the four components of school refusal behavior, identifying prevalence for this one is most problematic. Early prevalence estimates for school phobia included 1.7% by Kennedy (1965) and 3% by Eisenberg (1958), but the methods used to derive these figures were not made clear.

Granell de Aldaz, Vivas, Gelfand, and Feldman (1984) reviewed prevalence rates across 10 studies that evaluated children's fears and dislikes of school. The mean prevalence rate was 4.9% with a reported range of 0.01%–25.00%. Granell de Aldaz et al. also conducted their own study of 1,034 Venezualan children ages 3–14 years and found that 17.7% expressed intense fears of school. This contrasted, however, with parent (7.7%) and teacher (2.7%) reports that these children had such fears. Fearfulness was then combined with school nonattendance and ranged, across six sets of criteria, from 0.4% to 1.5% of the sample. Adding these six prevalence rates of fear of school and nonattendance, the authors provided a "liberal estimate" (p. 728) of fear–nonattendance at 5.4%. This rate is similar to the 4.9% mean derived from their review.

The clinical prevalence of school-related fear and anxiety was reported in early writings to be less than 8% (Chazan, 1962; Eisenberg, 1958; Kahn & Nursten, 1962). More contemporarily, Kearney and Beasley (1994) surveyed clinicians in the United States who treated children and adolescents with fear and anxiety disorders. The authors found, for youth referred for treatment, that 6.08% were referred because of absenteeism (6.17% for males and 5.95% for females). Of this group, 10% refused school because of fear of some specific object or situation. In addition, 35% refused school because of aversive, and possibly anxiety-provoking, social and evaluative situations. Honjo, Kasahara, and Ohtaka (1992) also reported a school refusal clinical prevalence rate of 16.5% at one Japanese hospital clinic.

Summary

What is the prevalence of school refusal behavior? To address this question, one could use general prevalence estimates derived here for complete and illicit absence from school (1.1%–4.0%), partial absence from school–class cutting (4.4%–8.8%), tardiness–morning misbehaviors to avoid school (4.4%–9.5%), and intense fear and anxiety of school (1.7%–5.4%). Simple addition of these four components reveals a gross estimated rate of 11.6%–27.7%. However, this rate is certainly fraught with incertitude and measurement error; it is only a general estimate. In particular, many youth in this population are uncounted, and it is unknown how this rate is affected by the number of youth with multiple aspects of school refusal behavior (e.g., tardiness and intense anxiety during school). In addition, the estimate is not fully reflective of societies in which school refusal behavior has not been a traditional problem (e.g., Japan; Iwamoto & Yoshida, 1997).

Perhaps a "best guess" is that 5%–28% of children and adolescents display some aspect of school refusal behavior. Whatever the exact rate, though, school refusal behavior is clearly a frequent problem that rivals prevalence rates for general childhood psychopathology (15.8%; Roberts, Attkisson, & Rosenblatt, 1998) and specific syndromes such as attention deficit hyperactivity (3.0%–6.0%; Barkley, 1996), conduct (1.0%–10.0%; Hinshaw & Anderson, 1996), depressive (0.4%–7.8%; Hammen & Rudolph, 1996), and anxiety (2.0%–21.0%; Albano, Chorpita, & Barlow, 1996) disorders.

DISTAL FACTORS AND SCHOOL REFUSAL BEHAVIOR

Much of this book concentrates on a child's deliberate and illicit refusal to attend school. This section, however, is a brief discussion of common distal variables that may spur absenteeism or be primary to the problem. These variables include homelessness, maltreatment, school victimization, teenage pregnancy, divorce, and child self-care. Although it is beyond the scope of this book to fully explicate the relationship between absenteeism and these distal variables, clinicians and educators must be wary of the possibility that a child is missing school because of more globally problematic or taxing situations at home or elsewhere.

Homelessness

Many instances of school absenteeism are due to general factors that are beyond a child's control. Homelessness, for example, reportedly affects 100,000 youth on a given night and 2,000,000 overall per year (Cwayna, 1993). According to the National Coalition for the Homeless, many youth become homeless following abuse, family and economic problems, lack of affordable housing, or discharge from foster care. Subsequent barriers to education for these youth include frequent relocation, school fees, lack of transportation to school, clothing and school supplies, and enrollment requirements such as guardianship and school and immunization records.

Homelessness in youth has been linked to educational problems such as school dropout, severe absenteeism, expulsion, higher risk of school failure, and poor achievement in reading and arithmetic (Rafferty, 1991). With specific respect to school attendance, Rafferty (1991; Rafferty & Rollins, 1989) reported that homeless children and adolescents attended elementary (74%), junior (64%), and high (51%) school at lower rates, respectively, compared with New York City averages (89%, 86%, and 84%, respectively). Overall, about 15%–57% of homeless school-age children do not attend school regularly (Rafferty & Shinn, 1991).

Maltreatment

School absenteeism may also be associated with child maltreatment. Sexual abuse, for example, has been linked with greater school nonattendance in youth (Asher, 1988; Beitchman, Zucker, Hood, daCosta, & Akman, 1991). In addition, some evidence indicates that child maltreatment may be associated with delinquent or status offender acts, including truancy (Famularo, Kinscherff, Fenton, & Bolduc, 1990; Kakar, 1996). The relationship between school absenteeism and maltreatment is often hard to pinpoint, however, and differs widely across individual cases. In one case, for example, a parent may abuse a child and then try to conceal this by keeping the child home from school. In another case, a parent may neglect a child's attendance or corruptively allow or encourage a child to miss school. Conversely, of course, a child could miss school as a result of the various sequelae of abuse, including physical problems and anxiety, depressive, dissociative, or other mental disorders. However, one must consider the possibility as well that a child will actually increase or rigidly maintain his or her school attendance to avoid an abusive situation at home.

School Victimization

Another type of child victimization, school victimization, may also provoke school refusal behavior. According to the NCES, rates of school victimization have remained steady but high. Many high school seniors, during their previous school year, are reportedly victims of theft (38.3%), deliberate property damage (25.9%), threat without a weapon (21.6%), threat with a weapon (13.2%), injury without a weapon (11.8%), and injury from a weapon (4.9%). With respect to the last, African American students report injury from a weapon (9.8%) at school at a rate that is 2.5 times higher than that for White students (3.7%). A related concern, of course, involves the school shootings that have taken place in many high schools in the United States. No data directly link such victimization to school refusal behavior, but it is logical to conclude that some youth miss school out of fear of potential harm while there (A. Cherry, 1992; Taylor & Adelman, 1990). A school's victimization rate may also induce parents, of course, to deliberately withdraw their child from that school.

Teenage Pregnancy

Another general factor that may hinder school attendance is teenage pregnancy, which occurs in about 10%–12% of American female adolescents aged 15–19 years (White, 7%, Hispanic, 14%, African American, 26%) and is associated with greater likelihood of school dropout before and after the birth (Becker, Rankin, & Rickel, 1998; Dennison & Coleman, 1998; Seitz & Apfel, 1999). This is especially true if a second child follows soon after the first (Seitz & Apfel, 1993).

Divorce

Divorce may also lead to poorer adjustment in some youth, including instances of school absenteeism. Single-parent families are disproportionately seen among children who refuse school, and divorce can lead to regressive, attention-seeking, depressive, or defiant reactions that include refusal to attend school (e.g., Torma & Halsti, 1975). However, differences between divorced and intact families are relatively small, and most youth of divorced parents adjust normally (Buchanan, Maccoby, & Dornbusch, 1996; Twaite, Silitsky, & Luchow, 1998). Important mediating factors include, among others, a child's age, gender, and social and cognitive development; social support; finances; parental conflict and coping skills; and the noncustodial parent's availability to the child (H. E. King, 1992; Wallerstein, 1987).

Child Self-Care

Another factor that may affect absenteeism is child self-care, or "latchkey" children who come home from school without parental supervision. No strong evidence has linked self-care with absenteeism or other problem behaviors (Benin & Chong, 1993), although some unsupervised youth may engage in more delinquent acts and school absenteeism. For example, some adolescents with a history of absenteeism may be more likely to skip classes if they know they will not be supervised during and after school. In general, maternal employment has not been linked with detrimental changes in child development or absenteeism (Gottfried & Gottfried, 1988; Harvey, 1999; Lerner, 1994). In fact, some evidence indicates that educated and employed mothers tend to have children who complete more schooling (D'Amico, Haurin, & Mott, 1983).

FEATURES OF YOUTH WITH SCHOOL REFUSAL BEHAVIOR

The following sections cover specific features of youth with school refusal behavior, including demographics, internalizing and externalizing symptoms, intelligence and academic achievement, and short- and long-term consequences of school refusal behavior. In reading these sections, recall that researchers often use, interchangeably, various terms regarding absenteeism (e.g., *school refusal* and *school phobia*; see chapter 1). In the following sections, terms used by the authors are adopted. Recall as well, however, that different authors often define the same terms somewhat differently.

Demographic and Related Variables

Age of Onset

Early researchers thought that most children who refused school were quite young (i.e., ages 5–10 years; e.g., T. B. Goldberg, 1953; Rodriguez,

Rodriguez, & Eisenberg, 1959; Thompson, 1948; Wallinga, 1959). However, later evidence indicated the most common age of onset of school refusal behavior to be in early adolescence. Hersov (1960a), for example, found a mean age of 11.8 years in 50 children with school refusal and 12.7 years in 50 children with truancy. Chazan (1962) reported a peak age of onset of 11–13 years in 33 cases of school phobia. In addition, S. L. Smith (1970) examined 63 cases of school refusal and reported that 49% began their current episode of absenteeism at ages 11–14 years. Torma and Halsti (1975) reported that 75.3% of their sample of youth with school refusal and truancy were ages 10–13 years.

This last finding has been generally supported over time. With respect to admissions to specialized clinics, for example, Last and colleagues reported means of 12.2, 13.5, 14.2, and 14.3 years with respect to anxiety-based school refusal–school phobia (Hansen, Sanders, Massaro, & Last, 1998; Last, Francis, Hersen, Kazdin, & Strauss, 1987; Last & Strauss, 1990; Last, Strauss, & Francis, 1987). With respect to 64 youth with general school refusal behavior also referred to a specialized clinic, Kearney and Silverman (1996) reported a mean age of 11.1 years. Among 180 school refusal behavior referrals, the mean age was 11.9 years with an $SD = 3.1$ years (Kearney, 2000).

These figures, however, may simply reflect time of referral and not necessarily true age of onset. For example, Last and Strauss (1990) and Hansen et al. (1998) reported that onset of school refusal was, on average, about 1–2 years prior to referral. In addition, the finding of an early adolescent age of onset may reflect a "wash" of different types of youth who refuse school. For example, separation anxiety and separation anxiety disorder are generally more common in younger children (Bell-Dolan & Brazeal, 1993), whereas conduct disorder or severe delinquent or antisocial behavior are generally more common in adolescents (Moffitt, 1993). In addition, school-related fears are generally more common in younger children, whereas social anxiety is generally more common in older children and adolescents (Vasey, 1995). Also, report card and failure anxiety are seen more in youngsters (Morris, Finkelstein, & Fisher, 1976), whereas general school absence is seen more in older youth (Rood, 1989). Adding all of these youth together produces a mean age somewhere in early adolescence.

Increased age does seem predictive of more severe absenteeism (Hansen et al., 1998). In addition, children are at greater risk for school refusal behavior during their first year at a new school, and most referrals for school refusal occur in the autumn months (Kearney & Albano, 2000). Years of particular risk thus include kindergarten, 6th or 7th grade, and 9th or 10th grade; among these, initial entry into middle–junior high school is usually most problematic (Makihara, Nagaya, & Nakajima, 1985). However, children of all ages refuse to attend school.

Gender

School refusal behavior occurs fairly evenly across boys and girls (W. B. Frick, 1964; Kearney, 1995). Like age, however, the relative evenness of gender in this population may somewhat reflect a "wash" of female students who tend to have more fear–anxiety symptoms and boys who tend to have more oppositional–conduct problems. For example, Morris et al. (1976) found that girls have greater school-related anxiety than boys. Granell de Aldaz et al. (1984) found that 20.3% of females and 15.0% of males reported intense fears of school. Across fear–anxiety-based school refusal samples, Last and colleagues (Hansen et al., 1998; Last, Francis, et al., 1987; Last & Strauss, 1990; Last, Strauss, & Francis, 1987) found that 51.5% were female. Bernstein et al. (1997) also found, among 44 adolescents with anxious–depressed school refusal, that 61.4% were female. However, Bernstein, Svingen, and Garfinkel (1990) found that 55.3% of their sample of youth with school phobia were male. Among so-called truant samples, conflicting findings have been reported regarding gender (Galloway, 1982; Levanto, 1975; Rood, 1989), although boys tend to have a poorer attitude about school attendance than do girls (Zieman & Benson, 1981).

Among mixed samples of youth with school refusal behavior, male students tend to be seen. For example, Hersov (1960a) found his samples of youth with school refusal and truancy to be 73.0% male. In addition, Torma and Halsti (1975) found their sample of youth with school refusal or truancy to be 74.0% male. Granell de Aldaz, Feldman, Vivas, and Gelfand (1987) found a sample of 57 Venezualan children with school refusal to be 56.1% male. Among adolescents with chronic school refusal, Bernstein and Garfinkel (1986) found that 57.7% were male. Bernstein and Borchardt (1996) also found a large sample of 134 children with school refusal to be 54.5% male, and Kearney and Silverman (1996) reported their sample of 64 youth with general school refusal behavior to be 59.4% male. In general, however, gender is not highly predictive of cases of school absenteeism.

Race

Few studies specifically examine racial characteristics of youth with school refusal behavior, although dropout rates are known to be substantially higher among Hispanic than African American or White students (see chapter 1). Some studies show, however, that absence from school is considerably higher among African American students than among White students (Levanto, 1975; Levine, Metzendorf, & VanBoskirk, 1986; Rood, 1989). One may also examine racial characteristics from studies of admissions to specialized clinics. Across five such studies (total $N = 305$), race was primarily White (90.5%) but also African American (5.6%), Hispanic (3.6%), and Asian American (0.3%; Bernstein & Garfinkel, 1986; Bernstein et al., 1997;

Hansen et al., 1998; Kearney, 2000; Last, Francis, et al., 1987; Last, Strauss, & Francis, 1987). However, this breakdown is not the best accounting because minorities were likely underrepresented in these clinical settings. No definitive statements may be made with respect to race and school refusal behavior, although some discuss the possible effects of race on school fearfulness (Rhine & Spencer, 1975).

Socioeconomic Status

Some studies report that school absence is associated with lower family income and material disadvantage (Berg et al., 1993; Reid, 1982). One may also examine socioeconomic status rates reported from admissions to specialized clinics. Across four such studies (total $N = 222$) that derived clear Hollingshead classes for their samples, socioeconomic status was primarily lower (47.3%) but also middle (31.5%) and higher (20.3%; Bernstein & Garfinkel, 1986; Bernstein et al., 1997; Hansen et al., 1998; Last, Strauss, & Francis, 1987). One (Kearney, 2000) sample of youth with general school refusal behavior had a mean familial annual income of $29,590. These figures reflect, of course, only those who sought outpatient help for their child's misbehavior.

Acute Versus Chronic

Many descriptions of acute versus chronic school refusal behavior have been made in the literature, but few have empirically derived the percentage of each in this population. Contemporarily, Bernstein, Svingen, and Garfinkel (1990) reported that 53.9% of their sample displayed school phobia for less than 2 years and 42.1% for more than 2 years (3.9% unknown). Recall, though, that this 2-year cutoff for acute–chronic school refusal behavior is different from the 1-year cutoff outlined in chapter 1. Therefore, by some standards, the ratio of chronic to acute cases of school refusal behavior may be higher.

Referral Source

Bernstein, Svingen, et al. (1990) also examined the referral sources of their sample of youth with school phobia. Specifically, youth were referred by a school (42.1%), social agency (22.4%), parents (13.2%), court (5.3%), or other source (17.1%). Stickney and Miltenberger (1998) also reported that the responsibility for identifying youth school refusal behavior fell to principals in over 80% of cases in select schools. In many cases of primary school refusal behavior, the referral is made jointly by several people on the "front lines" of the problem, most notably parents and school officials. In cases where school refusal behavior is mixed with other problems (e.g., depression, drug use), referral sources tend to be more varied.

School Characteristics

School characteristics have also been linked to absenteeism, albeit weakly and with great contradiction across studies. For example, some claim that private schools have less absenteeism than public ones (Concannon, 1980), but little data are available to support this claim. Bos et al. (1990), in evaluating 36 secondary schools in The Netherlands, found that absenteeism was not related to school location or size. However, absenteeism was most strongly correlated positively with a school's academic level and negatively with class size. A discussion of other school characteristics thought to be predictive of school refusal behavior or dropout is presented in chapter 10.

Internalizing Symptoms and Diagnoses

The study of school absenteeism has historically often been divided into two areas: (a) psychoneurotic truancy–school refusal–school phobia and (b) delinquent truancy. The first area is often associated with neurotic, internalizing symptoms, whereas the second is often associated with conduct-disordered, externalizing symptoms. Although this dichotomy is problematic, because most youth with school refusal behavior show a confluence of symptoms, a separate description of internalizing and externalizing symptoms is made here for the sake of simplicity. Internalizing symptoms often ascribed to this population include fear–phobia, anxiety, somatic complaints, depression, and general negative affectivity.

Fear–Phobia

Fears of school in children are common, often tenuous, and sometimes reality based (Berecz, 1980; N. J. King et al., 1996; Klungness & Gredler, 1984; T. H. Ollendick & Mayer, 1984). The construct of severe irrational fear, however, has been frequently associated with school refusal behavior since A. M. Johnson, Falstein, Szurek, and Svendsen's (1941) description of school phobia. Recall from chapter 1, however, that school phobia is only a part of what was known as psychoneurotic truancy–school refusal, which by itself is only a part of all youth who refuse to attend school. Phobia of school-related stimuli thus represents only a small minority of all youth with school refusal behavior. Fear can, however, be a significant and detrimental symptom for some youth in this population and must therefore be assessed in all cases of school refusal behavior.

Early work supported the presence of fear among some youth with school refusal–phobia (e.g., Hitchcock, 1956; A. M. Johnson et al., 1941; Suttenfield, 1954; Waldfogel, Coolidge, & Hahn, 1957; Warren, 1948). More contemporary studies have focused on diagnostic categories and indicate as well that simple or specific phobia is present in many youth with anxiety-based school refusal behavior. For example, Last and Strauss (1990) found that 30.2% of their sample displayed social phobia and that 22.2% displayed simple phobia. Last, Strauss, and Francis (1987) also found, in a sample of 73 children with anxiety disorders, that 15.1% displayed a phobic disorder related to school. Bernstein et al. (1997), in their sample of 44 adolescents with anxious–depressed school refusal, found that 68.6% met criteria for social phobia, although none met criteria for simple–specific phobia.

Certainly, some children are phobic of something related to school. But what would the something be, exactly? Hersov (1960b) found 26.0% of his sample of children with school refusal to be fearful overall, although several reported specific fears of harm to the mother (34.0%), academic failure (28.0%), ridicule or harm from peers (28.0%), or the teacher (22.0%). S. L. Smith (1970) also found that 41.3% of his sample had fears of violence, illness, leaving home, and failure. Granell de Aldaz et al. (1984) found that Venezualan children with severe fears of school were generally afraid of test failure (35.0%), poor grades (33.4%), visiting the principal (29.7%), tests (18.4%), being scolded at school (18.4%), going to the blackboard (13.5%), talking to a group or class (13.4%), being called on unexpectedly in class (12.5%), becoming ill at school (11.2%), and waiting to be picked up at school (11.0%).

Granell de Aldaz et al. (1987) similarly examined 57 Venezualan children who refused school and separated them into three groups: those with adaptation problems (49.1%), those with phobia (42.1%), and those with emotional problems (8.8%). Among these children, common fears included the teacher (43.9%), other children (21.1%), and separation from parents (21.1%). Severity of school refusal was significantly predicted by school-related fears; frequent changes of school; family history of school refusal; and emotional adjustment problems, such as depression.

As one evaluates these figures, it is apparent that fear is not a predominant aspect (i.e., >50%) of children with even anxiety-based school refusal behavior. In fact, Waldron, Shrier, Stone, and Tobin (1975) found that fearfulness and anxiety were less prevalent among children with school phobia compared with children with other neuroses. Hansen et al. (1998) also found that lower fear was predictive of more severe absenteeism in children with anxiety-based school refusal. In addition, Kearney, Eisen, and Silverman (1995) evaluated youth with school refusal behavior along the Fear Survey Schedule for Children—Revised (T. H. Ollendick, 1983). The mean rating for school-related items was only 2.02, or "some," on a 1–3 scale, suggesting that these youth did not have excessive or avoidance-provoking fear. In addition, other items were rated as similarly fear provoking (e.g., going to the hospital), but these fears have not been commonly or historically associated with school refusal behavior.

Kearney and Silverman (1996) also reported, from a sample of 64 youth with general school refusal behavior, that only 6.3% were diagnosed with primary simple phobia and 3.1% with social phobia. Recall as well that Kearney and Beasley (1994) found that only 10% of children referred to treatment for absenteeism displayed fear of some specific object or situation. In addition, Foreman, Dover, and Hill (1997) evaluated adolescents with school refusal behavior on emotional priming measures of information processing but found that they did not react to allegedly aversive words, such as *teacher* or *desk*, more so than a control group. The authors concluded that "with regard to school-refusing children, it seems unlikely that their dislike of school is based on any fear of it" (p. 858). Indeed, most children who refuse school cannot point to anything in particular that upsets them about school (Lall & Lall, 1979).

Anxiety

Anxiety or neurosis has for decades also been a constant descriptor of youth with school refusal behavior (Chotiner & Forrest, 1974; Coolidge, Hahn, & Peck, 1957; Eisenberg, 1958; A. M. Johnson et al., 1941; E. Klein, 1945; T. H. Ollendick, 1979; Suttenfield, 1954; Talbot, 1957; Wallinga, 1959). This applies especially to separation anxiety disorder, which has been found to be more prevalent in this population compared with children having other neurotic conditions (Goldenberg & Goldenberg, 1970; Waldron et al., 1975). However, it should be noted that in the early literature, separation anxiety and fear were often considered to be the same construct (Hersov, 1960b).

More contemporarily, Last, Francis, et al. (1987) examined 19 youth with a phobic disorder of school and found that 47.4% additionally met criteria for no diagnosis and 36.8% for overanxious disorder; 15.8% were unspecified. Last, Francis, et al. (1987) similarly evaluated 11 youth with a phobic disorder of school and found that they also met criteria for social (27.3%) and simple (18.2%) phobia as well as overanxious (18.2%), panic (18.2%), and obsessive–compulsive (9.1%) disorder. In addition, Last and Strauss (1990) found the most common anxiety disorders in their sample of children with anxiety-based school refusal to be separation anxiety (38.1%), panic (6.3%), and posttraumatic stress (3.2%) disorder. Bernstein et al. (1997), in their sample of 44 adolescents with anxious–depressed school refusal, found overanxious (93.2%) and avoidant (50.0%) disorder as well as agoraphobia (40.0%) and separation anxiety (29.5%) and panic disorder (8.6%) to be most prevalent. A summary of these four diagnostic studies for anxiety-based school refusal behavior is in Table 2.1.

Three other studies of note include that of Bernstein and Garfinkel (1986) who, in their sample of adolescents with chronic school refusal,

TABLE 2.1
Summary of Anxiety-Related Diagnoses From Four Diagnostic
Studies of Anxiety-Based School Refusal Behavior

Diagnosis	Prevalence (%)
Overanxious disorder[a]	36.5
Social phobia	33.6
Separation anxiety disorder	27.0
Avoidant disorder[a]	16.1
Simple–specific phobia	11.7
Agoraphobia	10.2
Panic disorder	6.6
Posttraumatic stress disorder	1.5
Obsessive–compulsive disorder	0.7
Unspecified or no anxiety diagnosis	8.8

[a] According to the *Diagnostic and Statistical Manual of Mental Disorders* (3rd ed. rev.; American Psychiatric Association, 1987).

found that 16 met criteria for an anxiety disorder, most notably separation anxiety (43.8%) or overanxious disorder (18.8%) or both (37.5%). In addition, among 78 youth with severe school attendance problems, Berg et al. (1993) found that 16.7% had an anxiety/mood disorder. Hayward, Taylor, Blair-Greiner, and Strachowski (1995) also found, among 40 girls who reported panic attacks, that several displayed mild (10.0%) or moderate (7.5%) school refusal.

Mixed samples of school refusal behavior also reveal strong rates of anxiety disorder. For example, Kearney and Silverman (1996), in their sample of youth with general school refusal behavior, found that 56.3% displayed a primary anxiety diagnosis. Regarding the entire sample, these included separation anxiety (18.8%), overanxious (18.8%), avoidant (7.8%), and posttraumatic stress (1.6%) disorder. Collectively, these studies indicate that anxiety is indeed a strong component in many cases of school refusal behavior. However, it is equally clear that many youth refuse school without anxiety and for other reasons.

Somatic Complaints

Somatic or physical complaints have also been frequently and historically associated with school refusal behavior, especially in children with emotional distress when attending school (e.g., Eisenberg, 1958; Hersov, 1960a; Leton, 1962; Levanthal & Sills, 1964; Talbot, 1957). For example, Stickney and Miltenberger (1998) found that 66% of youth with school refusal presented with somatic complaints, and Last (1991) found that children with anxiety disorders were more likely to refuse school if they had somatic complaints. Physical symptoms most commonly ascribed to youth who refuse school are headaches and stomachaches (Torma & Halsti, 1975).

Bernstein et al. (1997), in an extensive evaluation of somatic complaints in this population, examined 44 anxious and depressed adolescents with school refusal. The most common somatic complaints were headaches, sweating, lightheadedness, nausea or vomiting, stomach and back pain, chest pain and palpitations, blurred vision, trouble walking, shortness of breath, loss of voice, joint pain, trouble swallowing, and menstruation symptoms. A low but positive correlation (.27) was also found between somatic complaints and severity of school nonattendance. In addition, gastrointestinal symptoms and the absence of cardiovascular symptoms were predictive of separation anxiety disorder; muscular symptoms were predictive of *Diagnostic and Statistical Manual of Mental Disorders* (3rd ed. rev. [DSM–III–R]; American Psychiatric Association, 1987) avoidant disorder.

Depression

Depression and school refusal behavior have also been linked historically (e.g., Agras, 1959), and a review was conducted to examine this relationship (Kearney, 1993). Across seven studies that examined syndromes or diagnoses of depression and school refusal behavior, a mean comorbidity estimate of 31.4% was derived (Bernstein & Garfinkel, 1986, 1988; Hersov, 1960a; Kolvin, Berney, & Bhate, 1984; Last, Francis, et al., 1987; Last & Strauss, 1990; Last, Strauss, & Francis, 1987). However, across seven studies that examined *symptoms* of depression and school refusal behavior, a mean comorbidity estimate of 47.6% was derived (Atkinson, Quarrington, Cyr, & Atkinson, 1989; Baker & Wills, 1978; Campbell, 1955; S. Davidson, 1960; Kearney, Silverman, & Eisen, 1989; S. L. Smith, 1970; Waldron et al., 1975). In addition, Borchardt, Giesler, Bernstein, and Crosby (1994) compared inpatient and outpatient youth with school refusal and found the hospitalized group to have more depressive diagnoses, severe symptoms, and greater likelihood of single-parent families and physical abuse. Suicidal behavior is sometimes linked to school refusal behavior as well (Shaffer, 1974).

These studies, of course, were dominated by youth with anxiety- and depressive-based school refusal behavior. Depression is clearly a common occurrence in this particular subset of school refusal behavior but, as the overall figures indicate, not necessarily present in even a majority of these anxiety/depressive cases. Depression is not a condition that predominates in most cases of general school refusal behavior either. For example, Kearney and Silverman (1996), in their sample of youth with general school refusal behavior, found that only 6.3% displayed a primary diagnosis of major depression. Like fear and anxiety, depression in this population should be assessed but not assumed.

Internalizing Symptoms and General Negative Affectivity

Because fear, anxiety, somatic complaints, and depression seem characteristic of many youth with school refusal behavior, covert symptoms are often a high priority during assessment and treatment. However, the presence of well-defined fear and related syndromes, as well as children who readily identify specific, fearful school-related stimuli, are not typical of this population. Therefore, it may be untenable to focus specifically on diagnoses or other rigidly defined categories in this population. In fact, historically, researchers have struggled with this phenomenon when describing children with school refusal behavior. For example, loosely worded phrases such as "severe emotional upset" and "irrational/morbid dread" have been commonly used to describe children with anguish and physical complaints when attending school (Berg, Nichols, & Pritchard, 1969; De Sousa & De Sousa, 1980; Eisenberg, 1958; Kelly, 1973).

Many children show overlapping symptoms of fear, anxiety, and depression, and several researchers have evaluated this confluence of covert symptoms among youth with anxiety and other disorders. This condition is sometimes referred to as *negative affectivity* and refers to a global state or continuum of anxiety and depression or emotional distress (Kendall, Kortlander, Chansky, & Brady, 1992; N. J. King, Ollendick, & Gullone, 1991; Norvell, Brophy, & Finch, 1985; Watson & Clark, 1984). Other data suggest that fear, anxiety, and depression in clinical samples of children are somewhat more distinct (i.e., anxiety–negative affect, depression–low positive affect, fear–physiological hyperarousal), although each construct is still moderately correlated with one another (Chorpita, Albano, & Barlow, 1998).

The construct of negative affectivity, although it is evolving, may be useful for describing some youth who refuse school. Indeed, the construct allows for global or fluctuating emotional distress with somatic complaints and shies away from stricter categories, such as specific phobia, that require children to readily identify feared school-related stimuli. Kearney and Silverman (1996), in their taxonomy of children with school refusal behavior, contended that a subset refuse school to avoid objects, situations, or vaguely defined stimuli that provoke a general sense of negative affectivity and somatic complaints. This subset is discussed at more length in chapters 3–6.

Externalizing Symptoms and Diagnoses

Externalizing Symptoms Specific to School Refusal Behavior

Although researchers have focused heavily on internalizing symptoms with respect to children with school refusal behavior, various externalizing symptoms are also highly relevant to this population. The most common examples include verbal and physical aggression, noncompliance, clinging, refusal to move, hiding, running away from school or home, temper tantrums (including crying, screaming, and flailing arms and legs), lying, reassurance seeking and, occasionally, self-injury–mutilation (Kearney, 1995). Hersov (1960a) also identified wandering from home and stealing as strong indicators of children with truancy.

Externalizing behaviors can manifest themselves in various youth with school refusal behavior for different reasons. Oftentimes they are manifested in conjunction with internalizing symptoms. Following are some different scenarios under which youth with school refusal behavior commonly show externalizing symptoms:

- Externalizing behaviors may be an expression of covert symptoms. For example, a child could "freeze" or refuse to move out of sheer panic, or a child with depression could show oppositional, irritable, or uncooperative behavior (Kashani, Holcomb, & Orvaschel, 1986). Phobic reactions in children may also be marked by crying and tantrums (*DSM–IV*, American Psychiatric Association, 1994).
- Externalizing behaviors may be used to advertise the nature of an anxiety-based school refusal problem or to exaggerate discomfort. For example, a child with school refusal behavior may cling to a parent to make known a particular somatic complaint or to induce guilt and acquiescence.
- Externalizing behaviors may be used to avoid or ameliorate an anxiety-provoking situation. Examples include running away from school, pushing a parent out of the way to hide in a room, and continually asking the same questions (e.g., reassurance seeking) or making the same demands of parents.
- Externalizing behaviors may be used to garner attention from parents and others. For example, a child may throw a tantrum in the morning or harm him- or herself to draw attention from siblings and delay going to school.
- Externalizing behaviors may signify a test of parental resolve or an attempt to secure more tangible reinforcers. For example, a child may have learned that the best way to obtain privileges is get parents to bribe him or her to go to school following initial noncompliance to do so.
- Externalizing behaviors such as verbal or physical aggression may be used to intimidate parents or others into acquiescence.
- Externalizing behaviors such as aggression, noncompliance, tantrums, or other misbehaviors within a classroom may be used to force school officials to allow the child to contact (e.g.,

telephone call) parents for attention or reassurance–anxiety reduction. Classroom misbehaviors may also be shown to induce suspension or expulsion from school.

- Externalizing behaviors are often used as well to hide school refusal behavior from authority figures. Exiting school early and then lying about one's whereabouts or other important details are common behaviors to do so.

Conduct and Oppositional Defiant Disorder

The scenarios just mentioned do not necessarily qualify a youth for a formal disorder, but school refusal behavior is sometimes part of an overall conduct or oppositional defiant disorder. Bernstein and Garfinkel (1986), in their sample of adolescents with chronic school refusal–phobia, for example, found that 23.1% met criteria for conduct disorder. C. Pritchard, Cotton, and Cox (1992) also found that 20.4% of their sample of adolescents with truancy had fought with others and that 46.6% had engaged in vandalism. Berg et al. (1993), in a study of 78 youth with severe school attendance problems, found that 32.1% had a disruptive behavior disorder. Kearney and Silverman (1996), in their sample of youth with general school refusal behavior, found that 7.8% had a primary diagnosis of oppositional defiant or conduct disorder.

Substance-related disorder, a common correlate of conduct disorder, may also trigger or arise from school absence. Truancy has been linked, for example, to increased smoking and alcohol use as well as misuse of solvents; marijuana; and hard drugs such as cocaine, heroin, amphetamines, and others (Charlton & Blair, 1989; C. Pritchard et al., 1992). What remains unclear, however, is which condition—school absence or drug use—typically begins first.

Researchers have traditionally paid closer attention to internalizing behaviors among youth with school refusal behavior, but externalizing behaviors are just as, if not more, prevalent. In addition, parents and teachers often complain first about the obvious features of school refusal behavior and second about other externalizing problems (e.g., refusal to complete homework) that are peripherally related to absenteeism. Therefore, a large spectrum of potential behavior problems should be carefully assessed when addressing youth with school refusal behavior.

Other Mental and Medical Problems

Youth with school refusal behavior may display other mental disorders as well. Enuresis, for example, has been shown by some to be prominent in youth defined with truancy (Hersov, 1960a; Torma & Halsti, 1975), although less so in children who are anxious about going to school or those with general school refusal behavior (Kearney & Silverman, 1996; Waldron et al., 1975). In addition, some children show eating, sleeping, or related problems because of school-related stress, to manipulate parents or others, or to escape school. School refusal behavior has also been linked in some cases to severe problems, such as Tourette's syndrome (Linet, 1985), schizophrenia (Rubenstein & Hastings, 1980), bipolar disorder (Berg, 1992), and pervasive developmental disorder (Kurita, 1991).

Many youth with school refusal behavior also have no comorbid disorders or misbehaviors. For example, Bernstein and Garfinkel (1986), in their sample of adolescents with chronic school refusal–phobia, found that 11.5% met criteria for no mental disorder. In addition, Berg et al. (1993) found that 51.3% of those with severe school attendance problems had no mental disorder. Kearney and Silverman (1996), in their sample of youth with general school refusal behavior, found that 26.6% did not meet criteria for a mental disorder. These figures may reflect, however, children with symptoms of different disorders that do not rise to the level of formal diagnosis (i.e., subclinical cases).

Serious medical disorders may also plague youth with school refusal behavior. Asthma, for example, is closely associated with school absenteeism (see chapter 1). In addition, Iwatani et al. (1997) found that students with anxiety- or depressive-based school refusal had higher levels of blood glucose compared with controls, which may indicate a higher rate of glucoregulatory disorder in this population. Tomoda, Miike, Yonamine, Adachi, and Shiraishi (1997) also found that adolescents with school refusal display biorhythm desynchronization, especially with respect to body temperature and sleep–wake circadian rhythms. Of course, any other serious medical problem could cause a child to miss extensive periods of school as well (e.g., disease, traumatic brain injury or illness, gastrointestinal disorders such as recurrent abdominal pain; see Kearney, 2000; Rubenstein & Hastings, 1980; and Stein, 1996).

Intelligence and Academic Achievement

Controversy lingers over whether intellectual or academic problems trigger many cases of school refusal behavior. Learning problems could induce emotional distress and refusal to attend school in some cases (O'Brien, 1982), but data have not generally linked intellectual and academic problems to later school refusal behavior. In fact, with few exceptions (Thompson, 1948; Torma & Halsti, 1975), researchers have generally supported the notion that children who refuse school are of average or high average intelligence and display adequate academic achievement prior to their absenteeism (Berg, Collins, McGuire, & O'Melia, 1975; Chazan, 1962; T. B.

Goldberg, 1953; Hampe, Miller, Barrett, & Noble, 1973; Hersov, 1960a; Jacobsen, 1948; Jarvis, 1964; Leton, 1962; Rodriguez et al., 1959; S. L. Smith, 1970; Talbot, 1957; Van Houten, 1948; Waldron et al., 1975). Kearney and Silverman (1996) also found no comorbidity between school refusal behavior and learning disability in their sample. These data indicate that academic failure may be a consequence of, but not necessarily a common trigger of or precursor to, school refusal behavior.

One notable exception involved a comparison of predominantly depressed inpatient adolescents with a history of school refusal with those without such a history but with other psychiatric disorders (Naylor, Staskowski, Kenney, & King, 1994). No difference in overall intelligence was found, but the school refusal group displayed (a) lower verbal intelligence and academic achievement in math, reading, and writing and (b) greater prevalence of language impairments and learning disability. The predominance of depression, however, raises the possibility that depressive symptoms triggered school refusal behavior and subsequent learning problems in these youth.

Personality Characteristics

The study of personality characteristics of youth with school phobia–refusal has historically revolved around symptoms of fear, separation anxiety, and other mental conditions. However, other personality characteristics have been evaluated in this population. For example, Hersov (1960a) found that 52.0% of his sample of youth with school refusal were "excessively passive, dependent and inhibited" (p. 135). Berg and McGuire (1971) also found that youth with school phobia ages 11–15 years, especially girls, tended to be immature and asocial. The authors suggested that this was due to an overreliance on parents for different life tasks and a reluctance to discuss fears. Adams, McDonald, and Huey (1966) also found evidence of bisexual conflict among children with school phobia.

Other studies have shown less evidence for maladaptive personality characteristics in this population. For example, Berg and Collins (1974) compared children ages 11–15 years having school phobia with those with other disorders but found no differences with respect to oppositional behavior or "wilfulness." Similarly, Nichols and Berg (1970) compared children having acute and chronic school phobia with children with other conduct and neurotic disorders on a measure of self-evaluation–self-esteem. Children with chronic school phobia had slightly less positive self-evaluation, but no major differences between the groups were found. The authors thus disputed Leventhal and colleagues' claims (Leventhal & Sills, 1964; Leventhal, Weinberger, Stander, & Stearns, 1967) that school phobia was due primarily to elevated self-evaluation. Although some researchers have reported greater immaturity and dependency among youth with school refusal behavior, no consistent data support any particular personality profile in this population (Trueman, 1984).

SHORT- AND LONG-TERM CONSEQUENCES OF SCHOOL REFUSAL BEHAVIOR

Short-Term Consequences

School refusal behavior is one of the most disruptive conditions with which a child and family must contend during the developmental period. Common short-term consequences of school refusal behavior include severe child distress, problems with homework and declining grades, social alienation, increased risk of legal trouble, family conflict, severe disruption in a family's daily life routine, financial expense, and potential child maltreatment and lack of supervision. Many of these short-term consequences are described and addressed in greater depth throughout this book.

Long-Term Consequences and Prognosis

Early School Refusal–Phobia Follow-Up Studies

Long-term consequences of school refusal behavior have been identified in many follow-up studies. Rodriguez et al. (1959), for example, followed up 41 children with school phobia a mean of 3 years after initial clinic contact. Most (70.7%) of the sample attended school regularly, but this success rate differed substantially for those under age 11 (88.9%) and those over age 11 (35.7%) years. In addition, 79.3% of the successful group had made satisfactory academic and social progress. Among the nonsuccessful group, poor outcome was related to family problems (33.3%), schizophrenia (25.0%), inadequate treatment (25.0%), and "medical mismanagement" (16.7%, p. 543). Age and severity of psychopathology were therefore most important in determining long-term outcome. Warren (1960) also followed up 16 youth hospitalized for ongoing school refusal and found that 62.5% had severe phobic or neurotic conditions as adults.

Coolidge, Brodie, and Feeney (1964) followed up 47 children with school phobia and found that they gravitated toward three groups. The first group (27.7%), "those without limitation," displayed normal school achievement and improved independence. The second group (42.6%), those "moderately limited," improved somewhat but still had key social and academic problems. The third group (29.8%), those "severely limited or incapacitated" (p. 677), had psychotic, personality, or other disorders that negatively affected most areas of their life. Unlike the first two groups, this last group was predominantly male.

Weiss and Burke (1967) followed up a previously hospitalized group of 16 youth with school phobia 5–10 years later. Most of the sample (75%) was rated as excellent or good; the rest was rated as fair. Almost all had returned to school, but most were still anxious, depressed, phobic, and socially inhibited. It is interesting that most attributed their success to "the milieu aspect of treatment" and the authors reported that "only a few saw their problem in terms of fear of school" (p. 295).

Berg's School Refusal–Phobia Follow-Up Studies

Berg has conducted several follow-up studies in this area, including an examination of 21 youth with school phobia (mean age 13.7 years) hospitalized a mean of 9 months (Berg, 1970). The mean follow-up period was 13 months. Most of the sample maintained good attendance at either school (12 of 15; 80%) or work (4 of 6; 67%), although many continued to have problems adjusting at home (33.3%) and to peers (33.3%). Berg, Butler, and Hall (1976) also followed up 100 adolescents treated for school phobia in an inpatient unit. The sample was sorted into four groups of severity an average of 3 years after discharge. Among these groups, predictors of poor outcome included poor clinical state at discharge and, surprisingly, higher intelligence:

- The first group (17%) did not attend school at all, and several had severe symptoms of agoraphobia, depression, and other incapacitating conditions.
- The second group (18%) was slightly improved; half still had attendance problems, and several sought treatment for various mental conditions.
- The third group (38%) was a middle category in which 11 people were slightly improved less than 50% of the time and 27 were much improved more than 50% of the time. Half continued to have problems going to school.
- The fourth group (27%) had some neurotic symptoms but no need for additional treatment. Some (20%) continued to have attendance problems.

Berg and Jackson (1985) also followed up 143 adolescents a mean of 10.1 years after inpatient treatment for school refusal. Many of these youth required later treatment for an additional condition (44.8%) and generally had depression and poor social relationships and employment histories. Of those interviewed, only 43.6% were rated as well or as much improved, although significant predictors of good outcome included intelligence and treatment before age 14 years.

Other School Refusal–Phobia Follow-Up Studies

Baker and Wills (1979) examined 67 people ages 16–24 years who, as youth ages 6–16 years, had had school phobia and were seen at a child guidance clinic. Most (85.1%) were working or attending school full time. Those who had missed school, however, did not show a greater need for later psychiatric treatment, more serious diagnoses, or a certain gender. In contrast, Butcher (1983) reported a case of long-term school phobia that did lead to separation anxiety in adulthood.

Valles and Oddy (1984) followed up 34 youth with school refusal a mean of 7.2 years after discharge from an inpatient unit. Almost half (47.1%) had successfully returned to school following discharge, but the remainder had experienced continued problems attending school. A comparison of these groups revealed that the nonattenders tended to be older, (legally) convicted, and unmarried and to have conflictive and unstable families, difficulty in social relationships, longer admission histories, anxiety, and need for additional treatment. However, no differences were found with respect to current occupational status or early historical factors (e.g., separation problems, child or family psychiatric history, severity of school refusal, peer relationships, precipitants to school refusal).

Timberlake (1984) examined 64 children ages 6–11 years with school phobia who had undergone psychodynamically based social work intervention for 6 months to more than 2 years. Follow-up 10–20 years later revealed that a large majority (96.9%) had already completed or were completing their education, had no recurrence of school attendance problems (64.1%), participated frequently in social activities (98.4%), worked at least part time (90.6%), and had no work-related problems (100.0%). Regression analysis revealed several significant predictors of positive long-term functioning, including

> mutual agreement between the social worker and clients about termination, the lack of familial stress at intake, the mother's regular participation in treatment, less frequent contact with grandparents at intake, the rapidity of the child's return to school during treatment, the absence of a parental history of phobia or fearfulness, the father's regular participation in treatment, and the child's lack of apprehensiveness about many things at intake. (pp. 16–17)

Ohtaka et al. (1986) examined 40 Japanese adults who were treated for school refusal as adolescents. Follow-up an average of 14 years later revealed three groups: 47.5% displayed good social and occupational adjustment, 17.5% displayed fair adjustment, and 35.0% displayed poor adjustment. The latter group also had more family and psychiatric problems. Flakierska, Lindstrom, and Gillberg (1988) also examined, 15–20 years later,

35 Swedish children who were treated for school refusal at ages 7–12 years. This group was compared with matched controls, but no differences were found with respect to school attendance, physical health, social adjustment, criminal offenses, and inpatient care. The school refusal group, however, did have fewer children and had sought significantly more outpatient care for depression and separation anxiety disorder.

Buitelaar, van Andel, Duyx, and van Strien (1994) followed up 25 adolescents treated for anxiety- and depressive-based school refusal. Five years later 52.0% still met criteria for an anxiety, depressive, conduct–personality, or other disorder. Those who were still symptomatic also had higher levels of social fear, depression, and unsatisfactory social relationships compared with those no longer symptomatic. Silove and Manicavasagar (1993) also found that a history of school refusal was not predictive of adult panic disorder, although early separation anxiety was associated with school refusal in one's siblings or children. Finally, Gorman and Pollitt (1996), in a 20-year longitudinal study in Guatemala, found that children who remained in school longer were buffered cognitively against the effects of high-risk factors such as poor health conditions and low parental education.

Truancy Follow-Up Studies

Several authors have also looked at youth with truancy, which is usually defined in these studies as simple absence from school. A consistent finding, historically, is that poor school attendance is predictive of later occupational difficulties such as unstable job histories and unemployment (e.g., N. Cherry, 1976; Farrington, 1980; Gray, Smith, & Rutter, 1980). Others have found that early absenteeism is related to school dropout, leaving home early, early marriage and marital problems, having children with truancy, and various psychiatric and violence problems (Kandel, Raveis, & Kandel, 1984; Robins & Ratcliff, 1980).

Hibbett and colleagues (Hibbett & Fogelman, 1990; Hibbett, Fogelman, & Manor, 1990) examined adult outcomes of youth who were truant at age 11 years, 16 years, or both. A survey of 10,640 people and teacher ratings revealed that 0.4% were truant at age 11 years, whereas 19.4% were truant at age 16 years. At age 23 years, and compared with those who were not truant, those who were truant had more unstable job histories and total jobs, shorter length of jobs, lower family income, and greater likelihood of unemployment. In addition, those with past truancy tended to have later marital and psychological problems. This group had greater marital disruption; had more children, and at an earlier age; and were more likely to smoke and be depressed. These findings were largely independent of gender.

Summary

About one-third of youth in these follow-up studies continued to have serious adjustment problems later in life. Roughly another third showed only moderate adjustment over time. Although many youth do return to school, the effects of problematic absenteeism tend to linger. The variability of these effects, however, suggest that many youth with school refusal behavior adjust fine after absenteeism. Positive prognostic signs generally include younger age, female gender, early intervention, good functioning at the end of treatment, and less severe school refusal behavior and child–parent psychopathology.

FAMILIES WITH YOUTH WITH SCHOOL REFUSAL BEHAVIOR

Family Dynamics—Interaction Patterns

Early Research

The characteristics of families of youth with school refusal behavior are almost as heterogeneous as those of the youth themselves. Many psychodynamically oriented authors initially characterized these families as enmeshed or dominated by a problematic mother–child relationship (see chapter 1; A. M. Johnson et al., 1941). Common descriptors of the latter included dependent, hostile, vacillating, exploitative, and guilt inducing (W. B. Frick, 1964). In addition, fathers were often described as passive and unwilling to interfere in the lives of other family members. In case studies, school refusal behavior was largely associated with a hostile or self-perceived incompetent mother who rejected her child or who facilitated overdependency and school absenteeism.

Hersov (1960b) tried to evaluate these dynamics more empirically and purportedly identified three primary types of parent–child relationships in youth with school refusal. These types matched, to some extent, those from the early psychodynamic literature:

- "An over-indulgent mother and an inadequate, passive father dominated at home by a wilful [*sic*], stubborn and demanding child who is most often timid and inhibited in social situations away from home."
- A severe, controlling and demanding mother who manages her children without much assistance from her passive husband. The child is most often timid and fearful away from home and passive and obedient at home, but may become stubborn and rebellious at puberty."

- "A firm, controlling father who plays a large part in home management and an over-indulgent mother closely bound to and dominated by a wilful [*sic*], stubborn and demanding child, who is alert, friendly, and outgoing away from home." (p. 140)

Despite the questionable methodology of early studies of family dynamics in this population, the concept of enmeshment remained a powerful descriptor. For example, Berg and McGuire (1974) found that mothers of children with school phobia encouraged affection and communication with their youngsters to a much greater extent than control mothers. The authors concluded that these mothers were overprotective and preferred their children to be excessively dependent. In addition, Waldron et al. (1975) compared families of children with school phobia with families of children with other neuroses. The school phobia group had significantly more child–mother separation problems, parental failure to recognize a child's need for separateness, resentment of child demands, scapegoating of a child, and closer mother–child than mother–father bonds. In general, these problems affected mothers more so than fathers. Timberlake (1984), in her sample of 74 children with school phobia, also found that 68.9% of parents generally had an overprotective attitude toward their child.

Contemporary Research

More contemporary researchers have evaluated a wider swath of family dynamics in this population using more psychometrically sound instruments. Bernstein, Svingen, et al. (1990), for example, examined 76 families of children with school phobia using the Family Assessment Measure (FAM; Skinner, Steinhauer, & Santa-Barbara, 1983). The FAM consists of subscales for task accomplishment (TA), role performance (RP), communication (C), affective expression, affective involvement, control, and values and norms (VN). No dysfunctional patterns were initially seen, but a comparison of intact (62%) and single-parent (38%) families revealed more RP problems in the latter. This reflects problems in role adaptation, definition, and integration. A further analysis across child diagnosis revealed no dysfunctional patterns in an anxiety-disorder-only group; this compared with three dysfunctional patterns in a depressive-disorder-only (TA, RP, VN) group, four dysfunctional patterns in an anxiety-and-depressive-disorder (TA, RP, C, VN) group, and seven dysfunctional patterns in a no-anxiety-or-depressive-disorder group. The authors attributed the lack of problems in the anxiety-disorder-only group to the children's "quiet, compliant, and eager to please" (p. 29) nature.

Bernstein and Borchardt (1996) also evaluated families of children with school refusal and found two major types: mother only ($n = 40$) and two biological parents ($n = 61$). A comparison of these groups revealed that mother-only families displayed greater problems in communication and role performance. With respect to a school refusal population, the latter may indicate difficulty establishing boundaries for household tasks and school responsibilities. In addition, Bernstein, Warren, Massie, and Thuras (1999) examined 46 adolescents with anxious–depressed school refusal and found that many of the youth (50.0%), fathers (38.1%), and mothers (24.4%) classified their family as extreme (i.e., poor cohesion and adaptability). Such extremity was related to depression in the adolescents.

Kearney and Silverman (1995) provided a synopsis of historical literature and contemporary evidence in this area and contended that six patterns of family dynamics generally pervade families of youth who refuse school. The *enmeshed* family is characterized by parental overprotectiveness and overindulgence toward a child as well as dependency or less independence among family members. On the basis of Family Environment Scale (FES; see chapter 4) data, the authors reported that 32.8% of a sample of families in this population scored significantly lower than normative values on the Independence subscale. Although enmeshment is indicative of some families, particularly those with young children just starting to refuse school, the dynamic is not nearly as pervasive as once thought in this population.

Another pattern is the *conflictive* family, which is characterized by hostility, violence, and coercive processes (Patterson, 1982). This pattern pervades many families of youth with school refusal behavior, although it is not necessarily long standing in nature. On the basis of FES data reported by Kearney and Silverman (1995), 23.4% of families were classified as "conflict-oriented." Others have also confirmed the presence of a conflictive, violent family subtype in youth with school refusal behavior (Honma, 1986; Mihara & Ichikawa, 1986).

The *detached* family is characterized by poor involvement among family members in one another's lives. In many such cases, a child's misbehavior is not addressed until it is extreme. The *isolated* family is marked by little extrafamilial contact on the part of its members and may be less likely to seek treatment compared with other families. FES data reported by Kearney and Silverman (1995) indicated that 28.1% and 31.3% of families scored very low, respectively, on subscales of intellectual–cultural and active–recreational orientation.

The *healthy* family is characterized by cohesive, appropriately expressive members who solve problems effectively. FES data reported by Kearney and Silverman (1995) indicated that 39.1% of families were support oriented and characterized by cohesion and expressiveness. Finally, many families of this population show *mixed* familial profiles, or characteristics of two or more family patterns. Kearney and Silverman (1995) outlined how these familial patterns were related to different functions of school refusal behavior (see chapter 4).

Other Family Factors

Other family factors intermittently studied in this population include birth order, family size, marital problems and status, and parental psychopathology. S. L. Smith (1970), for example, found that 46.0% of his sample was the youngest child and that most children with school refusal (34.9%) came from families of two children. Similarly, Berg, Butler, and McGuire (1972) found that 55.0% of their sample of 100 youth with school phobia were only or youngest children and that the average number of children in these families was 2.93. Torma and Halsti (1975) also found that 43.8% of their sample of 73 children with school refusal and truancy were the only or the youngest child in their family and that 32.9% of the entire sample came from families of two or fewer children. Makihara et al. (1985) found that one third of their sample of 91 youth with school refusal were the only child in their family. Other researchers, however, found a higher prevalence of eldest children in their school refusal behavior samples (e.g., Baker & Wills, 1978; Warnecke, 1964). In general, children with school refusal behavior tend to be the only or eldest child or the youngest child in large families.

With respect to marital issues, Timberlake (1984) reported that 52.7% of parents of children with school phobia had admitted or some apparent marital problems, 79.7% of the families had communication problems, and 55.4% of families had one or more family stressors. It is interesting that all sets of parents were married. Torma and Halsti (1975) reported that only 45.2% of their sample lived with both parents, and that 16.4% of the children had a mother aged less than 21 years at time of birth. D. G. Ollendick (1979) also reported, from a sample of 177 4th-grade students, that boys from single-parent families were absent from school significantly more so than boys from two-parent families. A trend in this direction was also found for girls. In general, single-parent families tend to be overrepresented among children with school refusal behavior (Bernstein & Borchardt, 1996; Bernstein, Svingen, et al., 1990; Makihara et al., 1985; Reid, 1984; Sommer, 1985).

Some researchers have also evaluated the mental health of parents of children with school refusal. Berg, Butler, and Pritchard (1974) found that 44.0% of mothers and 13% of fathers of 100 youth with school phobia were "psychiatrically ill" (p. 466), primarily with affective disorder (29% of mothers). Torma and Halsti (1975) also reported that 80.8% of mothers and 47.9% of fathers of children with school refusal or truancy had at least fairly severe neurosis or immature personality. Severe disturbance in the form of psychosis, alcoholism, or asocial behavior was also present in 15.1% of mothers and 21.9% of fathers. Berg (1976) also found that the incidence of school phobia in young adolescents rose to 14% among mothers with agoraphobia. In addition, Timberlake (1984) found that many parents of children with school phobia themselves had medical problems or somatic complaints (62.2%), a history of fearfulness or phobia (59.5%), or social inactivity (67.6%). Last, Francis et al. (1987) also found, in their sample of children with school phobia, that many mothers met criteria for an anxiety (57.1%) or affective (14.3%) disorder or no disorder (35.7%).

Bernstein and Garfinkel (1988) also compared first- and second-degree relatives of six children having severe school phobia with those of five children with affective–anxiety disorders. Of 82 relatives in the school phobia group, 41.5% had an anxiety or depressive disorder, or both, compared with 24.6% of 57 relatives in the control group. Among the parents and siblings of these children, 72.7% displayed an anxiety or depressive disorder compared with 20.0% in the control group. In addition, parents of children with school phobia, compared with controls, had a higher rate of substance abuse and greater problems in role performance, communication, affective expression, and control. Finally, Martin, Cabrol, Bouvard, Lepine, and Mouren-Simeoni (1999) evaluated 51 youth with anxiety-based school refusal, dividing them into separation anxiety disorder and phobic groups. Mothers and fathers of children in the separation-anxiety disorder group had significantly less simple or social phobia (16.0% and 8.0%) compared with mothers and fathers in the phobic group (50.0% and 30.8%) but significantly more panic disorder or agoraphobia (56.0% and 27.3% vs. 19.2% and 0.0%).

ETIOLOGY OF SCHOOL REFUSAL BEHAVIOR

Family factors clearly influence many cases of school refusal behavior, but the complete etiology of this population is highly complex, variable and, quite frankly, often unknown. Even after a thorough assessment of a child with school refusal behavior, questions about what caused the problem in the first place are the most difficult to answer. Especially difficult questions are (a) whether a stressful life event, trauma, or mental disorder, such as depression or conduct disorder, triggered school refusal behavior and other problems; (b) whether comorbid problems developed simultaneously with school refusal behavior and currently help maintain the problem; or (c) whether primary school refusal behavior led to other problems, such as general noncompliance or academic failure. In essence, the classic "chicken and egg" dilemma fits this population well.

Knowing the full answer as to why a particular case of school refusal behavior began is often not necessary to start treatment. However, a working knowledge of some of the leading precipitating factors of school refusal behavior, as well as contemporary integrative models of constructs that are closely related to the problem, may be helpful and are presented here.

Precipitating Factors

As described earlier, school phobia–refusal was originally thought to be precipitated by some life event that threatened an overly dependent mother–child relationship (A. M. Johnson et al., 1941). Such events were thought to include illness, a move to a new neighborhood, changes in the family or school, hospitalization of the mother, marital strife, or some aversive incident at school, among others (Eisenberg, 1958; Hersov, 1960b). Contemporary work has not supported an overwhelming presence of enmeshment in this population, but evidence does indicate that specific precipitants, including concerns about separation, can be identified in many cases of school refusal behavior.

S. L. Smith (1970), for example, in 63 cases of youth with anxiety-based school refusal, found that major precipitants were newness or change at school (42.9%), a school-related frightening event (14.3%), legitimate absence from school (12.7%), family event (11.1%), starting school for the first time (4.8%), and fright unrelated to school (1.6%). It is interesting that 12.7% of the children had no precipitant for their school refusal behavior. Similarly, Torma and Halsti (1975), in 73 children with school refusal or truancy, found that major precipitants included change of teacher, class, or school (46.6%); serious illness in the family (34.2%); family's move to new place (26.0%); death in the family (21.9%); parental separation or divorce (21.9%); and parental marital crisis (19.2%).

Waldron et al. (1975) found in children with school phobia that major precipitants included frightening events at school (37.1%); threat to well-being at school (33.3%); perceived but not actual danger of death (17.9%); death of a family member (15.6%); and "absence, illness, separation, or depression in a parent" (21.7%, p. 806). No precipitant was identified in 42.4% of cases. Hersov (1960b) and Timberlake (1984) also reported no clear precipitant in 34.0% and 41.9%, respectively, of their samples of children with school refusal–phobia.

This heterogeneity of precipitating factors parallels the general symptom heterogeneity of this population. For children with anxiety-based school refusal behavior, school, family, and other life stressors almost certainly play a crucial role, as evidenced from the above studies. For children who refuse school for other reasons, however, precipitants are less clear. More ominous is the fact that a substantial percentage of children refuse school following no obvious precipitant. This helps explain why determining the etiology in many cases of school refusal behavior is a maddening task.

Etiological Models of Negative Affectivity and Antisocial Behavior

Negative Affectivity

An integral set of constructs related to school refusal behavior is fear–anxiety–depression or negative affectivity. Traditional etiological theories of these constructs are explicated at length elsewhere (e.g., Eisen & Kearney, 1995) and include psychodynamicism, classical and operant conditioning, two-factor theory, approach–withdrawal theory, observational learning, cognitive and affective models, psychosocial stressors, coping models, and preparedness theory, among others. Problematic attachment has also been linked specifically to school phobia (Bowlby, 1980). Etiological theories of fear–anxiety–depression also include biological factors, such as hyperventilation, neurotransmitter and brain dysfunction, mitral valve prolapse, and genetic transmission, among others.

An integrative theory of childhood fear and anxiety has also been proposed by Albano et al. (1996; see also Barlow, 1988). In this model, a child may have some biological vulnerability or temperamental–behavioral inhibition toward hypersensitivity to stress. With subsequent aversive life events, this may activate a general stress response involving hypothalamic–adrenocortical areas of the brain. This activation may provoke fear or a sense of psychological vulnerability marked by personal feelings of unpredictability or poor control over one's environment. This psychological vulnerability may also lead to fear or anxious apprehension, or it may be ameliorated by family dynamics, coping and interpersonal skills, social support, or other variables. This model may help explain childhood depression as well, although different cognitive misinterpretations are likely involved (Hammen & Rudolph, 1996).

This model could apply to some forms of school refusal behavior. A child who is biologically predisposed to stress could experience aversive events at school that trigger or precipitate additional stress and fear. This could be manifested by problems such as panic attacks, specific fear, or social anxiety. A child who feels he or she cannot control or cope with these stressors may then show various behaviors to avoid school. However, such refusal could be met and quashed immediately by a number of factors, including relief from the stressor (e.g., by switching classes) or early intervention to increase coping skills. In addition, of course, a child's anxiety may interact with some desire for attention. In this case, potential mediating variables to quash the behavior include firm, appropriate parenting or lack of attention to inappropriate conduct.

Antisocial Behavior

With respect to antisocial or disruptive behaviors, etiology is equally if not more complex than that of negative affectivity. Common etiological factors ascribed to antisocial behavior include, among others, the following (P. J. Frick, 1998; Henggeler, Schoenwald, Borduin, Rowland, & Cunningham, 1998; Hinshaw & Anderson, 1996):

- youth factors, such as low verbal and social skills, belief that others are hostile, reward dominance, positive attitude toward antisocial behavior, male gender, neuropsychological changes, attention deficits, and comorbid psychiatric conditions
- family factors, such as ineffective parenting and supervision, conflict, abuse, parental psychopathology, divorce, genetics, and detachment
- peer factors, such as association with deviant peers
- school factors, such as dropout, poor achievement, and a chaotic school environment
- neighborhood factors, such as disorganization, transience, high crime, lack of support, and poverty
- cultural factors, such as exposure to violence.

More integratively, Moffitt (1993) indicated that antisocial behavior may be conceptualized as either "adolescence-limited" or "life-course-persistent." Regarding the latter, Moffitt proposed that some infants with neurological deficits are predisposed for difficult temperament, poor self-control, and verbal and executive dysfunctions, among other problems. The effects of these deficits can then be exacerbated over time by inadequate parenting, familial dysfunctions, lack of social and academic skills, and general "criminogenic environments" (p. 683), among other variables. Many of these youth will then experience some behavior path (e.g., teenage pregnancy, drug use) later in life that further reduces opportunities for success. Ongoing, problematic interactions between a youth's traits and environment then serve to maintain antisocial behavior over the life span.

This model could potentially explain some cases of school refusal behavior, particularly those involving antisocial behavior or delinquency. For example, some children may be biologically predisposed toward low behavioral inhibition or even a callous and unemotional interpersonal style (P. J. Frick, 1998). These children may also have parents and families who respond to this impulsive, defiant style inappropriately or inadequately (e.g., inconsistent, harsh punishment or acquiescence). For example, many youth coerce their parents into bribing them to go back to school or into bowing to demands not to attend school by means of severe noncompliance or aggression (Patterson, 1982). In other cases, parents are overly permissive or simply ignore the problem and the child. Should these children look elsewhere for reinforcement, perhaps to a deviant peer group and outside of school, then school refusal behavior may flourish. Indeed, many youth refuse school for tangible reinforcement outside of school (Kearney & Silverman, 1996). Long-term absence, as noted earlier, could then impede future opportunities for success and maintain antisocial behavior.

Mixed Etiology

One should bear in mind that most children with school refusal behavior likely demonstrate a mixture of the precipitating and etiological factors just described. The characteristics of youth with school refusal behavior are diverse, heterogeneous, and likely reflective of many different causal paths. For example, some parents of children who are anxious about school acquiesce to the child's demands to avoid school and to have fun at home. In addition, some adolescents pursue tangible rewards outside of school with delinquent peers and are nervous about returning to school after a long absence. As stated earlier, the etiology of any particular case of school refusal behavior is usually complex, multifactorial, and indeterminable.

SUMMARY

School refusal behavior has as rich a pattern of symptomatology as history. Although it is clear that extended school refusal behavior is relatively prevalent and can lead to many problematic consequences, it is equally clear that no consistent profile of clinical symptomatology has yet been derived for this population. Much of this heterogeneity has also caused problems with respect to classification, a topic discussed in chapter 3.

3

CLASSIFICATION STRATEGIES

Brooke is a 10-year-old girl who struggles with her schoolwork and seems nervous during transitional periods of the day. She is also unmotivated at school and absent at least 2 days a week. Numerous parent–teacher conferences have not revealed any singular issue that causes these misbehaviors.

As indicated in chapters 1–2, children with school refusal behavior often show a complex mixture of symptoms. This mixture has led to a plethora of proposed systems to organize this population. In this chapter, a historical review and critique are presented on the major classification strategies that have been proposed for school refusal behavior. These strategies include psychoneurotic versus traditional truancy; neurotic versus characterological and acute versus chronic school refusal behavior; and empirical, diagnostic, and functional subtypes of school refusal behavior. More specific groupings that have been proposed by clinical researchers for this population are described as well.

Each classification strategy is scrutinized along several criteria. These criteria include assessment methodology, coverage, discriminant validity, clinical utility, and predictive validity. *Assessment methodology* refers to the use of reliable and valid measures to derive findings that serve as the basis for classification. *Coverage* refers to the ability of a classification system to apply to all youth with school refusal behavior. *Discriminant validity* refers to the ability of a classification system to clearly define and discriminate proposed groupings. *Clinical utility* refers to the value of a classification system to clinicians and educators who must choose appropriate assessment and treatment procedures. *Predictive validity* refers to the ability of a classification system to predict prognosis or treatment outcome.

PSYCHONEUROTIC VERSUS TRADITIONAL TRUANCY

Early Distinctions

As mentioned in chapter 1, one of the earliest distinctions made among children with problematic absenteeism focused on the dichotomy of (a) psychoneurotic truancy and (b) traditional, delinquent truancy. With respect to the former, Broadwin (1932) and A. M. Johnson, Falstein, Szurek, and Svendsen (1941) helped identify a subtype of children who refused school because of neuroses, problematic family relationships, or both. Each spurred the use of terms to describe emotionally wrought children in this population (i.e., "obsessional neurosis," Broadwin, 1932; "school phobia," A. M. Johnson et al., 1941), although neither provided a detailed taxonomy.

In contrast, Partridge (1939) evaluated 50 cases of school absenteeism and, on the basis of relatives' reports and clinical opinion, proposed five main groupings. The initial two were considered "simple" in nature, whereas the latter three were considered more complex:

- The *undisciplined* group (10%) referred to youth who missed school because of a lack of parental discipline and "out of control" delinquent behavior.
- The *hysterical* group (8%) referred to youth who simply ran away from difficulties at school; home; or other places, such as the dentist.
- The *desiderative* group (30%) referred to youth who were motivated to gain something tangible or intangible, such as attention. This group tended to be solitary, emotionally inhibited, and academically and intellectually limited. Home factors were thought to trigger truancy in this group by creating "unsatisfactory environments" (p. 68), and the children primarily sought "affection, personal interest, equality of rights in the home, reasonable freedom of expression, (and) continuity of these" (p. 57).
- The *rebellious* group (26%) referred to youth who developed from the desiderative group but displayed more severe delinquent behavior and attempts to hide absenteeism. Some were thought to rebel against home-based factors, whereas others rebelled against school-based factors. Three children (6%) were thought to be intermediate of the desiderative and rebellious groups.
- The *psychoneurotic* group (20%) referred to youth who were better adjusted to school but whose absenteeism rose from "pe-

culiar states of mind" (p. 68) and an overly emotional, overprotective mother–child relationship.

Partridge (1939) claimed that home-based factors were prominent in almost all cases of problematic absenteeism, whereas "dislike of the school" (p. 81) was prominent in only 8% of cases. None of these latter 8% were in the psycho-neurotic group. Although flawed in methodology, Partridge's observations supported the idea that children who refuse school do so for many different reasons, including escape from aversive events and for attention and amusements outside of school.

One should note that these early authors were essentially describing a general *syndrome* that was thought to be distinguishable from delinquency or simple absenteeism. For example, Broadwin (1932) stated that this form of truancy may be "a deep-seated neurosis" or "neurotic character of the obsessional type" (p. 254). In addition, Partridge (1939) stated that "the psycho-neurotic type of truancy must be construed as an attempt to find a solution to an emotional situation with which the patient is not able to cope" (p. 80). Finally, A. M. Johnson et al. (1941) called school phobia a "deep-seated psychoneurotic disorder" that "is not a clean-cut entity, for one finds overlapping of the phobic tendencies with other neurotic patterns" (p. 702). These authors contended not that one symptom adequately represented psychoneurotic truancy but rather that a heterogeneous mix of child-based symptoms and problematic family dynamics dominated this condition.

Later Distinctions

Following these early seminal articles, researchers tried to characterize in more detail the concepts of psychoneurotic truancy and traditional, delinquent truancy. Warren (1948) was among the first to do so, comparing the case histories of 8 children with "acute neurotic breakdown who refused to go to school" with 12 "truants without neurotic breakdown" (p. 268). In defining these categories, Warren claimed that the former displayed neurotic traits, possibly involving the entire family, that included anxiety, depression, fear, aggression, and disobedience. Children with truancy were thought to have no history of neurosis and were marked instead by a lack of discipline; a rebellious nature; delinquent symptoms, such as lying and stealing; and some "lack in the environment" for which the child attempted to compensate.

Warren's (1948) formal comparison revealed that children with acute neurotic breakdown were more likely to have maternal influence on their behavior, to be an only child, and to be overdependent; those with simple truancy were more likely to be in "bad homes or neighborhoods" and have too much "educational pressure." However, poverty was not evident in more than a third of each group. In addition, substantial overlap (i.e., at least 40% of each group) was evident for mental disturbance in close relatives, disturbed maternal and paternal attitude, lack of paternal influence, "material spoiling," and "frequent breaks and changes at home" (p. 268).

With respect to symptoms, children with acute neurotic breakdown were more likely to show disturbances in food fastidiousness, sleep, tension, anxiety, and depression. In addition, those with simple truancy were more likely to show disturbed paternal relationships, lying, stealing, and "truanting from home." However, several symptoms were not evident in more than a third of each group, including nocturnal enuresis, "gratification" and "assert-ive" habits, obsessions, hysteria, hypochondriasis, and ideas of reference. In addition, substantial overlap (i.e., at least 40% of each group) was evident for disturbed maternal and sibling relationships, "acute disturbance in relation to school," and disobedience (Warren, 1948, p. 268). Despite the small sample size and large amount of overlap, Warren concluded, almost astonishingly, that the "differences between these two groups are found to be considerable" (p. 272).

In a similar fashion, Hersov (1960a) compared 50 children with school refusal, or those with "a definite preference to remain at home while not in school," with 50 children with truancy, or those who had "no inclination to remain at home," potential association with truant peers, and absenteeism unknown to parents. Each child had these difficulties for at least 2 months, and the groups were compared with a control group of children without problematic absenteeism. Hersov examined case records and found no differences in age, gender, intelligence, or poor adjustment at school. However, children with truancy had significantly more problematic school reports and schoolwork and frequent changes of school. With respect to environmental factors, those with school refusal had significantly more maternal overprotectiveness, whereas those with truancy had significantly more maternal and paternal absence during childhood and inconsistent discipline at home.

With respect to symptoms, no differences were found in tics and stammering, encopresis, gratification and tension habits, aggression, destructiveness, and inappropriate sexual activity. However, children with school refusal showed significantly more eating and sleep disturbance, gastrointestinal problems, and fears. In addition, those with truancy displayed significantly more enuresis, lying, stealing, wandering from home, and juvenile court appearances. Finally, with respect to diagnoses, children with school refusal displayed significantly more anxiety reactions, whereas those with truancy displayed significantly more conduct disorder. However, no differences were found with respect to depressive or hysterical reactions, obsessional or character disorder, or "reactive behaviour disorder with some neurotic features" (Hersov, 1960a, p. 136).

Hersov (1960a, 1985) concluded that two groups were largely delineated; school refusal was "one manifestation of a psychoneurosis," whereas truancy was indicative of a "conduct disorder which often involves other delinquent behavior" (1960a, p. 135). This study is noteworthy for many reasons, including the fact that it helped spur the use of the term *school refusal* to represent what had previously been labeled "psychoneurotic truancy" or "school phobia." As a result, psychoneurotic truancy, school phobia, and school refusal have come to represent essentially the same condition: a child with problematic absenteeism that is due to emotional and family factors.

Torma and Halsti (1975) also compared 39 children with school phobia–refusal (SPR), defined as those with a predominant "neurotic development tendency," with 34 children with truancy, defined as those with "immaturity (as) the dominant trait in personality" (p. 210). On the basis of case records, children with SPR were found to display significantly more somatic complaints, cohesive–dual-parent families, older mothers, overprotective or possessive parents, and less asociality than children with truancy. However, no significant differences were found with respect to organic etiology, depression, sibling or socioeconomic status, stability of maternal or paternal relationships, or school performance.

Torma and Halsti (1975) also analyzed 18 variables that might discriminate SPR from truancy, but only 7 were found to do so. These included nature of mother and father relationship (closer in the SPR group), age of father (younger in the SPR group), mother's and father's mental health (milder disturbance in the SPR group), changes in father relationship (more permanent in the SPR group), and concept formation (poorer in the SPR group). The authors made no theoretical conclusions from their data, however.

Galloway (1983) compared 31 youth with truancy (i.e., parents seldom or occasionally knew their child's whereabouts during school absence) with 48 youth classified as "other absentees" (i.e., parents knew their child's whereabouts during school absence, p. 607). Youth classified with truancy displayed significantly more stealing, lying, and wandering from home on evenings and weekends, and were more influenced by peers than "other absentees." Youth classified as "other absentees" also displayed significantly more concern about their academic future, fear of harm to parents, and anxiety about leaving home than those with truancy. No differences were found between the groups with respect to difficult social relationships, eating and sleep disturbances, and enuresis. With respect to parent–family variables, those classified as "other absentees" had significantly more overprotective parents, dependency, satisfactory parent–child relationships, and higher reading age than those with truancy. No differences between the groups were found with respect to tense child–parent relationships, passive–inadequate parenting, firm–controlling parenting, intelligence, committed offenses, and attendance rates.

M. Cooper (1986) also tried to characterize differences between 37 youth with school refusal and 39 youth with truancy using case study reports. Among 19 family background and personal characteristics, only 4 represented a majority of at least one group. These included protective mother (51% of school refusal group and 15% of truancy group), broken family (24% and 59%), antisocial (3% and 59%), and disruptive (0% and 67%). Substantial overlap or minority percentages in each group were found for protective father, close relationship with mother and father, neglected by mother or father, poor relationship with mother, use of corporal punishment, criminal family, ill–anxious–depressed mother or father, isolated–lonely, immature, depressive, anxious, bullied by peers, and aggression–violence. Cooper concluded that a primary difference between these two groups was the amount of dependence in the child–parent relationship (i.e., high in school refusal and low in truancy).

Assessment Methodology

Certainly a key historical distinction made among youth with problematic absenteeism has been psychoneurotic truancy–school refusal–school phobia versus traditional, delinquent truancy. The distinction and the articles from which it came remain widely cited today. In making this distinction, however, one should note that most authors relied on their own clinical observation, archival data, or case records or studies to examine differences between groups. Little data were given to support the psychometric strength of the assessment methods that helped produce the findings. A prime example is Hersov (1960a), who is widely credited for helping distinguish school refusal from truancy but who relied on archival data and reports that were not supported by any reliability or validity data. In addition, several authors (e.g., Hersov, 1960a; Torma & Halsti, 1975; Warren, 1948) relied on undefined diagnostic criteria for conditions such as depression. Such criticism, however, may be made of almost all school refusal behavior studies prior to 1980. Finally, no standardized definitions of school refusal or truancy were used, making comparisons across these studies very difficult. Issues of poor assessment strength and definitional consistency thus limit the validity of findings and conclusions regarding these subtypes.

Coverage

Like the issue of inadequate assessment methodology, an overwhelming majority of early school refusal behavior studies do not empirically address the issue of coverage. An early exception was Hersov's (1960b) attempt to categorize children with school refusal into a tripartite familial classification scheme (see chapter 2). However, only 60% of families described in the study could be classified into Hersov's three categories, a figure close to Blashfield and Draguns's (1976) 50% cutoff for restricted taxonomic usefulness. Empirical studies to be discussed later also show that school refusal and truancy represent only about one third of all children with severe school attendance problems. Although a popular distinction, school refusal–truancy seems to apply only to a limited subset of all youth with school refusal behavior.

Discriminant Validity

An additional concern is whether there is a clear difference between youth with psychoneurotic truancy–school refusal–school phobia and those with simple absenteeism or delinquent truancy. Data from the above studies would seem to suggest considerable overlap among these distinctions. For example, if one examines the total number of variables thought to distinguish school refusal–phobia from truancy in these studies, only 45.7% (59 of 129) actually do. The fact that a majority (54.3%) of variables flow freely across each category is evidence of the dubiousness of the distinction.

Other studies also do not support a school refusal–phobia–truancy dichotomy and, in fact, provide evidence against the distinction. M. G. Cooper (1966a), for example, in a review of the literature confirmed that investigations of school refusal behavior generally center on children with school phobia or truancy. She concluded, however, that these "two broad categories, inevitably, have been found to overlap" (p. 115). Common features across the subtypes include absenteeism, somatic complaints, overdependence, and parental knowledge of the disorder. M. G. Cooper (1966b) compared 40 children with school phobia and 40 children with truancy across several child, familial, and school variables. Some minor differences were found—for example, children with phobia clung more to home and experienced more vigilant parenting styles than children with truancy—but no differences were evident on several measures of social withdrawal and other variables (e.g., size or type of school). The author concluded that "much emotional ground [is] common to both types of 'school refusal' " (p. 229).

Tyerman (1968), in an exhaustive review, also found that many well-defined cases of school nonattendance from the psychodynamic literature were "extreme and atypical" (p. 103) in nature. The construct "school phobia" was criticized on several grounds, including inadequate empirical support (e.g., interrater reliability) and poor differentiation from truancy. Tyerman noted that children with school phobia and those with truancy share many symptoms, such as anxiety, shyness, and peer withdrawal. Similarly, the term *truancy* was criticized for carrying with it the "implication of delinquency" (p. 33). Tyerman also expressed concerns that a diagnosis of "school phobia" implied a singular etiology, possibly leading to neglect of other causal factors. He concluded that school phobia and truancy are "extremes which shade into one another" and that distinguishing the two is "rarely accurate or desirable" (p. 24). Rubenstein and Hastings (1980) similarly concluded that school phobia and truancy become highly blurred during adolescence. Specifically, they indicated that the presence of many "neurotic conflicts" in both groups makes this distinction questionable.

Evidence also disputes Hersov's (1985) conclusion that children with truancy display "more often conduct than emotional disorder," whereas children with school refusal "are highly unlikely to display antisocial behavior and the great majority show clear evidence of emotional disorder" (p. 383). Studies of general clinical child samples show significant comorbidity of "supradomain" anxiety–affective and behavior–conduct symptoms. For example, Woolston et al. (1989) found that 51% of children in their sample displayed at least one affective–anxiety diagnosis (e.g., dysthymia) and one behavior diagnosis (e.g., conduct disorder). Other reports of substantial supradomain comorbidity have been reported as well (e.g., Anderson, Williams, McGee, & Silva, 1987; Biederman, Newcorn, & Sprich, 1991; Kashani & Orvaschel, 1990; Mitchell, McCauley, Burke, & Moss, 1988) and may in fact underestimate a "true" rate of overlapping symptoms (Caron & Rutter, 1991).

Such heterogeneity among affective–anxiety and conduct problems has also been shown in studies of children with school refusal behavior. Tennent (1969; see also Tennent, 1971), for example, found symptoms of anxiety and affective disorders in children with truancy, prompting Hersov (1985) to suggest the "coexistence of neurotic and conduct disorders in boys on remand for school nonattendance" (p. 383). In addition, subsequent studies (e.g., Bernstein & Garfinkel, 1986; Kearney & Silverman, 1996) indicate significant comorbidity of assigned anxiety–affective and conduct diagnoses among children with school refusal behavior. These data contradict arguments for school refusal–truancy homogeneity.

The substantial blur among school refusal, school phobia, and truancy obstructs a better understanding of this population. The problem is particularly troublesome because it impedes information retrieval (e.g., what topic to seek in a library), provides clinicians with a muddied view of the situation, and impairs communication among mental health professionals and researchers. When a school official or pediatrician consults a clinical psychologist about a child with an elimination disorder, the psychologist has a decent taxonomic base for quickly narrowing and conceptualizing the problem (e.g., nocturnal vs. diurnal, primary vs. secondary). When a case of school "phobia" or "refusal" or "truancy" is similarly presented, however, a psychologist likely has little initial idea about the clinical picture until many questions are asked. A nomothetic approach to classifying absenteeism on the basis of a school refusal–truancy distinction is neither homogeneous nor adequate.

Problems in demonstrating the discriminant validity of psychoneurotic truancy–school refusal–school phobia and traditional truancy have prompted some to rely more on subtle differences. In particular, school refusal–phobia is sometimes characterized by parental knowledge of the child's school refusal behavior, whereas truancy is often considered to be unknown to parents (e.g., Berg, Brown, & Hullin, 1988; Brulle, McIntyre, & Mills, 1985). For example, Berry and Lizardi (1985) stated that "both disorders [truancy and school phobia] have 'school absence' as a common characteristic . . . [but] a truant is usually thought of as a child who is absent from school without his or her parent's or the school's permission" (p. 66).

The distinction between school refusal and truancy based on parental knowledge of the problem may be relevant to some cases but is far too fine for general clinical usefulness. No researchers of treatment outcome studies for school refusal behavior have assigned therapy using this distinction, and clinicians likely do not base treatment primarily on whether a child's parents were initially cognizant of the problem. After all, once the child is in treatment, his or her parents are usually aware of the problem. Distinguishing school refusal and truancy on the basis of one detail and ignoring all the variables that blend the two is taken as further evidence of the dichotomy's fallibility.

Clinical Utility

Given the limited nature of school refusal–truancy in describing most children with school refusal behavior, and given that the constructs overlap considerably, it is no surprise that detailed assessment and treatment protocols based on this distinction have not been produced. Instead, the clinical utility of this distinction may be found in one or two variables that seem to discriminate the groups. Overdependent child–parent relationships, for example, appear to be more prevalent in school refusal groups than in truancy groups and may help form the basis for a more general familial taxonomy for this population. In particular, enmeshment is a key aspect of some families of children with school refusal behavior, and specific recommendations for addressing this family dynamic have been proposed (Kearney & Silverman, 1995). At present, however, the clinical utility of a school refusal–truancy distinction remains unsatisfactory.

Predictive Validity

Because no detailed treatment options based on a school refusal–truancy distinction have been delineated, predictive validity has not been demonstrated either. Some recommendations regarding treatment and treatment outcome have been made (e.g., Warren, 1948), but no empirical studies to test these hypotheses are available. Perhaps clinicians target school nonattendance as a key characteristic in both school refusal and truancy with little regard for the alleged differences between the two. Between two children with school refusal behavior, for example, one who refuses to leave home in the morning and another who leaves school during the afternoon, clinicians are likely to address noncompliance, child and parental skills, and related variables in both cases regardless of previously assigned labels such as "school refusal" or "truancy."

Commentary on the Focus and Use of "School Phobia"

During and after the development of the school refusal–truancy dichotomy, fear became an increasingly popular construct for describing youth with problematic absenteeism. Why is this the case when, as discussed in chapters 1–2, fear is not even a predominant aspect of most cases of school refusal behavior? Perhaps because the concept of school phobia has been altered over time.

Recall that school phobia was originally meant to represent a general syndrome or cluster of symptoms that loosely consisted of a child's forms of emotional distress, problematic family relationships, and other issues (A. M. Johnson et al., 1941). Although eventually dismissed as a misnomer by its own creator (A. M. Johnson, 1957), school phobia was widely used in the 1950s as a replacement for the awkward phrase psychoneurotic truancy. In addition, school phobia became synonymous with school refusal after the publication of articles by Hersov (1960b) and Kahn and Nursten (1962). This synonymity has persisted in different forms. For example, Berg (1983) used his own school phobia criteria to define school refusal; Atkinson, Quarrington, Cyr, and Atkinson (1989) classified youth with school refusal using Berg, Nichols, and Pritchard's (1969) criteria for school phobia; and youth with school phobia and those with school refusal are often lumped together as one diagnostic research group (e.g., Torma & Halsti, 1975).

Though originally conceived as a general syndrome, school phobia became narrowed by some who viewed the problem more as a specific phobia or symptom (e.g., Suttenfield, 1954). This narrowing was accelerated by behavioral researchers in the 1960s and early 1970s who successfully desensitized children with specific phobias of school-related stimuli (e.g., Garvey & Hegrenes, 1966; Lazarus, Davison, & Polefka, 1965; P. M. Miller, 1972).

Although a highly significant advance in clinical child psychology, these studies had the wide-ranging effect of limiting the original concept of "school phobia" to a much more specific area of study, namely fear and avoidance of school. This limitation is not necessarily bad, nor is it surprising given increased desire at the time to assign greater operational definition to psychological phenomena, including school refusal behavior. Given the heterogeneity of school refusal behavior and lack of historical support for clear dichotomies, researchers may have been drawn to the idea of assigning circumscribed labels of fear or avoidance to the amorphous emotional distress often seen in this population. Perhaps fear and avoidance were viewed as pathognomonic signs that could be simply assessed in all kinds of children with problematic absenteeism.

The danger in limiting the study of school phobia to fear and avoidance is that it deprives researchers and clinicians of the full richness that was originally meant to be part of the construct. Indeed, many symptoms other than fear and avoidance were thought by early clinical researchers to compose "psychoneurotic truancy–school phobia." Later researchers, in an attempt to explain the mechanisms of this problem, have perhaps overemphasized fear and avoidance as the primary ingredients of problematic absenteeism. Indeed, skewed attention has historically been given to school-related fears (Graziano & DeGiovanni, 1979).

As discussed in chapter 1, it is not uncommon for many professional and laypeople to interchangeably use the terms *school phobia, school refusal,* and *school refusal behavior* (Elliott, 1999; M. Pritchard, King, Tonge, Heyne, & Lancaster, 1998). This likely reflects confusion as to how each term should be used or applied to different children. This confusion has perhaps led to, or partially been the result of, the popular use of the *Diagnostic and Statistical Manual of Mental Disorders* (DSM; American Psychiatric Association, 1980, 1987, 1994), which does not deem general school refusal behavior a "clinically significant behavioral or psychological syndrome" (American Psychiatric Association, 1994, p. xxi). Instead, if a child avoids school, but this is his or her only presenting symptom, he or she would not fully qualify for a diagnosis such as separation anxiety or conduct disorder (although the child could be assigned either anxiety or disruptive behavior disorder not otherwise specified). Instead, the full DSM category most pertinent to a child with some emotional distress and who avoids school is specific phobia of school. This diagnostic structure may be amenable to a reliable assessment procedure, because fear and avoidance can be quickly evaluated, but it fails to recognize or discriminate alternative etiological or maintaining factors of school refusal behavior. What about, for example, all the children who refuse to go to school and have little or no emotional distress?

An emphasis on school phobia as a leading factor in general school refusal behavior has led to a widespread and erroneous assumption that most cases of problematic nonattendance are fear or avoidance based. Discussions of problematic school nonattendance disproportionately emphasize school refusal and school phobia, which may provide clinicians with the inaccurate notion that fear–avoidance symptoms are generally characteristic of the absentee population. Fear and avoidance are important aspects of cases of overall school refusal behavior, but they are only two components of a multifaceted syndrome.

As a result, the concept of school phobia should be abandoned in favor of more descriptive and clinically accurate concepts. Dispensing with the term would help alleviate confusion among mental health professionals and educators and pave the way for standard definitions and taxa. In addition, the work of clinicians and researchers would be more comparable and thus speed the improvement of assessment and treatment processes for youth with absenteeism.

NEUROTIC VERSUS CHARACTEROLOGICAL SCHOOL REFUSAL BEHAVIOR

In conjunction with a school refusal–phobia–truancy distinction, researchers began to focus on neurotic–characterological and acute–chronic subtypes. The major proponents of the former distinction were Coolidge, Hahn, and Peck (1957), who evaluated 27 cases of youth with school phobia and divided them into neurotic (18) and characterological (9) groups. Those in the neurotic group were generally female and younger, whereas those in the characterological group were generally male and older. A descriptive analysis based on case histories indicated as well that the neurotic group was characterized by "fairly sound personality" (p. 305), intact peer relationships, overdependent mother–child relationships, and "acute regressive reaction." In contrast, the characterological group was characterized by "deeper character disturbance" (p. 297), longer length of the problem, and more insidious onset.

Kennedy (1965, 1971) expanded on Coolidge et al.'s (1957) neurotic–characterological distinction, postulating that children with school phobia could be divided into Type 1–neurotic crisis and Type 2–way-of-life phobia groups. Differential diagnosis was proposed on the basis of any 7 of the 10 symptoms listed for each group. However, no direct comparisons of Type 1 versus Type 2 children were made. From case records, Type 1 children were thought to be characterized by

- initial episode of school phobia
- Monday onset following illness the previous Thursday or Friday
- acute onset

- lower grades
- expressed concern about death
- perceived or actual illness in the mother
- good parental communication
- generally well-adjusted parents
- mother–father competitiveness with respect to household management
- parents who readily understand the dynamics of their case.

In contrast, Type 2 children were thought to be characterized by

- second, third, or fourth episode of school phobia
- no prevalence of Monday onset or previous illness
- insidious onset
- higher grades
- no concern about death
- no perceived or actual maternal illness
- poor parental communication
- maternal neurotic disorder and paternal character disorder
- little paternal interest in the household or children
- difficulty in working with parents.

Others have also developed theories parallel to Coolidge et al.'s (1957) neurotic–characterological distinction. On the basis of case observations, for example, Sperling (1967) made a distinction between *common* and *induced* school phobia, either of which could be acute or chronic in nature. Sperling claimed that common acute school phobia was generally marked by little history of prior school phobia, "traumatic neurosis," anxiety, and a clear precipitating event. In contrast, induced acute school phobia was marked by no clear precipitating event and more insidious onset. Features character-istic of both types, however, included potential onset at any time of the school year, problematic family relationships, and "preoedipal fixations" (p. 390). Chronic school phobia of either type was thought to be marked by "serious personality disturbance" (p. 389). Treatment cases based on this classification system were presented by C. Goldberg (1977).

In similar fashion, on the basis of case studies Marine (1968) proposed four categories of school refusal that were partially based on length of the problem:

1. *Simple separation anxiety*, which referred to young children experiencing initial separation from the mother. Common symptoms included crying, clinging, and asocial behavior that usually remitted within 1 week.
2. *Mild acute school refusal*, which was quite similar to Coolidge et al.'s (1957) neurotic and Kennedy's (1965) Type 1 school

phobia groups. This group was marked by acute and dramatic onset of school phobia that was persistent in nature.

3. *Severe chronic school refusal,* which was quite similar to Kennedy's (1965) Type 2 school phobia and was marked by older children with insidious onset of the problem and more complex psychopathology.

4. *Childhood psychosis with school refusal symptoms,* which referred to youth whose school refusal was enveloped in more severe psychopathology related to depression, social withdrawal, somatic reactions, phobias, or rituals.

Shapiro and Jegede (1973) also classified children with school refusal along a bipolar behavior continuum. At one pole were ego alien behaviors that included phobia, anxiety, clinging, and somatic complaints. At another pole were ego syntonic behaviors that included truancy sometimes parentally reinforced by criticism of teachers. In the middle of the continuum was dawdling behavior.

ACUTE VERSUS CHRONIC SCHOOL REFUSAL BEHAVIOR

At a level more fundamental than neurotic–characterological, some researchers chose to evaluate the validity of a specific acute–chronic dichotomy for school refusal behavior. Berg et al. (1969), for example, evaluated 29 children with school phobia using their definition outlined in chapter 1 (i.e., severe trouble attending school, emotional distress, staying at home with parental knowledge, and lack of antisocial behavior). Those with acute school phobia ($n = 19$) had at least a 3-year history of "trouble-free attendance" (p. 124) before the onset of their symptoms; those with chronic school phobia ($n = 10$) did not have this distinction.

A comparison along several variables indicated that the chronic group was significantly younger, more dependent and affectionate, more likely to act alone, more depressed and maladjusted at school, and had greater preference for parents and friends than the acute group (Berg et al., 1969). No differences were found between the groups, however, with respect to socioeconomic status; maternal age or separation; number of siblings; missing school without parental knowledge; "suicidal gestures, somatic symptoms, onset or exacerbation of symptoms on transfer to secondary school"; and frequency of birth complications, severe illness, accidents, and operations (p. 127). In addition, no differences were found regarding weekend activities, child–parent introversion–extroversion, child "unforthcomingness" (p. 131), and overall intelligence.

Using the same definitional criteria as Berg et al. (1969), Baker and Wills (1978) evaluated 99 cases of children with acute ($n = 63$) or chronic

(n = 36) school phobia. Those in the chronic group showed significantly more parental mental illness and had a higher number of siblings. Those with acute school phobia were significantly more likely to be the youngest child, be depressed, have a "normal character structure" prior to school phobia, have known precipitating factors, and "be seen within three months of the appearance of the symptoms" (p. 495). No differences between the groups, however, were found with respect to overall socioeconomic status, parental physical illness, maternal age, family situations (i.e., "illegitimacy, fostering, death [of] or desertion by a parent, or second marriage," p. 494), child age, intelligence, psychosis or other neurosis, or treatment outcome. Like Berg et al. (1969), Baker and Wills offered no theoretical conclusions about their results.

As with school refusal–phobia–truancy, enduring dichotomies of problematic absenteeism include neurotic–characterological or acute–chronic. These latter distinctions, although rephrased in several ways (e.g., Type 1–Type 2, common–induced), are usually linked closely with school refusal–phobia–truancy. In general, two subtypes of individuals with school refusal behavior have been proposed: (a) younger children with acute onset of school refusal behavior involving emotional distress or phobia and (b) older children and adolescents with insidious onset of school refusal behavior involving acting out or conduct problems.

Assessment Methodology

As with early studies that evaluated a school refusal–truancy distinction, lack of reliable and valid assessment techniques to derive information plague examinations of neurotic–characterological and acute–chronic school refusal behavior. One exception was Berg et al. (1969), who reported 89.7% interrater agreement as to whether cases of school phobia were acute or chronic. Most authors, however, did not address the consistency of their ratings or procedures.

Coverage

As with assessment procedures, studies of neurotic–characterological school refusal behavior do not address empirically the issue of coverage. Coverage may be better assumed using a simple acute–chronic distinction, which is based on length of the problem and where all youth with school refusal behavior are necessarily covered (e.g., length of problem less or greater than 3 years). The problem in this distinction lies more in the cutoff used to distinguish acute from chronic. Berg et al. (1969), for example, used 3 years, but this is viewed by some clinicians and researchers as overly stringent. For example, Kearney and Silverman (1996; see also chapter 1) defined chronic cases of school refusal behavior as those lasting more than 1 year, whereas others (Bernstein & Garfinkel, 1986) have used a 2-year cutoff. Attempts at coverage for this population based on neurotic–characterological symptomatology have been largely unsuccessful, but the simple delineation of length of problem as a classification tool has some merit and is likely predictive of severity of absenteeism (Hansen, Sanders, Massaro, & Last, 1998) or treatment outcome (Kearney, 1995).

Discriminant Validity

The discriminant validity of neurotic–characterological school refusal behavior was questioned virtually as the distinction was proposed. For example, A. M. Johnson (1957) thought the distinction was superfluous to theories that already existed. In addition, Coolidge et al. (1957) themselves conceded that there may be little difference between the groups. Specifically, they stated that "the hypothesis that we may be dealing with a continuum and that the children in the characterological group may be no different qualitatively from the children in the neurotic group could be considered" (p. 298).

Questionable discriminant validity may also apply to Kennedy's (1965) Type 1–Type 2 distinction. Although Kennedy relied primarily on clinical observation to make this distinction, he did advocate a rapid, forced school attendance treatment procedure to eliminate Type 1–acute school phobia. Parents were encouraged to bring their children to school and keep them in the classroom for the entire day. Kennedy reported a 100% success rate, although several factors may have mediated the effect. For example, mothers were allowed to remain in the hallway outside a child's classroom. Kennedy questioned the validity of his own model, however, by stating that "perhaps what is called Type 1 School Phobia is not really a severe phobic attack at all, but borders on malingering of a transient nature which would spontaneously remit in a few days anyway" and that "there is little reason to doubt that the majority of cases would eventually return to school whatever treatment was undertaken" (p. 289).

It is possible that Kennedy (1965) was describing children whose school refusal was "self-corrective" (Type 1) versus those whose school refusal was acute or chronic in nature (Type 2) and required treatment. My clinical experience and existing research data support this hypothesis. Regarding my referrals of children with recent school refusal behavior, approximately one quarter to one third cancel their assessment or (1 week later) consultation session because the problem has quickly dissipated. In addition, an examination of school attendance in participants receiving placebo medication (e.g., Bernstein, Garfinkel, & Borchardt, 1990; Gittelman-Klein & Klein, 1971) reveals that approximately half return to school without any active treatment. These observations and data help support the distinction proposed in chapter 1 among self-corrective, acute, and chronic school refusal behavior.

Perhaps because of these problems, others have focused simply on an acute–chronic distinction. This distinction is not without its own problems, however. For example, several researchers have reported findings contrary to earlier research that led to this distinction. For example, Berg et al. (1969) and Baker and Wills (1978) found children with acute school phobia to be older than those with chronic school phobia, a finding opposite to that of Coolidge et al. (1957). Berg et al. also noted that a higher percentage of children with acute than with chronic school refusal missed school without parental knowledge. This contradicted earlier research that found that children with chronic truancy are more likely to surreptitiously avoid school (e.g., Hersov, 1960a). Kolvin, Berney, and Bhate (1984) found as well that very few empirical discriminants supported an acute–chronic distinction. In addition, referral bias associated with this distinction has not been generally considered. For example, demographic and other factors may influence when parents refer a child for assessment and treatment, and this may affect who presents as acute or chronic.

Clinical Utility

In contrast to the school refusal–truancy dichotomy, an acute–chronic distinction likely has better clinical utility for clinicians and educators. For example, knowing the length of school refusal behavior may help one understand its severity. Children who are out of school for a long period of time, especially longer than 1 academic year, likely have a more generalized problem with comorbid conditions and are more difficult to treat than those who are out of school for a short period of time (Kearney, 1995).

Predictive Validity

Despite its potential clinical utility, however, problems of predictive validity mark an acute–chronic distinction. For example, Baker and Wills (1978) used various treatments for youth with acute or chronic school phobia, but positive (i.e., good or fair) treatment outcome was nearly identical (86% vs. 83%), and return to school was identical (89%), across the groups. Our knowledge of whether a child with school phobia presents with new or chronic symptoms does not yet allow for the prediction of specific treatment techniques that are best suited to him or her. Instead, only vague references are available to longer duration treatment for those with chronic school refusal behavior (e.g., A. M. Johnson, 1957; Shapiro & Jegede, 1973; Sperling, 1967).

EMPIRICAL SUBTYPING OF SCHOOL REFUSAL BEHAVIOR

Following early studies of school refusal behavior that identified only rudimentary subtypes, attempts were made to more empirically or statistically distinguish subtypes in this population. These empirical–statistical studies generally center on two strategies: (a) analyses of problematic behaviors with implications for school refusal behavior in youth along overcontrolled–undercontrolled or internalizing–externalizing dimensions and (b) analyses of characteristics more representative of school refusal behavior. For clarity, these are discussed separately.

Analyses of General Problematic Behaviors in Youth

Achenbach and Edelbrock (1978), in reviewing empirical efforts to classify childhood psychopathology, noted that factor analyses of parent, teacher, and mental health worker reports often result in overcontrolled and undercontrolled broadband factors (see chapter 1). They also noted the lack of assessment techniques derived from multivariate analyses of childhood behavior, claiming that researchers had not developed measurements of use to most clinicians. As a result, they identified several syndromes or sets of correlated problematic behaviors from factor analyses of parent and teacher ratings of children and adolescents. Subsequent measures based on these analyses include the Child Behavior Checklist (CBCL; Achenbach, 1991a), an inventory of parent ratings of social competence and 118 behaviors in children and adolescents; the Teacher's Report Form (TRF; Achenbach, 1991b), a similar device to solicit teacher ratings of misbehavior; and the Youth Self-Report (Achenbach, 1991c), a similar device to solicit an adolescent's ratings of his or her own misbehavior. Broadband (internalizing–overcontrolled and externalizing–undercontrolled) and several narrowband (e.g., withdrawn, somatic complaints, anxious–depressed, delinquent and aggressive behavior) factors have been identified for boys and girls ages 2–3, 4–11, and 12–18 years.

Related to this dichotomy, a distinction between "internalizing school refusal disorders" and "externalizing truant disorder" has been hypothesized (Young, Brasic, Kisnadwala, & Leven, 1990) as a "trial classification" (p. 202) for youth with problematic school nonattendance. Those with internalizing school refusal are described as showing "evidence of conflict, anxiety, distress about the symptoms, and symptoms of other emotional disorders." Children with phobia, separation anxiety, depression, and somatic complaints are subsumed under this category. In contrast, those with externalizing truant disorder are thought to show "impulsive, defiant, manipulative, noncompliant behavior, and other symptoms of a conduct disorder or delinquency, including nonattendance at school (with) little anxiety" (p. 202).

Analyses of Problematic Behavior Specific to School Refusal

Proactive attempts to empirically–statistically subtype behaviors more pertinent to school refusal have also been reported. For example, Kolvin et al. (1984) evaluated 51 children with school phobia with or without depression. Discriminant function analyses were conducted on 10 background features and symptoms. Five potentially useful dichotomies of school phobia were assessed, including acute–chronic, male–female, preadolescent–adolescent, attends–does not attend school, and depressed–nondepressed. However, a significant number of discriminants (five) was found only for the depressed–nondepressed distinction. These included living with only one biological parent and "organic features," which were seen more frequently in the depressed group (p. 351). Kolvin et al. concluded that at least two primary groupings could be identified in children with school phobia: "depression" and "residual school refusal syndrome" (p. 355).

Examining a broader set of variables, Berg et al. (1985) conducted a principal-components factor analysis of parent ratings of 64 children with severe school attendance problems. A truancy component accounted for 20% of the variance and included items such as "child not with parent or at home," "parent does not know who the child is with or when the child is off school," "parent discovered school absence from an education officer," and "school contacted for help." In addition, a school refusal component accounted for 15% of the variance and included items such as "refuses to go to school," "stays home," "resists parents' efforts to secure attendance," "social services contacted for help," and "tearful on school mornings." Overall, children were classified as having truancy only (31.3%), school refusal only (18.8%), truancy and school refusal (14.1%), or neither (35.9%). Despite this overlap, Berg et al. concluded that "children taken to juvenile court because of failure to attend school may show either some of the features of truancy or some of the characteristics of school refusal" (p. 163).

Atkinson et al. (1989) subjected to statistical analysis data from the clinical files of 100 children with school refusal (using Berg et al.'s, 1969, criteria for school phobia). Four discernible groups were culled from an initial factor analysis, including

- "general fearfulness and extensiveness of disorder," which includes "general fearfulness, extensiveness of disorder, depression, age, significant separation–loss, school failure, maternal depression, feelings of maternal incompetence" (17.3% of variance)

- "mutual separation anxiety," which includes "separation anxiety, maternal overprotection, child slept longer than is usual with parents, mother–child interdependence" (12.0% of variance)
- "perfectionism and fear of failure," which includes "child's perfectionism–fear of failure, depression, domination of mother, and mother's emotional deprivation as a child" (9.4% of variance)
- "manipulative," which includes "manipulative (and) failed at least one school year" (8.5% of variance; p. 193).

Factor scores were then entered into a cluster analysis that yielded three groups: separation anxiety (15% of children), perfectionistic (28%), and extensively disturbed (29%). The last group was thought to parallel Kennedy's (1965) Type 2 distinction and was characterized by older age, depression, pervasive fear, academic and maternal problems, and loss of parent or grandparent. Many youth (28%) remained unclassified.

Finally, Bools, Foster, Brown, and Berg (1990) examined 100 children with severe school attendance problems and, using cluster analysis, found their sample to fall into three groups: nonclinical (68%), refusal (21%), and truancy (11%). Those in the refusal group tended to have more "morning symptoms" and "general neurotic disturbance," whereas those in the truancy group tended to be male and have more antisocial behavior (p. 175). No age or family differences were found.

Assessment Methodology

Achenbach's (1991a, 1991b, 1991c) empirical classification model has several important benefits for clinicians and educators, including its flexibility; replicability; reflection of developmental changes over time; and excellent reliability, construct, and criterion-related validity. The presence of a continuum of internalizing, mixed, and externalizing symptoms for most childhood psychopathology is well established (Achenbach & McConaughy, 1997). However, Young et al. (1990), in proposing their classification system for school refusal behavior based on this model, did not provide supporting data regarding its reliability or validity.

With respect to studies that provided statistically based subtypes for specific school refusal behaviors, psychometric strength was not apparent. Authors tended to rely on unstructured interviews (Berg et al., 1985; Bools et al., 1990) and archival data (Atkinson et al., 1989; Kolvin et al., 1984) that were not generally supported by reliability or validity data. In addition, variables that were entered into these analyses were not well defined, and so conclusions from these studies must be considered suspect at best.

Coverage

Achenbach's (1991a, 1991b, 1991c) empirical classification model covers a wide variety of potential childhood behavior problems. Its coverage for different school refusal behaviors has not been specifically addressed but is probably good. As described in chapter 2, children with school refusal behavior present with many different internalizing and externalizing symptoms, and these forms of behavior are well represented in Achenbach's system.

With respect to statistically based subtypes for specific school refusal behaviors, however, their coverage must be considered incomplete because of substantial amounts of unexplained variance. In looking at Berg et al.'s (1985) and Bools et al.'s (1990) studies, for example, 65%–68% of youth with school refusal behavior could not be statistically defined as "school refusal" or "truancy." Indeed, the procurement of empirical subtypes of specific school refusal behaviors only confirmed earlier descriptions regarding the heterogeneity of this population.

Discriminant Validity

The primary problem of Achenbach's system with respect to school refusal behavior is its discriminant validity. In particular, each narrow—band factor contains several traditional school refusal-related behaviors. The CBCL (boys ages 4–11 years), for example, includes the following behaviors: (a) unhappy, sad, or depressed; (b) withdrawn, doesn't get involved with others; (c) secretive, keeps things to self; (d) headaches and stomachaches or cramps; (e) cries a lot; (f) feels he/she has to be perfect; (g) nervous, high strung, or tense; (h) too fearful or anxious; (i) worries; and (j) clings to adults or too dependent (Achenbach, 1991a). These behaviors are represented across several different internalizing or mixed factors: Withdrawn, Somatic Complaints, Anxious–Depressed, and Social Problems. In addition, the item "fears going to school" does not load on any of these factors and is instead listed separately with Other Problems.

In a similar fashion, traditional school refusal-related behaviors include the following: (a) poor school work, (b) hangs around with others who get in trouble, (c) lying or cheating, (d) truancy, skips school, (e) argues a lot, (f) demands a lot of attention, (g) disobedient at school, (h) sudden changes in mood or feelings, and (i) temper tantrums or hot temper (Achenbach, 1991a). These behaviors are represented across several different mixed or externalizing factors: Attention Problems, Delinquent Behavior, and

Aggressive Behavior. Internalizing and externalizing school refusal behaviors are also evident on related teacher and self-report scales (Achenbach, 1991b, 1991c).

Kearney and Silverman (1996) presented CBCL and TRF data regarding children and adolescents with school refusal behavior. With respect to both measures, boys and girls did not show clinical levels of internalizing and externalizing behaviors, although younger children had scores barely in the clinical range for internalizing problems. All gender and age groups showed more internalizing than externalizing behavior, however. This suggests that the only differentiation for this population is a lessened gap between overcontrolled and undercontrolled scores from childhood to adolescence. When parent and teacher data are taken together, no clear clinical picture or distinctions are found among youth with school refusal behavior. A mixed clinical profile is provided even when evaluating broadband factor scores. This was further evidenced by a significant correlation ($r = .59$) between all internalizing and externalizing scores (Kearney & Silverman, 1996).

Several authors (e.g., Hinshaw, 1992) have noted a high correlation between internalizing and externalizing behaviors when psychopathology is broad, as is generally true for youth with school refusal behavior. The information presented by Kearney and Silverman (1996) does not support the ability of the CBCL–TRF-based empirical model to provide discriminantly valid subtypes particular to school refusal behavior. Indeed, factor analyses of childhood behavior problems sometimes yield a separate School Avoidance factor (Lambert, Weisz, & Thesiger, 1989), suggesting that the heterogeneity of this population is too extreme to permit classification even as broadly as overcontrolled or undercontrolled.

Youth with school refusal behavior are essentially represented in almost all narrow-band factors, so none is pathognomonic or highly representative of this population. A muddied clinical picture results (Kearney & Silverman, 1996). This is further exemplified by Young et al.'s (1990) proposed groupings of "internalizing school refusal disorder" and "externalizing truant disorder," which likely have intermingling symptoms. For example, children with internalizing school refusal certainly show nonattendance at school, and children with externalizing truancy usually evidence some symptoms of negative affectivity.

With respect to the discriminant validity of empirical analyses of specific school refusal behaviors, substantial heterogeneity remains problematic. For example, Kolvin et al. (1984) stated that "instead of two separate groups [depression and school phobia], we may be dealing with a spectrum of severity" (p. 355). Kolvin et al.'s study is also criticized for the presence of significantly higher cerebral insult in children of the depressed group (Kearney, 1993) and the liberal use of statistical procedures, given the small number of participants (Atkinson, 1986). Thus, the validity of a depressive subtype to school phobia remains largely speculative (Weinberg, Emslie, & Wilkes, 1986).

Other statistically based studies in this area exhibit significant heterogeneity as well. For example, Berg et al. (1985) found, on the basis of a principal-components factor analysis, that 54.7% of their sample had either school refusal and truancy or neither school refusal nor truancy. In general, the "school refusal and truancy group" was found to be more troubled than children in either category alone, and little difference was seen between those with school refusal and those with truancy. In addition, Atkinson et al. (1989) reported no differences on a behavioral measure between their separation-anxiety and fear-of-failure clusters and found no differences among any of their three clusters with respect to delinquency. Finally, Bools et al. (1990) found, on the basis of cluster analysis, that 68% of their sample fell into their largest group of children with attendance problems; this group represented a mixture of those with school refusal, truancy, both, or neither. In general, therefore, statistical analyses of children with problematic absenteeism have generally yielded clusters of mixed subtypes that lack good discriminant validity.

Clinical Utility

Certainly there is intuitive appeal in trying to divide children with school refusal behavior into empirically derived subtypes, but the overwhelming heterogeneity of this population automatically puts a damper even on this process. Too many children with school refusal behavior present with a combination of symptoms, family problems, and other issues. Still, knowing all the forms of a child's behavior when he or she refuses school is important, and Achenbach's assessment instruments are commonly used to evaluate this population (see chapter 5). Unfortunately, detailed clinical recommendations from proponents of statistically derived subtypes of specific school refusal behaviors have not been proposed.

Predictive Validity

The predictive validity of empirical models of school refusal behavior also remains controversial. Burke and Silverman's (1987) contention is still true that this empirical information gives "no indication of how to choose an approach to treatment on the basis of the differences found" (p. 357). This applies both to internalizing–externalizing and specific school refusal behavior statistical models, none of which have been linked to detailed treatment recommendations or prognostic outcome.

DIAGNOSTIC SUBTYPING OF SCHOOL REFUSAL BEHAVIOR

In conjunction with empirical models of school refusal behavior, diagnostic models have also been proposed for this population. Diagnostic subtyping of youth with school refusal behavior was conducted to some extent prior to 1980, but it suffered from a lack of definitional clarity and comparability to similarly titled syndromes in other studies. With the advent of a more detailed *DSM* (American Psychiatric Association, 1980), however, a more uniform and extensive diagnostic system became available to categorize subpopulations of children, including those with school refusal behavior. This section focuses on studies that best illustrate attempts to diagnostically classify this population.

Attempts to isolate categories of school phobia–refusal using the *DSM* system include those of Bernstein and Garfinkel (1986, 1988), who contended that children with school phobia could be divided into four subgroups:

1. those with affective disorder only
2. those with anxiety disorder only
3. those with both affective and anxiety disorders
4. those with neither an affective disorder nor an anxiety disorder.

Bernstein and Garfinkel (1986) reported that children with school phobia most often met criteria for an affective disorder (e.g., depression) and an anxiety disorder (i.e., separation anxiety or overanxious disorder, 50.0%), an affective disorder only (19.2%), an anxiety disorder only (11.5%), or neither an affective disorder nor an anxiety disorder (19.2%). Bernstein and Garfinkel (1988) also found that children with school phobia primarily met criteria for an anxiety or affective disorder, as did many of their family members. However, the authors noted several caveats to forming conclusions from these data, including small sample size, heterogeneity among diagnostic classes, difficulty determining primary versus secondary symptoms, clinically indistinct symptoms between those with severe anxiety disorders and those with depression, and unclear cause and effect regarding chronic absenteeism and anxiety–depression.

Last and colleagues have also provided some data to support Bernstein and Garfinkel's diagnostic classification for school phobia. For example, Last, Francis, et al. (1987) found that children with a phobic disorder of school tended to meet criteria for another anxiety (52.6%) or affective (31.6%) disorder or no disorder (36.8%). Similarly, Last, Strauss, et al. (1987) and Last and Strauss (1990) reported that children with school phobia had additional diagnoses of anxiety disorder, major depression and dysthymia, and oppositional defiant or no mental disorder. In addition, Last, Strauss, et al. and Last and Strauss have concluded that separation anxiety and phobia are the primary diagnostic subtypes of anxiety-based school refusal.

Assessment Methodology

With the advent of *DSM–III* and its descendants, assessment techniques such as structured interviews have become more common and gradually more reliable and valid (see chapter 5). Examples from the aforementioned studies include the Diagnostic Interview for Children and Adolescents (Herjanic & Campbell, 1977), the Interview Schedule for Children (Last, Francis, et al., 1987), and a children's version of the Schedule for Affective Disorders and Schizophrenia (Puig-Antich, Orvaschel, Tabrizi, & Chambers, 1980). Various child self-report and parent–family measures also have been used, including the Revised Children's Manifest Anxiety Scale (C. R. Reynolds & Paget, 1983), the Beck Depression Inventory (Beck, Rush, Shaw, & Emery, 1979), and the Family Assessment Measure (Skinner, Steinhauer, & Santa-Barbara, 1983). Overall, the assessment methodology used in contemporary diagnostic studies of school refusal behavior has been strong.

Coverage

In contrast with assessment methodology, the coverage of diagnostic subtypes for youth with general school refusal behavior has been problematic. This is largely because researchers have specifically emphasized children with anxiety-based school refusal behavior at the expense of other, non-anxiety-based samples. For example, Bernstein and Garfinkel (1988) selected participants who "had the highest scores on anxiety and depression scales" (p. 70), and Last, Francis, et al. (1987) examined only children with separation anxiety disorder or phobic disorder of school. Despite the fact that children and adolescents without anxiety-based school refusal behavior represent at least half this population, these youth are typically excluded from diagnostic studies in this area.

Furthermore, within samples of youth with general school refusal behavior, more than one-fourth do not meet criteria for any mental disorder (Kearney & Silverman, 1996). As mentioned earlier, the *DSM* does not allow for full diagnoses in youth whose primary, singular behavior is refusal to go to school, so these youth are generally excluded from diagnostic models of classification. Diagnostic coverage for all youth with school refusal behavior is therefore incomplete at this time.

Discriminant Validity

Youth with school refusal behavior certainly present with a variety of psychiatric diagnoses. The most common among those with anxiety-based school refusal behavior appear to be simple–specific and socially oriented phobias, separation anxiety disorder, and depression. Any proposed taxonomy for this population should thus incorporate these diagnostic subtypes for youth who are actually phobic of some school-related object or situation, and some have done so (e.g., Kearney & Silverman, 1996).

If one examines youth with more general school refusal behavior, however, the diagnostic picture becomes messier. For example, Kearney and Silverman (1996) presented data on 64 children and adolescents with acute school refusal behavior that revealed considerable overlap of administered diagnoses. In particular, a large percentage of youth met criteria not only for multiple anxiety disorders but also for others, such as depression and oppositional defiant and conduct disorder. No clear diagnostic profile was evident for this sample.

Diagnostic studies generally reveal, again, the heterogeneity of this population. Youth with school refusal behavior often present with no mental disorder or overlapping anxiety, affective, and conduct-related diagnoses. Although certain children may be more anxious, or more depressed, or more disruptive, or none of the above, it is difficult to predict a diagnostic profile for one particular child with school refusal behavior. Discriminantly valid classification schemes for this population based on diagnosis thus remain elusive.

Clinical Utility

Advantages to diagnostic subtyping include its popularity, near-uniform use among clinicians, assistance in educating clients about a certain disorder, and facilitation of third-party payments. However, using diagnostic systems such as the *DSM* is linked to a host of potential problems as well, including stigmatization and peer ridicule; reinforcement of negative parental attitudes toward a child; lack of clarity; questionable reliability and validity; and "prejudice, discrimination, restriction of opportunity, emphasis on behavior deficits, and neglect of a child's individual characteristics" (Kearney & Sims, 1997, p. 377). In addition, information about assessment, treatment, course of a disorder, and other important clinical variables are not generally available from commonly used diagnostic systems. Therefore, the clinical utility of these systems, especially with respect to school refusal behavior, is debatable.

Predictive Validity

With respect to diagnostic models of school refusal behavior, it is best to recall Last and Strauss's (1990) statement that "psychosocial and psychopharmacological outcome studies with 'school phobic' children have failed to distinguish among them by diagnosis, and thus have not determined whether treatment response is related to diagnosis" (p. 35). Knowing even a general diagnosis of a child with school refusal behavior does not yet permit the assignment of an appropriate treatment strategy. In general, the predictive validity of childhood anxiety disorders and school refusal behavior based on diagnostic subtypes has been poor (Kearney & Sims, 1997).

SUMMARY

Many classification strategies have been proposed for youth with school refusal behavior and are typically based on some dichotomy or other division of demographic, symptom, and family variables. Unfortunately, classification systems in this area have generally failed to (a) provide reliable, homogeneous descriptions of disorder subtypes that allow clinicians to retrieve information about them; (b) ease communication among mental health professionals by providing agreed-on terminology; (c) integrate with clinically useful and psychometrically sound assessment techniques; and (d) predict prognosis or individual response to treatment (Kearney & Silverman, 1996). Such taxonomic failure is derived from problems in assessment methodology, coverage, discriminant validity, clinical utility, and predictive validity.

Because of these deficiencies, practitioners likely are using clinical judgment for many cases of school refusal behavior, possibly relying on a universal treatment strategy for all. What is needed for this population is a classification system that clearly outlines different types of children who refuse school without relying solely on symptoms to do so. More important, what is needed is a subtyping system that is linked closely to an effective assessment and decision-making strategy to help professionals choose or prescribe appropriate treatments (Burke & Silverman, 1987; Paccione-Dyszlewski & Contessa-Kislus, 1987). One classification system that does incorporate these features involves the functional subtyping of school refusal behavior, and this model is described at greater length in chapter 4.

4

UNDERSTANDING THE FUNCTIONS

Evan is a 7-year-old boy who cries every morning on the playground before entering school. He clings to his mother and complains that he doesn't want to go to school and "get hurt." Evan was victimized by a bully earlier in the year and has since missed a third of his school days. Although the situation regarding the bully was resolved (he was moved to another school), Evan insists on being allowed to stay home with his mother and play.

Researchers have tried to classify cases such as Evan's for decades, with variable success. Traditional systems to classify youth with school refusal behavior (see chapter 3) have generally involved either categorical or dimensional models. Categorical models of classifying behavior are usually geared toward separating phenomena into discrete sections or categories; these categories are typically meant to be present or absent (i.e., one either has the behavior or not) and relatively separate from one another (e.g., depression vs. schizophrenia). For school refusal behavior, examples of proposed categories include school refusal/phobia–truancy, neurotic–characterological, acute–chronic, and various diagnoses. A supposed advantage of categorical approaches is that a primary problem is identified (e.g., chronic truancy–conduct disorder) and then addressed. As noted in chapter 3, however, categorical models for classifying youth with school refusal behavior are marked by considerable problems in definition and discriminant validity—many youth have symptoms that overlap greatly among the proposed categories.

Dimensional models of classification, in contrast, are usually geared toward a continuum or profile of phenomena. Depression, for example, may be viewed along a continuum of functioning that includes people who are not depressed, people with minor depressive symptoms, people with major depressive symptoms that interfere with daily functioning, and people with suicidal urges and attempts. Examples of dimensional approaches include Achenbach's (e.g., 1991a) internalizing–externalizing model and, more pertinent to school refusal behavior, Young, Brasic, Kisnadwala, and Leven's

(1990) internalizing school refusal–externalizing truancy proposal. An advantage of dimensional approaches is that a profile of strengths and weaknesses can be derived about a particular person. However, as discussed in chapter 3, extant dimensional models have not applied well to youth with school refusal behavior.

A CATEGORICAL–DIMENSIONAL APPROACH
BASED ON FUNCTION

Kearney and Silverman (1996) stated that a better approach to classifying youth with school refusal behavior might involve aspects of both a categorical model and a dimensional model. In this approach, a primary problem is identified along with a profile of other problems that may have to be addressed in treatment. For example, one could find that a child's primary problem is depression but that conduct problems, anxious behavior, and family conflict are secondary concerns that also interfere with the child's daily functioning.

The question remains, however, on what to base this categorical–dimensional model. Kearney and Silverman (1996) stated that because classification systems based on the forms of school refusal behavior have been so problematic, it may be better instead to focus on the functions of school refusal behavior. *Function* refers to what maintains a child's school refusal behavior or what motivates a child to continue to refuse school. Another way of describing this is to ask what a child is getting out of the school refusal behavior—what reinforcement or reward serves to maintain the child's behavior over time? Although children show many different forms of school refusal behavior, the functions or reasons why children demonstrate these behaviors may be relatively few. Therefore, a classification system based on function may be more manageable and useful than prior systems based on form.

Kearney and Silverman (1990, 1991, 1993, 1996, 1999) have outlined a functional model of school refusal behavior that focuses more on the maintaining variables or motivating conditions of the problem than on specific symptoms. Specifically, they proposed that children refuse school for one or more of four reasons, or functions. These functions are grouped broadly into domains of negative reinforcement and positive reinforcement. *Negative reinforcement* generally refers to the termination of an aversive event, whereas *positive reinforcement* generally refers to the administration of a tangible or intangible reward. Either or both sets of reinforcement can motivate or maintain behavior, including school refusal behavior.

As discussed previously, some youth certainly refuse school to get away from unpleasant or aversive events there. As they avoid or escape such events or stimuli, the unpleasantness of the situation and subsequent negative feelings generally fade. Relief from this unpleasantness is, of course, very rewarding and a form of negative reinforcement. As a result, one may continually refuse school to dodge unpleasant situations and feelings there. Within a functional model of school refusal behavior, children who refuse school for negative reinforcement are thought to do so more specifically to (a) avoid stimuli that provoke a sense of general negative affectivity or somatic complaints, (b) escape aversive social or evaluative situations, or (c) both.

Many youth also refuse school for intangible or tangible rewards outside of school that are more powerful than those within school. Intangible rewards may include things such as verbal attention and reassurance, whereas tangible rewards may include things such as sleeping late, drug use, and playing with friends. Within a functional model of school refusal behavior, children who refuse school for positive reinforcement are thought to do so more specifically to gain (a) attention from parents or significant others, (b) tangible reinforcement outside of school, or (c) both.

In the sections that follow, a synopsis is presented of each of the four proposed functions for school refusal behavior. The initial two are negatively reinforcement based, whereas the second two are positively reinforcement based. These separate sections do not imply, however, that children necessarily refuse school for only one of these conditions—any number of functions can apply to any child with school refusal behavior.

During a discussion of each function, summaries are offered of contemporary data from my sample of 166 youth with general school refusal behavior (Tillotson & Kearney, 1998). These youth, referred to specialized clinics, were sorted according to function using child and parent versions of the School Refusal Assessment Scale (SRAS; see chapter 5 for a full description of all assessment measures described here). The SRAS allows for the descriptive identification of the primary function(s) or maintaining variable(s) of a particular child's school refusal behavior. Of these 166 youth, (a) 56 were classified as refusing school primarily to avoid stimuli that provoke general negative affectivity, (b) 13 were classified as refusing school primarily to escape aversive social or evaluative situations, (c) 39 were classified as refusing school primarily for attention, and (d) 58 were classified as refusing school primarily for tangible reinforcement outside of school.

Child self-report measures were associated with child reports from the SRAS; parent measures were associated with parent reports from the SRAS; composite *Diagnostic and Statistical Manual of Mental Disorders* (3rd ed. rev. [DSM–III–R], American Psychiatric Association [APA], 1987; 4th ed.

[DSM–IV], American Psychiatric Association, 1994) diagnoses were associated with composite reports from the SRAS. Some youth did receive more than one diagnosis. Diagnoses of disorders not otherwise specified are excluded here. Illustrative case examples are also provided.

NEGATIVE REINFORCEMENT

Avoidance of Stimuli That Provoke a Sense of General Negative Affectivity

Some youth certainly refuse school to avoid unpleasant stimuli near or at school. In some cases these children readily point to something that troubles them—examples include a bus, fire alarm, teacher, or animal in the classroom. Most children who refuse school to avoid unpleasantness, however, cannot identify specific fear-related stimuli. Instead, these children say they are unsure as to why they do not like school—they just have feelings of general "malaise" or "misery" when at school. These are youth who refuse school to avoid stimuli that provoke negative affectivity (SPNA; see chapter 2 for a description of negative affectivity).

Many of these typically younger children report general symptoms of anxiety, sadness, and somatic complaints. Youth who refuse school to avoid SPNA show significantly elevated scores on the Revised Children's Manifest Anxiety Scale (C. R. Reynolds & Paget, 1983), the State–Trait Anxiety Inventory for Children (Spielberger, 1973), and the Daily Life Stressors Scale (DLSS; Kearney, Drabman, & Beasley, 1993) compared with children who refuse school for positive reinforcement. In addition, there is a trend toward significance with respect to depressive symptoms on the Children's Depression Inventory (CDI; Kovacs, 1992): Youth who refuse school for negative reinforcement in general, and to avoid SPNA in particular, tend to have higher CDI scores than those who refuse school for positive reinforcement. Finally, although there are no major differences with respect to overall fearfulness, youth who refuse school to avoid SPNA do report more fear on school-related items on the Fear Survey Schedule for Children–Revised compared with youth of other functions.

With respect to parent data from the Child Behavior Checklist (CBCL; Achenbach, 1991a), youth who refuse school to avoid SPNA have no significantly elevated scores on internalizing factors compared with youth of other functions. However, children who refuse school to avoid SPNA are rated significantly lower with respect to attention problems and delinquent and aggressive behavior compared with youth who refuse school for tangible reinforcement.

Data from the Family Environment Scale (FES; Moos & Moos, 1986) indicate that youth who refuse school to avoid SPNA have families with relatively normal levels of achievement orientation, active–recreational orientation, control, expressiveness, intellectual–cultural orientation, moral–religious emphasis, and organization. However, levels of independence are one standard deviation below the mean. Still, families of these children are much more cohesive compared with families of children of other functions. These data collectively indicate that youth who refuse school to avoid SPNA come from mostly healthy families (Kearney & Silverman, 1995).

Following are composite *DSM–III–R/DSM–IV* diagnoses for youth who primarily refuse school to avoid SPNA. These data help support the idea that many children refuse school with a confluence of severe school-related fear and panic, general anxiety, depressive symptoms, and overall stress.

- overanxious–generalized anxiety disorder, 35.7%
- no disorder, 28.6%
- depression–dysthymia, 21.4%
- separation anxiety disorder, 19.6%
- social phobia–anxiety disorder, 17.9%
- panic disorder, 10.7%
- specific phobia, 10.7%
- avoidant disorder, 8.9%
- agoraphobia, 5.4%
- attention deficit hyperactivity disorder, 5.4%
- oppositional defiant disorder, 5.4%
- posttraumatic stress disorder, 5.4%
- enuresis, 1.8%.

As a case example, Joshua is a 7-year-old boy referred for a 2-month episode of school refusal behavior. Although he has missed only 3 school days since September, his parents report that Joshua is becoming increasingly difficult to get to school on Monday and Tuesday mornings. On most Sunday nights, he becomes sullen and asks his parents not to send him to school. When asked why, Joshua cries and says that he does not know but that "I just don't want to go back." He also complains of stomachaches and some diarrhea in the morning, although a recent visit to the pediatrician revealed no physical problems. He has asked for home schooling, and his parents are considering that option. Joshua's teacher reports that her student is usually very quiet and occasionally cries during class but cannot point to anything in particular that would have upset Joshua. His classmates have been generally supportive, but Joshua's distress and somatic complaints have not abated over time. His sullenness and withdrawal are also beginning to sour his grades.

Escape From Aversive Social or Evaluative Situations

Youth may also refuse school to escape more specific situations than those claimed by children who refuse school to avoid SPNA. In particular, many older children and adolescents refuse school to escape aversive social or evaluative situations at school. These situations can include any number of things, but common examples include public speaking, interactions with others, walking in hallways or into class or school, tests and graded situations, writing on the blackboard, being called on in class, and classes that regularly involve some performance before others (e.g., physical education, choir, driving classes; Beidel, Turner, & Morris, 1999). In addition, these children may be refusing school to avoid certain people there, including teachers, peers, crowds, or others.

Many youth of this group show elevated levels of general and social anxiety, overall stress, depressive symptoms, and some somatic complaints, although many do not. Youth who refuse school to escape aversive social or evaluative situations show significantly more elevated scores on the Revised Children's Manifest Anxiety Scale and the State–Trait Anxiety Inventory for Children compared with those who refuse school for positive reinforcement. In addition, there is a trend toward significance with respect to the DLSS and depressive symptoms on the CDI: Children who refuse school for negative reinforcement in general, and to escape aversive social or evaluative situations in particular, tend to have higher DLSS and CDI scores than those who refuse school for positive reinforcement. Levels of social anxiety are also somewhat higher in this group compared with those who refuse school for positive tangible reinforcement.

With respect to parent data from the CBCL, youth who refuse school to escape aversive social or evaluative situations show significantly higher scores on the Withdrawn and Somatic Complaints factors, as one might expect, compared with youth of other functional conditions. A trend toward higher scores on the Anxious–Depressed factor is also seen for this group. In addition, youth who refuse school to escape aversive social or evaluative situations tend to have lower delinquent behavior scores compared with children who refuse school for positive reinforcement (Tillotson & Kearney, 1998).

Data from the FES indicate that children who refuse school to escape aversive social or evaluative situations have relatively normal levels of familial achievement orientation, conflict, control, expressiveness, intellectual–cultural orientation, moral–religious emphasis, and organization. However, this group is almost one standard deviation below the mean with respect to active–recreational orientation, cohesion, and independence. These data may indicate that substantial family detachment marks much of this functional group (Kearney & Silverman, 1995).

Following are composite *DSM–III–R/DSM–IV* diagnoses for youth who primarily refuse school to escape aversive social or evaluative situations. These data help support the idea that many children refuse school with a confluence of severe school-related social and general anxiety and depressive symptoms.

- overanxious–generalized anxiety disorder, 61.5%
- social phobia–anxiety disorder, 61.5%
- depression–dysthymia, 53.8%
- avoidant disorder, 46.2%
- oppositional defiant disorder, 23.1%
- specific phobia, 15.4%
- conduct disorder, 7.7%
- separation anxiety disorder, 7.7%.

As a case example, Samantha is a 13-year-old girl in eighth grade referred for a 3-month episode of school refusal behavior. Specifically, she has adamantly refused to go to school on days when she has to be in large crowds, such as assemblies or physical education class; she has 4 full absences and 18 partial absences. Samantha reports great anxiety during these situations, although she is unsure exactly why. Her parents describe their daughter as a "loner" who is overweight and who does not make friends readily. She often "keeps to herself" and prefers to read a book or stand in the corner rather than introduce herself to others. Unfortunately, Samantha's school refusal behavior is worsening as the year progresses and more social and evaluative academic performances are required. Samantha's teachers report that she is an average student but one who is clearly withdrawn and somewhat depressed. She does respond well to adults who draw her out a bit, but she sometimes becomes overdependent on them.

POSITIVE REINFORCEMENT

Attention-Seeking Behavior

Youth may also refuse school for positive reinforcement outside of school, including intangible rewards such as attention or sympathy from parents or others (e.g., grandparents, older siblings, neighbors). This group often consists of younger children who demonstrate various misbehaviors in the morning to get attention and stay home from school. These misbehaviors often include tantrums, screaming, clinging, locking oneself in a room or car, reassurance seeking, guilt-inducing behavior, exaggerated complaints of physical symptoms, noncompliance, and running away (usually temporarily), among others. These children may have some separation anxiety as well, but this is often subsumed under manipulative, controlling behavior designed to solicit attention.

These attention-seeking children often appear little different from youth in other functional groups. In fact, elevated levels of overall fear and social anxiety are sometimes seen in this group (Tillotson & Kearney, 1998). This finding may reflect the younger age of this group (mean age 9.6 years) or that these children exaggerate internalizing symptoms to make themselves appear more dysfunctional than they are. It is interesting that these children also report the lowest level of overall stress on the DLSS compared with youth of other functional groups. Such variability in measures may reflect some of the manipulativeness of this group, although this is only speculative at this point.

With respect to parent data from the CBCL, children who refuse school for attention are rated fairly low for Withdrawn and Somatic Complaints and moderate for Anxiety–Depression. The latter finding may reflect true anxiety or simply parental beliefs of the child's claims. Low to moderate levels of externalizing behaviors are also present. However, on one externalizing CBCL item, "demands a lot of attention," children who refuse school for attention are rated by their parents substantially higher than youth of other functional groups.

Data from the FES indicate that children who refuse school for attention generally have families of normal achievement orientation, active–recreational orientation, conflict, control, expressiveness, intellectual–cultural orientation, moral–religious emphasis, and organization. Most striking, however, is that these families are marked by low levels of cohesion and very low levels of independence. These latter findings support the contention that many families of this functional group are enmeshed (Kearney & Silverman, 1995).

Following are composite *DSM–III–R/DSM–IV* diagnoses for youth who primarily refuse school for attention. These data indicate that many of these children may have some level of separation anxiety but also that many have some level of defiance or no disorder.

- Separation anxiety disorder, 66.7%
- Overanxious–generalized anxiety disorder, 33.3%
- No disorder, 20.5%
- Avoidant disorder, 12.8%
- Oppositional defiant disorder, 12.8%
- Specific phobia, 12.8%
- Attention deficit hyperactivity disorder, 5.1%
- Social phobia–social anxiety disorder, 5.1%
- Agoraphobia, 2.6%

- Enuresis, 2.6%
- Panic disorder, 2.6%
- Sleep terror disorder, 2.6%.

As a case example, Natalie is a 6-year-old girl referred for a 1-month episode of school refusal behavior. Almost every morning, Natalie refuses to get out of bed or runs from her parents as they are trying to dress her and otherwise prepare her for school. Natalie reports that she does not like school, but her parents and teacher say she relishes school once she gets there. Natalie has been able to force her parents to allow her to stay home on seven occasions so far this year, and her misbehavior is getting more severe. Her mother, who is home during the day, reports that Natalie enjoys helping her with chores, fixing lunch, and going shopping. Natalie has no behavior problems outside of 6:00 a.m. to 8:30 a.m. and is otherwise a splendid child and student. Her parents are especially concerned, however, by the fact that Natalie kicked her father recently during an attempt to stay home from school.

Pursuit of Tangible Reinforcement Outside of School

Many youth also refuse school for tangible reinforcement outside of school. Many of these older children and adolescents either skip classes, whole sections of the school day (e.g., an afternoon), or the entire day to pursue reinforcers that are more powerful than those at school. Outside reinforcers are manifold, of course, but common examples include watching television, playing video games or sports, accessing the Internet, sleeping late, visiting with friends on the telephone or in person, eating off the school campus, engaging in drug use, going to day parties, shopping, attending casinos, or working, among others.

Youth who refuse school for tangible reinforcement outside of school tend to have lower levels of general and social anxiety, depression, fear, and overall distress compared with youth of other functions (Tillotson & Kearney, 1998). This group is therefore the best example of non-anxiety-based school refusal behavior. This does not imply, however, that these youth never have symptoms of negative affectivity—in fact, many do show these symptoms after having been out of school for a long time—but rather that such symptoms are less likely to be seen in this group compared with other groups.

With respect to parent data from the CBCL, youth who refuse school for tangible reinforcement outside of school tend to have more attention problems and delinquent and aggressive behavior than children who refuse school for negative reinforcement. Again, these youth tend to have more externalizing, non-anxiety-based problems compared with youth of other functional conditions (Tillotson & Kearney, 1998).

Data from the FES indicate that children who refuse school for tangible reinforcement outside of school tend to have families of relatively normal levels of achievement orientation, active–recreational orientation, control, expressiveness, intellectual–cultural orientation, independence, moral–religious emphasis, and organization. However, these families are significantly more conflictive than other groups and show low levels of cohesion (Kearney & Silverman, 1995).

Following are composite *DSM–III–R/DSM–IV* diagnoses for youth who primarily refuse school to pursue tangible reinforcement outside of school. These data indicate that many of these youth are defiant or have no disorder:

- Overanxious–generalized anxiety disorder, 27.6%
- Oppositional defiant disorder, 25.9%
- No disorder, 25.9%
- Conduct disorder, 10.3%
- Depression–dysthymia, 10.3%
- Separation anxiety disorder, 8.6%
- Specific phobia, 8.6%
- Avoidant disorder, 6.9%
- Social phobia, 6.9%
- Attention deficit hyperactivity disorder, 3.4%
- Enuresis, 3.4%
- Agoraphobia, 1.7%
- Panic disorder, 1.7%.

As a case example, Saul is a 15-year-old boy referred for a 7-month episode of school refusal behavior. He has missed 20 days of school so far as well as numerous classes on days he does attend. Saul reports that he usually "hangs out with my friends" when they leave the school campus to eat lunch or play basketball. He is currently failing one class but has Cs or better in all of his other classes, which prompts Saul to wonder why he has to attend so much. Saul's parents are extremely frustrated by his overall defiance and refusal to attend school and have reportedly had numerous fights with him about this subject. Fortunately, Saul has not yet engaged in any severe delinquent behavior, but his parents worry that his friends are a bad influence on him. Saul's teachers report that he is quiet and a little withdrawn in class but not disruptive in any way. They all confirmed, however, that unless his attendance and make-up work improve soon he is in danger of failing 10th grade.

FUNCTIONS OF SCHOOL REFUSAL BEHAVIOR

As mentioned earlier, the initial two functional conditions refer to youth who refuse school to get away from something aversive at school; these children refuse school for *negative reinforcement*. The second two functional conditions refer to youth who refuse school to pursue something more reinforcing outside of school; these children refuse school for *positive reinforcement*. Of course, some children also refuse school for multiple reasons. For example, a child may initially have negative affectivity when attending school and persuade his parents to let him stay home. When home during the day, the child may enjoy rewarding amenities such as watching television or sleeping late. A child like Evan, for example (whose case is described at the beginning of this chapter), may then refuse school both to avoid school and to pursue pleasantries at home.

SUMMARY AND ADVANTAGES

Because of the innumerable forms of school refusal behavior, a classification, assessment, and treatment system based on fewer functions may be preferable. An advantage of this evolving functional model is its link to a clear definition of school refusal behavior as well as self-corrective, acute, and chronic distinctions (see chapter 1). In addition, the model covers all youth who refuse to attend school, and discriminant validity among the reinforcement dimensions has been shown (Kearney & Silverman, 1991, 1993). Another advantage of the functional model is its link to a formal assessment strategy that is outlined in greater depth in chapter 5. This includes the SRAS, a measure that assesses the relative strength of the four functional conditions (Kearney & Silverman, 1993). As indicated earlier, the highest scoring condition from the SRAS is considered the primary maintaining variable of a particular child's school refusal behavior.

Perhaps the strongest advantage of the functional model is its direct link to prescriptive treatment and prediction of treatment outcome. The model is designed to provide therapists and others with a systematic and objective clinical strategy for assessing a child with school refusal behavior and for assigning the best treatment package to return the child to school without distress. My colleagues and I (Kearney & Albano, 2000; Kearney & Silverman, 1990, 1996, 1999) have formulated prescriptive therapeutic options for each function of school refusal behavior. Initial outcome evaluations have shown that treatment can be successfully predicted and implemented for this population using a functional model (e.g., Chorpita, Albano, Heimberg, & Barlow, 1996; Kearney & Silverman, 1990, 1999):

- For youth who refuse school to avoid a general sense of negative affectivity, prescriptive treatment includes child-based psycho-education, somatic control exercises, and re-exposure to the school setting.
- For youth who refuse school to escape aversive social or evaluative situations, prescriptive treatment includes child-based psychoeducation, modeling and role play, cognitive restructuring, and behavioral exposures.
- For youth who refuse school for attention, prescriptive treatment includes parent-based training in contingency management and, potentially, forced school attendance.
- For youth who refuse school for tangible reinforcement outside of school, prescriptive treatment includes family-based therapy in contingency contracting, communication skills training, peer refusal skills training, and escorting youth to school, to classes, or both.

An ongoing description of the functional model for school refusal behavior is presented throughout the remainder of this book. More specifically, in chapter 5, assessment techniques and a strategy for identifying the primary function of a child's school refusal behavior are described. In chapters 6–9, treatment strategies based on the four functions outlined are delineated. In chapter 10, extreme cases and prevention and relapse prevention strategies most amenable to the functional model are discussed.

5

ASSESSING YOUTH
WITH SCHOOL
REFUSAL BEHAVIOR

Jasmine is a 16-year-old girl who spends time with her friends later in the day whenever she can't get out of bed and go to school in the morning. On days she does attend school, she is often unmotivated or skips out early. School officials have informed the family of their intent to refer Jasmine's case to the juvenile court system and have urged the family to seek counseling.

In cases such as Jasmine's where many factors could and likely do impinge on her behavior, a thorough and systematic assessment process is necessary. In this chapter, primary methods are reviewed for assessing youth with school refusal behavior. These methods include interviews, youth self-report and parent–teacher measures, direct observation, daily monitoring, school official reports, and other methods. Note that it is beyond the scope of this chapter to completely evaluate all measures that theoretically could apply to as heterogeneous a population as youth with school refusal behavior. Indeed, almost any assessment measure could apply to these youth and their families. Therefore, measures that are most relevant and helpful, previously used for this population, psychometrically strong, or pertinent to a functional model of assessment are described here.

Within a functional model of school refusal behavior, general goals of assessment are to (a) identify the primary forms of the behavior, (b) identify the primary functions of the behavior, and (c) integrate all information to help choose the best treatment option. Therefore, for each major assessment method described here, separate discussions surround the evaluation of form and function. Later, a strategy and case example are outlined for synthesizing information to choose treatment. Prior to descriptions of formal assessment, however, a brief discussion follows here with respect to screening cases of potential school refusal behavior.

SCREENING YOUTH WITH POTENTIAL
SCHOOL REFUSAL BEHAVIOR

When screening a referral with potential school refusal behavior, it is best to carefully ask certain questions to ensure that a valid problem does exist. In many cases, immediate formal assessment is unnecessary because a child's absenteeism is limited or potentially short lived in nature. Therefore, an important question to ask at this time is whether the child has just begun to refuse school, especially at the very beginning of the school year. Although many parents contact a therapist or school official as soon as their child refuses school, many children of this population display self-corrective school refusal behavior—they return to school on their own after sporadic attempts to stay home. If the school refusal problem has lasted less than 2 weeks, especially after an extended break, then formal assessment may be delayed until it is clear the child has a true case of acute school refusal behavior.

This does not mean, however, that every school refusal case lasting less than 2 weeks should be deferred. For example, if a child is displaying very severe behavior (e.g., self-injury) to avoid school, if a family is in considerable turmoil and confusion because of the problem, or if the child has a history of such behavior, then formal assessment should begin as soon as possible. Clinical judgment is obviously necessary in such cases, and erring on the side of caution is recommended; when in doubt, conduct an immediate formal assessment.

A second important screening question surrounds the child's primary behavior problem. In particular, one should ascertain whether the child's school refusal behavior is (a) the primary or only problem or (b) related to or subsumed by some other problem. With respect to the latter, for example, a child's school refusal behavior may be symptomatic of some larger problem, such as panic or social anxiety disorder, depression or suicidal behavior, learning disability, oppositional defiant or conduct disorder, substance abuse, or simple lack of motivation in all activities. Knowing whether school refusal behavior is a primary or secondary problem may not be important for simply deciding to schedule a client for formal assessment, but it may be useful for tailoring the assessment methods used (e.g., hopelessness measures, intelligence testing, drug screen). In addition, knowing whether a child's school refusal behavior is circumscribed or part of a more general syndrome will help one consider, initially, the necessary scope of treatment. However, this is less relevant in cases where, regardless of overall syndrome, absenteeism is the first and foremost problem that parents and youth want to address.

During initial investigation of the nature of a child's school refusal behavior, many parents overemphasize externalizing behaviors, such as noncompliance and running away, and de-emphasize internalizing behaviors, such as anxiety and depression. However, all relevant behaviors should be covered and, if possible and as appropriate, others (e.g., teachers) who may have additional information should be contacted. During the screening process, some parents and some school officials may become frantic and overblow the severity of the problem (Kearney & Sims, 1997). In this situation, a therapist should serve as a calm role model and proceed methodically with the screening.

A third important set of screening questions surrounds other medical or familial variables that may influence a child's school refusal behavior. Primary physical conditions such as asthma, pain, or ulcers, for example, may be present and mandate a referral for medical examination before or during psychological assessment. In other cases, less severe somatic complaints or other health concerns coexist with school refusal behavior. Consultations with physicians are important to know whether a child's physical symptoms are real and anxiety based or exaggerated and attention seeking in nature. In still other cases, consultations with child psychiatrists are necessary to help manage comorbid conditions such as attention deficit hyperactivity disorder or severe anxiety or depression. As mentioned in chapters 1 and 2, clinicians and educators should also be wary of school withdrawal, when a parent deliberately removes a child from school, and carefully consider other distal–familial variables that could be influencing a child's school refusal behavior.

Finally, knowing the child's age may lead to initial hypotheses about factors important for addressing school refusal behavior. One factor is the reason why the child is refusing school. Younger children tend to refuse school more to avoid general negative affectivity and somatic complaints or for attention, whereas adolescents tend to refuse school more to escape aversive social or evaluative situations or for tangible reinforcement outside of school (see chapter 4). This is not always the case, however—any child may refuse school for any reason, and many children refuse school for multiple reasons. In addition, knowing the child's age may help somewhat with treatment selection. For example, the feasibility or desirability of forced school attendance is better with younger children, whereas cognitive–verbally based therapies tend to be more effective with older children and adolescents.

FORMAL ASSESSMENT OF YOUTH WITH SCHOOL REFUSAL BEHAVIOR

After the screening process, formal assessment may indeed be considered appropriate. When conducting a formal assessment of youth with school refusal behavior, given the heterogeneity of this population, it is extremely important to use multiple methods and solicit multiple sources of information. As mentioned earlier, formal assessment should be structured to fully evaluate both the *form* and the *function* of a child's school refusal behavior. Of course, familial, school-related, and other variables most pertinent to a specific case should be fully examined as well. In this section the most prominent assessment methods for youth with school refusal behavior—the methods that are most relevant, helpful, previously used, psychometrically strong, and pertinent—are outlined with respect to form and function.

Interview

The Form of School Refusal Behavior

When collecting information about the form of a child's school refusal behavior, the interview is, of course, a very common assessment tool for clinicians and educators. Interviews may be relatively structured or unstructured depending on the desire for rigor and consistency across cases. Structured interviews used in research settings for youth with school refusal behavior and their families have included, in alphabetical order, the Diagnostic Interview for Children and Adolescents (Herjanic & Campbell, 1977), Family History Research Diagnostic Criteria (Endicott, Andreasen, & Spitzer, 1975), Interview Schedule for Children (see Last, Francis, et al., 1987; and Last, Strauss, & Francis, 1987), Schedule for Affective Disorders and Schizophrenia (Kiddie–SADS; Puig-Antich, Orvaschel, Tabrizi, & Chambers, 1980), and the National Institute of Mental Health Diagnostic Interview Schedule for Children (Shaffer et al., 1996). Other common structured interviews include the Child and Adolescent Psychiatric Assessment (Angold & Costello, 2000), Child Assessment Schedule (Hodges, Kline, Stern, Cytryn, & McKnew, 1982), Children's Interview for Psychiatric Syndromes (Weller, Weller, Fristad, Rooney, & Schecter, 2000), Dominic–R (Valla, Bergeron, & Smolla, 2000), and Pictorial Instrument for Children and Adolescents (Ernst, Cookus, & Moravec, 2000).

The School Absence Questionnaire (Huffington & Sevitt, 1989), which is based on the classic school phobia/refusal–truancy dichotomy (see chapters 1 and 3), has also been used to interview parents in this population. Seven yes–no questions are asked, including

- Do you always know whether your child is at school or not?
- Do you feel your child's absence from school is justified?
- Does your child, in your opinion, experience difficulty in attending school?
- When your child is not at school, do you know where he or she is?
- If the answer (to the previous question) is yes, is your child at home?

- Does your child get emotionally upset at the prospect of going to school (i.e., showing misery, fear, undue tempers, complaints of feeling ill)?
- Has your child shown any serious antisocial behavior?

A disadvantage of most structured interviews is their lack of specific attention to school refusal behavior. An exception is the Anxiety Disorders Interview Schedule for Children (Silverman & Albano, 1996), a structured diagnostic interview with separate versions for children and parents (ADIS–C, ADIS–P). Composite diagnoses from these reports are derived for anxiety and other disorders, such as depression, oppositional defiant and conduct disorder, substance abuse, enuresis, and attention deficit hyperactivity disorder, among several others. The ADIS–C and ADIS–P have displayed good interrater and test–retest reliability (Silverman & Eisen, 1992; Silverman & Nelles, 1988), and a kappa coefficient of .75 has been reported for overall anxiety disorder using combined information from each (see Rapee, Barrett, Dadds, & Evans, 1994, for kappa coefficients specific to each anxiety disorder).

The ADIS–C and ADIS–P contain sections for both school history and school refusal behavior, and parts of these are reproduced in Exhibits 5.1 and 5.2. Questions of school history surround history of and current attendance, academic grades, past need for a home tutor, and days missed from school because of anxiety. Questions of school refusal behavior surround whether the child has problems attending school, gets nervous about or scared of going to school, stays home because of nervousness or fear, contacts parents from school because of nervousness or fear, and visits the nurse or complains of illness at school. Questions also concern what makes school difficult for the child, whether the child misses school because he or she prefers to be home, whether the child gets upset if he or she does not do well in school, what the child does when not in school during the week, family member reactions, parental methods to induce school attendance, medication the child has taken for school refusal behavior, and length of school refusal behavior. In addition, fear and interference ratings on a 0–8 severity scale are solicited for various stimuli that may provoke school refusal behavior.

The ADIS–C and ADIS–P are commonly used to assess children with school refusal behavior and their parents (e.g., Kearney & Silverman, 1990, 1996, 1999), but a key limitation is that it clearly focuses on children with emotional distress related to school nonattendance. For example, fear and avoidance ratings are taken in the school refusal behavior section, but ratings of noncompliance, acting-out behaviors, and related problems are not. Interviewers are informed that school refusal behavior should be fully examined within the context of all *Diagnostic and Statistical Manual of Mental Disorders*

EXHIBIT 5.1
ADIS–C Section on School Refusal Behavior

Initial Inquiry

1. **Do you get very nervous or scared about having to go to school?** ☐ Yes ☐ No ☐ Other

2. **Do you stay home from school because you are nervous or scared?** ☐ Yes ☐ No ☐ Other

   If "Yes," **How many times has that happened this year?**_____

   Calculate percentage of days missed in the present school year.

   How many times did that happen last year? _____

   Calculate percentage of days missed during the last school year.

3a. **Do you get very nervous or scared when you are in school?** ☐ Yes ☐ No ☐ Other

   If the child responds "Yes," ask Questions 3b and 3c. Otherwise, skip to Question 4.

3b. **When you are scared in school, do you ever go to the school nurse or counselor?** ☐ Yes ☐ No ☐ Other

   If "Yes," **How often?** _____

3c. **When you are scared at school, do you or does someone from school, such as the school nurse, ever call your mom or dad?** ☐ Yes ☐ No ☐ Other

   If "Yes," **How often has that happened this school year?**

   Ask the child to elaborate on any "Yes" responses to Question 3a, 3b, or 3c. Inquire about patterns of reassurance seeking.

(4th ed. [*DSM–IV*]; American Psychiatric Association, 1994) categories, but no questions are asked about days missed from school for other than anxiety-based concerns.

Many other questions should thus be asked when interviewing youth with general school refusal behavior and their families. In particular, reports should be obtained about a child's history and episodes of all types of school refusal behavior (including severity and duration), interpersonal and academic functioning, health and physical functioning, developmental and

EXHIBIT 5.2
ADIS–P Section on School Refusal Behavior

In this section, record as "No" responses that reflect "typical" child school-related anxiety and that do not appear to be excessively interfering (e.g., "a little nervous before tests," "a little nervous when he or she forgets his or her homework," etc.).

1. **Does your child have problems attending or staying in school?** ☐ Yes ☐ No ☐ Other

2. **Does your child get very nervous or scared about having to go to school?** ☐ Yes ☐ No ☐ Other

3. **Does your child stay home or try to stay home from school because** (he or she) **is nervous or scared?** ☐ Yes ☐ No ☐ Other

4. **Does your child ever tell you that** (he or she) **is nervous or scared when** (he or she) **is in school?** ☐ Yes ☐ No ☐ Other

   If "Yes," **Has your child ever left school early because of this, has** (he or she) **made phone calls to you during school hours, or has anyone from the school ever called during school hours on behalf of your child?** ☐ Yes ☐ No ☐ Other

   If "Yes," **How many times has that happened this year?** _____

5. **To your knowledge, does your child often go to see the nurse or often complain of feeling sick while in school?** ☐ Yes ☐ No ☐ Other

   If "Yes," **How many times has that happened this year?** _____

psychiatric history, mental status, and all relevant externalizing behaviors and distal variables. With respect to the family, full reports should be obtained about previous treatment attempts by parents and professionals, daily family routines, effects on daily functioning, social support and current resources, relevant cultural variables, family members' perceptions of and reactions to the problem, urgent issues or crises, and marital–family history and dynamics. The family's reasons for seeking help now and their motivation for following through in treatment should be assessed as well. Finally, because each case of school refusal behavior is so unique, it is best to be flexible in an interview and allow for many other potentially pertinent questions.

The Function of School Refusal Behavior

When interviewing children, parents, school officials, and others about a child's school refusal behavior, specific questions should also be geared toward the function of the behavior. These questions may surround the four functions described in chapter 4, although more general functional interviews are available (see Lee & Miltenberger, 1996). Although the following questions are listed separately per function, it is best to ask each question to (a) rule out a function that may not be particularly influential and (b) see if a child is refusing school for two or more functions. In the latter case, questions should also surround which function is most prominent.

Regarding the first function, avoidance of stimuli that provoke negative affectivity, interview questions could involve some variant of the following:

- How often does the child refuse school specifically because he or she is generally distressed or upset about school?
- Is the child upset about school much more so than most children his or her age?
- Are there any school-related items that the child prefers to avoid (e.g., bus, classroom item, school setting, teacher, fire alarm)?
- Has the child informed anyone of recent negative life events, or has the child suddenly changed his or her behavior in any way?
- Has the child expressed any specific emotions or had any physical symptoms in regard to going to school?
- Do these problems generally occur every day, or primarily on school days?
- Is the child more likely to attend school if certain items or activities are not present?

Regarding the second function of school refusal behavior, escape from aversive social or evaluative situations, interview questions could involve some variant of the following:

- How often does the child refuse school specifically because he or she wants to escape social situations or school situations in which he or she might be evaluated?
- Does the child escape these situations much more so than most children his or her age?
- What social or evaluative situations does the child prefer to avoid (e.g., writing or speaking in front of others, meeting new people, peer interactions, recitals, tests, athletic contests, being in or approaching groups of people)?
- Has the child informed anyone of recent negative social or evaluative events, or has he or she suddenly changed his or her social behavior in any way?

- Has the child expressed any specific emotions or had any physical symptoms in regard to interacting in social or evaluative situations?
- Do these problems generally occur in all social or evaluative situations, or primarily in school-related ones?
- Would the child be more likely to attend school if certain people or evaluative situations were not present?

Regarding the third function of school refusal behavior, attention seeking, interview questions could involve some variant of the following:

- How often does the child refuse school specifically because he or she wants attention from a parent or a significant other?
- Does the child seek attention much more so than most children his or her age?
- In what specific behaviors does the child engage to get attention (e.g., clinging, reassurance seeking, refusal to move, tantrums, making telephone calls, protests, verbal demands, guilt-inducing behavior, running from school to home)?
- Has the child had any recent negative life events, or has he or she suddenly changed his or her behavior in any way?
- Has the child expressed any specific emotions or had any physical symptoms in regard to interacting with, or being away from, significant others?
- Do these problems generally occur in most daily life situations, or primarily in school-related situations?
- Would the child be more likely to attend school if a significant other (e.g., parent, sibling) attended school with him or her?

Regarding the fourth function of school refusal behavior, pursuit of tangible reinforcement outside of school, interview questions could involve some variant of the following:

- How often does the child refuse school specifically to pursue something tangible from some source outside of school?
- Does the child pursue tangible rewards outside of school much more so than most children his or her age?
- What specific things does the child leave school to pursue (e.g., time with friends, alcohol–drug use, television or games at home, bicycling, shopping centers or casinos)?
- Has the child had any recent negative life events, or has he or she suddenly changed his or her behavior in any way?
- Has the child expressed any specific emotions about being in or leaving school?

- Does the child pursue tangible rewards in many daily life situations, or primarily during school hours?
- Would the child be more likely to attend school if school were more fun or if certain pleasures outside of school were no longer available?

When interviewing families in this population, it is usually best to interview the child before parents and others. This helps build rapport and credibility with the child, who has likely been targeted as the "problem," and allows a therapist to immediately explain his or her confidentiality policy. Interviewing at this stage can also be used as a forum to convey to the child that everyone's reasonable point of view is considered and that part- or full-time school attendance will likely be a key goal of future treatment.

Youth Self-Report Measures and Parent–Teacher Questionnaires

Many youth self-report measures and parent–teacher questionnaires have also been used to assess families and their youth with school refusal behavior. These measures are particularly useful for gathering information not fully derived from an interview because of lack of time, unwillingness to share information, poor memory, or other reasons.

The Form of School Refusal Behavior

Youth self-report measures. Youth self-report measures are particularly applicable to older children and adolescents with good verbal and reading skills and those with internalizing problems. The most prominent self-report measures for assessing youth with school refusal behavior include, alphabetically, the following:

- Children's Depression Inventory (CDI; Kovacs, 1992), a 27-item measure of depressive symptoms within the past 2 weeks. The CDI is useful in determining whether depression is primary or secondary to school refusal behavior. The scale is also useful for assessing youth who refuse school to avoid general negative affectivity or to escape aversive social or evaluative situations. Common related measures include the Children's Depression Scale (Tisher & Lang, 1983), Kandel Depression Scale (Kandel & Davies, 1982), and Reynolds Child/Adolescent Depression Scale (W. M. Reynolds, 1986, 1989). A clinician rating scale, the Children's Depression Rating Scale–Revised (Poznanski, Freeman, & Mokros, 1985), has also been used for this population (e.g., Bernstein et al., 1997).
- Daily Life Stressors Scale (DLSS; Kearney, Drabman, & Beasley, 1993), a 30-item measure of distress that a child might

experience from common, everyday events. In using the DLSS for youth who refuse school for negative reinforcement, attention, or both, a particular focus should be made on morning and school-related events. A common related measure is the Children's Hassles Scale (Kanner, Feldman, Weinberger, & Ford, 1987).

- Fear Survey Schedule for Children–Revised (T. H. Ollendick, 1983), an 80-item measure of general fearfulness. Although most youth with school refusal behavior do not show specific fears related to school, this measure is useful for those who do. Special attention should be paid to school-oriented items, such as fears of getting lost, looking foolish, having to go to school, getting poor grades or a report card, being sent to the principal, giving an oral report, being teased or criticized by others, taking or failing a test, putting on a recital, being alone, being in a fight, getting sick at school, staying after school, doing something new, making mistakes, meeting people, playing rough games, being called on by the teacher, riding in a car or bus, being in a big crowd, closed places, and loud sirens (Kearney, Eisen, & Silverman, 1995). Common related measures include the Fear Survey Schedule for Children–II (Gullone & King, 1992) and the Louisville Fear Survey Schedule (L. C. Miller, Barrett, Hampe, & Noble, 1972).

- Multidimensional Anxiety Scale for Children (MASC; March, 1997), a 45-item measure of physical anxiety, harm avoidance, and social and separation anxiety. The MASC is most useful for assessing youth who refuse school for negative reinforcement and, in some cases, attention.

- Negative Affect Self-Statement Questionnaire (NASSQ; Ronan, Kendall, & Rowe, 1994), which measures the strength of self-statements reflective of general anxiety and depression. Versions have been developed for those age 7–10 years and 11–15 years. The NASSQ is most useful for assessing youth who refuse school to avoid negative affectivity. A common related measure is the Children's Negative Cognitive Error Questionnaire (Leitenberg, Yost, & Carroll-Wilson, 1986).

- Revised Children's Manifest Anxiety Scale (RCMAS; C. R. Reynolds & Paget, 1983), a 37-item yes–no inventory that targets physiological anxiety, worry, and concentration difficulties. However, the scale appears more predictive of depression than anxiety (March & Albano, 1998). It is most useful for assessing youth who refuse school for negative reinforcement. A related measure for youth with school refusal behavior is the

School Anxiety Questionnaire (Morris, Finkelstein, & Fisher, 1976). A clinician rating scale, the Anxiety Rating for Children–Revised (Bernstein, Crosby, Perwien, & Borchardt, 1996), has also been used for this population.

- Social Anxiety Scale for Children–Revised (SASC–R; La Greca & Stone, 1993), a 22-item measure of social anxiety with specific subscales for fear of negative evaluation, pervasive social avoidance and distress, and social avoidance and distress in new situations or with unfamiliar peers. The SASC–R is most useful for assessing youth who refuse school to escape aversive social or evaluative situations. Common related measures include the Social Interaction Self-Statement Test (R. L. Johnson & Glass, 1989), Social Phobia and Anxiety Inventory for Adolescents (Clark et al., 1994), and Test Anxiety Scale for Children (S. B. Sarason, Davidson, Lighthall, Waite, & Ruebush, 1960).
- State–Trait Anxiety Inventory for Children (STAIC; Spielberger, 1973), a 40-item instrument that measures situationally based anxiety as well as more characterological anxiety. The STAIC is most useful for assessing youth who refuse school for negative reinforcement. A common related measure is the Cognitive and Somatic Trait/State Anxiety Inventory (Fox & Houston, 1983).
- Visual Analogue Scale for Anxiety–Revised (Bernstein & Garfinkel, 1992), an 11-item instrument that measures anxiety by asking children to place a mark on a continuum.
- Youth Self-Report (YSR; Achenbach, 1991c), a 118-item measure that solicits an adolescent's ratings of his or her own internalizing and externalizing behavior problems. The YSR is designed for 11- to 18-year-olds and is useful for assessing all adolescents who refuse school. A common related measure is the Conners Wells' Adolescent Self-Report Scale (Conners, 1997).

The reader is cautioned about using measures of internalizing symptoms because, although they are technically strong psychometrically, controversy remains as to exactly which constructs are being measured (see Perrin & Last, 1992). Indeed, care should be taken when using these measures outside of controlled research studies. Still, it may be useful to administer several of these questionnaires to gather the flavor of a particular case, to assess the overall level of negative affectivity, or both.

Parent–teacher questionnaires. Although self-report measures are useful for evaluating youth with school refusal behavior, younger children are often unable to complete them, and few measures are available for noncompliant or other externalizing behavior problems. As a result, parent and teacher measures are commonly used to derive such information about a child as well as relevant family and classroom variables that might influence the child's school refusal behavior. Prominent parent and teacher measures for assessing youth with school refusal behavior include, alphabetically, the following:

- Child Behavior Checklist (CBCL; Achenbach, 1991a), a 118-item measure that solicits parent ratings and provides symptom profiles of various internalizing and externalizing behaviors, including those related to school refusal behavior. These behaviors are listed across several empirically derived factors, namely, Social Problems (withdrawn, somatic complaints, anxious–depressed), Thought Problems, and Attention Problems. Common related measures, some of which contain school nonattendance items, include the ACQ Behavior Checklist (Achenbach, Howell, Quay, & Conners, 1991), Behavior Assessment System for Children (C. Reynolds & Kamphaus, 1992), Children's Symptom Inventory (Gadow & Sprafkin, 1995), Comprehensive Behavior Rating Scale for Children (Neeper, Lahey, & Frick, 1991), Eyberg Child Behavior Inventory (Eyberg, 1992), Louisville Behavior Checklist (L. C. Miller, 1984), Personality Inventory for Children–Revised (Lachar & Gruber, 1991), and Revised Behavior Problem Checklist (Quay & Peterson, 1987).
- Conners Rating Scales–Parent Version Revised (CRS–PVR; Conners, 1997), which also measures various internalizing and externalizing behaviors in youth but is quite a bit shorter than the CBCL (long form: 80 items; short form: 27 items). Subscales include Oppositional, Hyperactive–Impulsive, Perfectionism, Psychosomatic, ADHD Index, Cognitive Problems, Anxious–Shy, Social Problems, DSM–IV Symptoms Subscales, and Global Index. Like the CBCL, the CRS–PVR is useful for assessing any child with school refusal behavior.
- Conners Rating Scales–Teacher Version Revised (CRS–TVR; Conners, 1997), which is similar in scope to the CRS–PVR, with similar subscales (no Psychosomatic scale; long form: 59 items, short form: 28 items).
- Family Adaptability and Cohesion Evaluation Scale (FACES II; Olson, Bell, & Portner, 1982; cf. Bernstein, Warren, Massie, & Thuras, 1999), a 30-item measure of two family dimensions:

cohesion (enmeshed to disengaged) and adaptability (flexible to rigid). Overall family type (balanced, mid-range, extreme) is also derived.

- Family Assessment Measure (Skinner, Steinhauer, & Santa-Barbara, 1983), a 50-item measure of family functioning along seven subscales: Task Accomplishment, Role Performance, Communication, Affective Expression, Affective Involvement, Control, and Values and Norms.

- Family Environment Scale (FES; Moos & Moos, 1986), is a 90-item measure of family functioning along 10 subscales: Cohesion, Expressiveness, Conflict, Independence, Achievement Orientation, Intellectual–Cultural Orientation, Active–Recreational Orientation, Moral–Religious Emphasis, Organization, and Control. Several subscales are related to functions of school refusal behavior (Kearney & Silverman, 1995; see chapter 4).

- Measures of parenting practices (Alabama Parenting Questionnaire; Shelton, Frick, & Wootton, 1996) and expectancies (Parental Expectancies Scale; Eisen, Spasaro, Kearney, Albano, & Barlow, 1996) are also relevant to many families of children with school refusal behavior.

- Self-Administered Dependency Questionnaire (Berg, 1974), which measures maternal dependency and overprotectiveness along subscales of affection, communication, assistance, and travel. Related checklist measures of separation anxiety include the Parent Anxiety Rating Scale–Separation, Teachers' Separation Anxiety Scale (Doris, McIntyre, Kelsey, & Lehman, 1971), and Teacher Rating of Separation Anxiety (Hall, 1967; cf. Barrios & Hartmann, 1997). A checklist measure of attachment is the Parent Reunion Inventory (Marcus, 1997).

- Symptom Checklist–90–Revised (Derogatis, 1994), a 90-item self-report symptom inventory of nine dimensions: Somatization, Obsessive–Compulsive, Interpersonal Sensitivity, Depression, Anxiety, Hostility, Phobic Anxiety, Paranoid Ideation, and Psychoticism. Common related measures include the Beck Anxiety/Depression Inventory (Beck, Brown, Epstein, & Steer, 1988; Beck, Rush, Shaw, & Emery, 1979), Fear Questionnaire (Marks & Mathews, 1979), Hamilton Depression Inventory (W. M. Reynolds & Kobak, 1995), Millon Multiaxial Clinical Inventory (Millon, Millon, & Davis, 1994), and the Minnesota Multiphasic Personality Inventory (Hathaway & McKinley, 1989). Measures of parental psychopathology are sometimes highly relevant to cases of youth with school refusal behavior.

- Teacher Report Form (Achenbach, 1991b), which is similar in scope to the CBCL but solicits ratings from a teacher, school counselor or psychologist, or another official who is most familiar with a particular child with school refusal behavior.

Parent–teacher measures are typically invaluable for assessing children with school refusal behavior. However, care should be taken in cases in which bias may be likely, the child shows substantial changes in behavior across situations, or both. Many children with school refusal behavior, for example, have many behavior problems at home, but only during the morning, and none at school. The aforementioned scales may not detect the subtleties of this behavior pattern. Still, it may be useful to administer several of these questionnaires to gather the flavor of a particular case or to assess for overall level of internalizing and externalizing behaviors and family functioning.

The Function of School Refusal Behavior

Youth self-report and parent-based measures can also be used to assess the function of a child's school refusal behavior, although development in this area is still rather new. Such descriptive functional analysis involves soliciting child and parent ratings of why a child is refusing school and integrating these ratings with other sources of information (e.g., interviews, direct observation, teacher reports). This integration can then help one decide about treatment assignment.

Kearney and Silverman (1993) devised a systematic descriptive functional analysis for school refusal behavior. They developed the School Refusal Assessment Scale (SRAS), the original version of which is a 16-item measure of the relative influence of the four functional conditions for school refusal behavior (see Kearney & Albano, 2000). Four items are devoted to each condition, and items are scored on a 0–6 scale that ranges from *never* to *always*. Child (SRAS–C; see Exhibit 5.3) and parent (SRAS–P; see Exhibit 5.4) versions have been developed, and a revision of the scale is underway (Kearney & Tillotson, 1998). The SRAS is based on the Motivation Assessment Scale, a measure used to help derive the function of self-injurious and other maladaptive behaviors (Durand & Crimmins, 1988). The SRAS has demonstrated good reliability and validity.

Recall that four functions have been hypothesized to potentially maintain a child's school refusal behavior. With respect to the first function, avoidance of stimuli that provoke a general sense of negative affectivity, SRAS Items 1, 5, 9, and 13 generally surround difficulty attending school

EXHIBIT 5.3
School Refusal Assessment Scale (Child)

Your name: _____

Date: _____

Please circle the answer that best answers the following questions:

1. How often do you have trouble going to school because you are afraid of something in the school building (for example, a fire alarm, room, etc.)?

Never	Seldom		Half the Time	Usually		Always
0	1	2	3	4	5	6

2. Do you have trouble speaking with the other kids at school?

Never	Seldom		Half the Time	Usually		Always
0	1	2	3	4	5	6

3. Do you often do things to upset or annoy your family?

Never	Seldom		Half the Time	Usually		Always
0	1	2	3	4	5	6

4. How often do you go out of the house when not in school during the week (Monday to Friday)?

Never	Seldom		Half the Time	Usually		Always
0	1	2	3	4	5	6

5. Are you afraid of the teachers or others at school?

Never	Seldom		Half the Time	Usually		Always
0	1	2	3	4	5	6

6. Do you feel embarrassed or scared in front of other people at school?

Never	Seldom		Half the Time	Usually		Always
0	1	2	3	4	5	6

7. How often do you feel that you would rather be with your parents than attend school?

Never	Seldom		Half the Time	Usually		Always
0	1	2	3	4	5	6

8. Do you ever talk to or see other people when not in school during the week (Monday to Friday)?

Never	Seldom		Half the Time	Usually		Always
0	1	2	3	4	5	6

9. Do you feel more nervous with your friends at school than with your friends somewhere else (e.g., at a party or at home)?

Never	Seldom		Half the Time	Usually		Always
0	1	2	3	4	5	6

10. Do you have trouble making friends?

Never	Seldom		Half the Time	Usually		Always
0	1	2	3	4	5	6

11. Do you ever think about your parents or family when in school or when they are away from you?

Never	Seldom		Half the Time	Usually		Always
0	1	2	3	4	5	6

12. Do you enjoy doing different things when not in school during the week (Monday to Friday)?

Never	Seldom		Half the Time	Usually		Always
0	1	2	3	4	5	6

13. Do you feel scared about school when you think about it on Saturday and Sunday?

Never	Seldom		Half the Time	Usually		Always
0	1	2	3	4	5	6

14. Do you often stay away from places where you would have to talk to someone?

Never	Seldom		Half the Time	Usually		Always
0	1	2	3	4	5	6

15. Do you ever refuse to go to school in order to be with your parents?

Never	Seldom		Half the Time	Usually		Always
0	1	2	3	4	5	6

16. Do you ever skip school because it's more fun to be out of school?

Never	Seldom		Half the Time	Usually		Always
0	1	2	3	4	5	6

ANA	ESE	AGB	PTR
1. _____	2. _____	3. _____	4. _____
5. _____	6. _____	7. _____	8. _____
9. _____	10. _____	11. _____	12. _____
13. _____	14. _____	15. _____	16. _____
Total score = _____			
Mean score = _____			

EXHIBIT 5.4
School Refusal Assessment Scale (Parent)

Your name: _____

Date: _____

Please circle the answer that best answers the following questions:

1. Does your child seem extremely fearful of something at or within the school building (for example, a fire alarm, room, etc.)?

Never	Seldom		Half the Time	Usually		Always
0	1	2	3	4	5	6

2. Does your child have problems speaking with the other kids at school?

Never	Seldom		Half the Time	Usually		Always
0	1	2	3	4	5	6

3. Does your child seem to upset or annoy you to gain attention?

Never	Seldom		Half the Time	Usually		Always
0	1	2	3	4	5	6

4. Does your child go out of the house when not in school during the week (Monday to Friday)?

Never	Seldom		Half the Time	Usually		Always
0	1	2	3	4	5	6

5. Does your child seem frightened of the teachers or others at school?

Never	Seldom		Half the Time	Usually		Always
0	1	2	3	4	5	6

6. Does your child say to you that he/she feels uncomfortable or embarrassed in front of other people at school?

Never	Seldom		Half the Time	Usually		Always
0	1	2	3	4	5	6

7. How often does your child wish to be with you or your spouse rather than attend school?

Never	Seldom		Half the Time	Usually		Always
0	1	2	3	4	5	6

8. Does your child often speak to or see other people when not in school during the week (Monday to Friday)?

Never	Seldom		Half the Time	Usually		Always
0	1	2	3	4	5	6

9. Does your child seem more nervous with his/her friends when in school than with his/her friends somewhere else (e.g., at a party or at home)?

Never	Seldom		Half the Time	Usually		Always
0	1	2	3	4	5	6

10. Does your child say that he/she has trouble making friends?

Never	Seldom		Half the Time	Usually		Always
0	1	2	3	4	5	6

11. Does your child say that he/she thinks of you often when you are away?

Never	Seldom		Half the Time	Usually		Always
0	1	2	3	4	5	6

12. Does your child enjoy doing various activities when not in school during the week (Monday to Friday)?

Never	Seldom		Half the Time	Usually		Always
0	1	2	3	4	5	6

13. Does your child seem scared about school on the weekends?

Never	Seldom		Half the Time	Usually		Always
0	1	2	3	4	5	6

14. Does your child seem to avoid social situations where talking to others is likely?

Never	Seldom		Half the Time	Usually		Always
0	1	2	3	4	5	6

15. Does your child ever refuse to attend school just to be with you or your spouse?

Never	Seldom		Half the Time	Usually		Always
0	1	2	3	4	5	6

16. Does your child skip school because he/she has more fun outside of school?

Never	Seldom		Half the Time	Usually		Always
0	1	2	3	4	5	6

ANA	ESE	AGB	PTR
1. _____	2. _____	3. _____	4. _____
5. _____	6. _____	7. _____	8. _____
9. _____	10. _____	11. _____	12. _____
13. _____	14. _____	15. _____	16. _____
Total score = _____	_____	_____	_____
Mean score = _____	_____	_____	_____

because of fear or nervousness. In a revised version of the SRAS, these items will likely reflect less fear and more negative affectivity. With respect to the second function, escape from aversive social or evaluative situations, SRAS Items 2, 6, 10, and 14 generally surround difficulty with social interactions at school or with making friends.

With respect to the third function, attention seeking, SRAS Items 3, 7, 11, and 15 generally surround annoying (manipulating) one's parents and desires to be with one's parents instead of in school. Finally, with respect to the fourth function, pursuit of tangible reinforcement outside of school, SRAS Items 4, 8, 12, and 16 generally surround how often the child leaves school because it is more fun to be out of school. The development of the SRAS remains in a state of evolution, so the reader should be aware of future revisions.

During a descriptive functional analysis for school refusal behavior, a child and his or her parents separately complete the SRAS–C and SRAS–P, respectively. This takes about 10 minutes. For young children just learning to read, SRAS items can be presented verbally, and the children can answer on their own. Ideally, SRAS ratings are obtained from the child, the mother, and the father if all are available (if not, any available ratings are used as long as at least one adult is included). A teacher version of the SRAS has been developed but not published; teacher data regarding the function of school refusal behavior are often incomplete because of the child's nonattendance or, following morning misbehaviors at home, lack of misbehavior at school.

Following the completion of each relevant version of the SRAS, item means are derived for each function. On the original version of the SRAS–C and each SRAS–P, therefore, scores are added for

- Items 1, 5, 9, and 13 (first function)
- Items 2, 6, 10, and 14 (second function)
- Items 3, 7, 11, and 15 (third function)
- Items 4, 8, 12, and 16 (fourth function).

These four total scores are then each divided by four or the number of items answered in each set. For example, if a child's total rating score across the

- first item set was 10, then the item mean would be 2.50 ($10 \div 4$)
- second item set was 13, then the item mean would be 3.25 ($13 \div 4$)
- third item set was 22, then the item mean would be 5.50 ($22 \div 4$)
- fourth item set was 3, then the item mean would be 0.75 ($3 \div 4$).

This process is done separately for ratings from the child, mother, and father. Subsequently, these mean item scores for each functional condition are averaged themselves across all administered SRAS versions. For example, if

- the child's mean item scores from the SRAS–C were 2.50, 3.25, 5.50, and 0.75
- the mother's mean item scores from the SRAS–P were 3.75, 4.00, 5.50, and 1.00
- the father's mean item scores from the SRAS–P were 3.50, 4.00, 4.75, and 1.25,

then

- the overall mean for the first function would be 3.25 (2.50 + 3.75 + 3.50 ÷ 3)
- the overall mean for the second function would be 3.75 (3.25 + 4.00 + 4.00 ÷ 3)
- the overall mean for the third function would be 5.25 (5.50 + 5.50 + 4.75 ÷ 3)
- the overall mean for the fourth function would be 1.00 (0.75 + 1.00 + 1.25 ÷ 3).

In this particular case, the functional profile is 3.25–3.75–5.25–1.00. Three main statements can be made about this profile:

1. Because the highest scoring function is considered to be the primary reason why a particular child is refusing school, it seems likely that this child is refusing school mostly for attention (i.e., 5.25, Function 3). However, this is only a hypothesis that should be confirmed using other information, especially from direct observation.
2. The weakest influence on the child's school refusal behavior appears to be a desire for tangible reinforcement outside of school (i.e., 1.00; Function 4). As a result, this may not necessarily be a major treatment concern.
3. Two functions appear to be of secondary concern to attention. Functions 1 and 2 (avoidance of stimuli provoking negative affectivity and escape from aversive social or evaluative situations) present with mean scores of 3.25 and 3.75, respectively. This could mean, during treatment, that the child's concerns about school could eventually become an important factor. This may be especially so if the attention component is addressed. In addition, these two functions (1 and 2) may be considered relatively comparable in strength. In past uses of

the SRAS, scores within 0.50 point of one another have been considered equivalent in nature (Kearney & Silverman, 1990, 1999).

The SRAS should be considered only one tool for deriving hypotheses about the function of a child's school refusal behavior (Daleiden, Chorpita, Kollins, & Drabman, 1999). If time is short, or an experimental analysis cannot be conducted, then prescriptive treatment may be assigned on the basis of this descriptive procedure. However, this should be done only with extreme caution. Ideally, one should confirm the descriptive analysis by engaging in the observational procedures described next.

Direct Behavioral Observation

An excellent measure of the form and function of a child's school refusal behavior is direct behavioral observation. This observation should ideally take place (a) early in the morning as the child prepares him- or herself for school and then enters the school building, and (b) during the school day. Parents often claim that their child "is a different person" in the morning compared with an afternoon or evening interview, so direct observation is helpful in deriving a vivid picture of resistive and anxiety-based child behaviors as well as reactions of family members and school officials. In addition, close observation of the child during the school day can help pinpoint when the child leaves school and when he or she is most distressed and avoidant. Although many behavioral observation systems have been developed for conditions related to absenteeism (e.g., active and passive Behavioral Avoidance Tests, Lang & Lazovik, 1963, Murphy & Bootzin, 1973; Child's Game–Parent's Game, Forehand & McMahon, 1981; Family Interaction Coding System, Patterson, 1982), this section describes a proposed method for observing and evaluating *specific* school refusal behaviors in youth.

The Form of School Refusal Behavior

A structured scrutiny of the child and family's morning activities can help one form opinions about treatment targets. General suggestions for such an observation include the following:

- Prior to the observation, discuss some rating scale (e.g., 0–10) with the child and parents. This rating scale can be used for whatever behavior seems most prominent (e.g., refusal to get out of bed, tantrums, child distress, dawdling). Solicit ratings at different points of the morning routine and as the child enters school.
- Arrive at the family's home at a predetermined time in the morning and record the amount of time the child resists any

activity necessary for on-time school attendance. These activities include, among others, rising from bed, dressing, washing, eating breakfast, preparing materials for school, and going to the car or bus. Resistance can come in many forms, including refusal to move, noncompliance, tantrums, dawdling, clinging, throwing objects, arguing, crying, locking oneself in a room, running away, and aggression. Verbalizations or vocalizations that serve as expressions of school refusal behavior (e.g., "Can't I just go to school tomorrow?") should be noted as well.

- Record any parental or family member reactions, especially maladaptive ones, to the child's school refusal behavior. Examples include attending inappropriately to a child's misbehavior, acquiescence, or abusive behavior.
- Record any discrepancies between the observation and what family members reported in an interview or from another measure.
- Record any verbal or physical child resistance to entering school. Many children prepare for school without any problem but refuse to enter the school building once there.
- At the end of the school day, contact the child's teachers, school attendance officer, or other relevant official to record any time missed during the day.

During any direct observation, close attention should be paid to certain behaviors and other variables. These include (a) behavioral avoidance (e.g., clinging, noncompliance with commands to go to school, running away), (b) somatic complaints, (c) cognitive distortions or verbalizations, (d) sudden changes in child or parental behavior, (e) pleas to end the observation and return home, (f) increased family conflict, and (g) teacher reports of misbehavior at school. However, like the interview, an observation may be tailored to uniquely fit a particular case of school refusal behavior.

The Function of School Refusal Behavior

To confirm information from a descriptive functional analysis, it is best to observe the child, family, and relevant others (e.g., grandparents, school officials) under different conditions. This differs somewhat from the general observation just discussed; here, certain circumstances are established to test a hypothesis about a function of school refusal behavior. This may be done by comparing the child's school refusal behavior on typical school days with the child's behavior under conditions more or less "favorable" to him or her—in other words, under conditions the parent–child claims, or therapist–educator believes, would enhance or further hinder school attendance. If substantial changes occur in the child's behavior or attendance between a regular and an "enhanced" school day, for example, then evidence for a particular function might be assumed. In this section, proposed observations are discussed for each function.

For youth suspected of refusing school to avoid stimuli that provoke somatic complaints and negative affectivity, it may be useful to compare the child's school refusal behavior on regular days with his or her behavior on days when he or she is asked to attend school under ostensibly more favorable conditions. For example, the child may be asked to go to school only during reportedly stress-free times (e.g., lunch, playground) or only on days when he or she lacks a certain class (e.g., physical education). Should the child attend school more willingly under these conditions but no other, then evidence is available that he or she is indeed avoiding school because of certain stimuli that provoke negative affectivity and possibly somatic complaints. This observation could also help rule out other functions. For example, if the child readily attends lunch with peers without a supporting adult (e.g., parent), this would help rule out school refusal behavior to escape aversive social or evaluative situations or to get attention or tangible reinforcement outside of school. Other scenarios to more definitively rule in or out certain functions could be established as well.

For youth suspected of refusing school to escape aversive social or evaluative situations, it may be useful to compare the child's school refusal behavior on regular days with his or her behavior when asked to attend school when only a few or even no people are present (e.g., after normal school hours). If the child more willingly enters and attends school independently during this time, then the social aspect of school may indeed be most problematic. In addition, the child may be asked to attend school on certain days when no tests, oral presentations, or athletic or other performances are required. Many children attend school without difficulty, for example, if they are allowed to "fade into the woodwork," and this may indicate that school refusal behavior is indeed maintained by a desire to escape aversive social or evaluative situations. If the child otherwise attends school without any problem and by him- or herself, this would also tend to rule out other functional conditions.

For youth suspected of refusing school for attention, it may be useful to compare the child's school refusal behavior on regular days with his or her behavior when (a) accompanied by his or her parents into the classroom or (b) under conditions that allow the child to contact his or her parents at any time during the school day and come home. Children who truly refuse school for attention often attend school more willingly under these conditions but not without direct or indirect contact with their parents. In fact, these children generally attend school if their parents are there, even under various stressful conditions and social interactions. In addition, these children often refuse to attend school alone despite large tangible bribes to do so. If so in a particular case, this would tend to rule out school refusal behavior due to negative rein-forcement or a desire for tangible reinforcement.

For youth suspected of refusing school for tangible reinforcement out-side of school, it may be useful to compare the youth's school refusal behavior on regular days with his or her behavior when a very large incentive (e.g., privilege, money) is temporarily given for attendance and then removed. If the youth attends school more readily during the incentive period but refuses again after its withdrawal, then evidence is available that outside incentives are indeed more powerful than school-based ones. The youth's attendance during this time would also serve to rule out high levels of anxiety and desires for attention. Another interesting observation might involve drastically lowering positive reinforcers if school is missed; for exam-ple, eliminating social activities after dinner. If a child is refusing school simply for tangible reinforcement outside of school, attendance may increase to remove this restriction. However, this strategy may generate substantial conflict within the family and should therefore be used only with great caution.

Finally, more complex observations are necessary for youth suspected of refusing school for multiple reasons. For example, if a child is suspected of refusing school for both attention *and* tangible reinforcement outside of school, then attendance of a parent or guardian at school and powerful incentives may have to be interwoven into the observation. One idea would be to increase only parent or guardian attendance for 2 days, increase only tangible reinforcement for 2 days, and increase both together for 2 days. Likewise, in a child suspected of refusing school to avoid stimuli that provoke general negative affectivity and to escape aversive social or evaluative situa-tions, attendance under various school-related conditions (i.e., different classes, groups of people) over several days may have to be monitored.

In some cases, formal experimental analyses are simply not feasible because of the severity of the case, time limitations, or other restrictions. If so, therapists and school officials can still evaluate key behaviors in session that may help confirm why a child is refusing school. Of course, these simpler observations can only lead to general suppositions about function and should be integrated with other formal assessment methods as much as possible:

- Youth suspected of refusing school because of stimuli that pro-voke negative affectivity may display tearfulness, passivity, and withdrawal during assessment. This function, however, is most difficult to assess by means of simple observation in an office setting, unless the setting is at school.
- Youth suspected of refusing school to escape aversive social or evaluative situations may show discomfort when interacting

with others in a clinic or office setting. However, many youth in this group interact more readily with adults than with peers, so this must be considered.

- Youth suspected of refusing school for attention may have trouble separating from a parent or show tantrums or other misbehaviors to avoid speaking alone with a therapist or school official.
- Youth suspected of refusing school for tangible reinforcement outside of school may argue intensely with parents to resist changes in their social lifestyle. These youth may also be less forthcoming and less likely to attend treatment because of potential changes to their favorable status quo.

Monitoring School Refusal Behavior on a Daily Basis

In addition to formal observation, the form and, to some extent, the function of school refusal behavior can be monitored by children and adults on an ongoing daily or weekly basis. For children who refuse school with substantial emotional distress, formalized daily ratings of fear or anxiety have been developed. Prime examples include the following:

- The Daily Diary (Beidel, Neal, & Lederer, 1991), which assesses "situational parameters related to the occurrence of anxious events, including time of day, location, specific anxiety-producing event, and behavioral responses to the event" (p. 508). The Daily Diary is most useful for youth refusing school for negative reinforcement.
- A fear thermometer has been used in different studies in different formats (e.g., Kelley, 1976; Lang & Lazovik, 1963; Melamed, Yurcheson, Fleece, Hutcherson, & Hawes, 1978). The fear thermometer, pictured as an actual thermometer, contains a 1–5 or 1–10 scale of fearfulness to which a child can readily point. This technique would be primarily useful, however, for the minority of children with a specific fear related to school.
- The Subjective Units of Distress/Disturbance Scale (SUDS; Wolpe, 1969) is a 0–100 rating scale of general distress that has been used to assess emotional distress in youth with school refusal behavior (Kearney & Silverman, 1990, 1999). The SUDS is particularly useful for deriving hourly ratings from children whose emotional distress is variable during the school day (e.g., higher during certain classes).

These three measures are predominantly child based and relevant only to youth who refuse school with some degree of emotional stress. In addition, school attendance itself is not measured. For children with more general school refusal behavior involving a confluence of symptoms, I and my colleagues (Kearney & Albano, 2000; Kearney & Silverman, 1999) have devised simple logbooks for children and parents. These logbooks solicit ratings of a child's daily level of anxiety, depression, overall distress–negative affectivity, noncompliance, disruption to the family's daily life routine, other child behavior problems, and time missed from school. Ratings are made on a 0–10 scale on which 0 = *none* and 10 = *an extreme amount*. Children and parents are briefly taught how to complete the logbooks, and questions are regularly addressed. In one treatment outcome study, child–parent inter-rater reliability with respect to anxiety and depression ratings was .62 ($p <$ .01; Kearney & Silverman, 1999).

Because the form of school refusal behavior is highly complex and variable, daily monitoring procedures should be reviewed regularly (e.g., each treatment session). Such monitoring is an excellent way of gauging motivation for and compliance with homework assignments; enhancing family member awareness of a child's behavior; and measuring progress, or lack thereof, over time. Because the function of a child's school refusal behavior sometimes changes over time as well, periodic readministrations of the SRAS and formal observations may also be necessary.

Contacting School Officials

Youth and parents are certainly the backbone of assessment in most cases of school refusal behavior, but school officials are also a rich source of information that should not be overlooked. Pertinent officials include regular and specialized teachers, school psychologists and social workers, guidance counselors, principals, nurses, librarians, and school attendance officers, among others. During assessment and treatment, specific types of information should be derived regularly from these sources.

Important information from these sources include actual past and present school attendance; reports or ratings of a child's distress or noncompliance or other misbehavior; a child's interactions with others; academic schedules and work; procedures and timelines for, and obstacles to, reintegrating a child into school; policies and rules about absenteeism and conduct; alternative academic programs; feedback regarding the effectiveness of treatment procedures; advice given to parents regarding a child's school refusal behavior; and parent–school official conflict. Of course, any other information pertinent to a certain child with school refusal behavior should be regularly sought as well.

During the assessment process, therapists should start to develop and nurture a strong and positive working relationship with school officials. Multidisciplinary cooperation is usually essential in resolving cases of school refusal behavior, and discord among parents, educators, therapists, and others can be disastrous in this population (Will & Baird, 1984). Fostering good therapist–school official contact can also serve as an appropriate model for parents during treatment.

OTHER METHODS OF ASSESSMENT

Other methods of assessment may also be pertinent to some children with school refusal behavior. For example, physiological assessment in the form of respiration, heart rate and blood pressure, and sweating have been commonly used in the past to evaluate children with emotional distress (N. J. King, 1994). In addition, formal psychological assessment methods, such as intelligence tests, are useful for ruling out cognitive dysfunctions or learning disability or for identifying a child's verbal ability for treatment (Eisen & Kearney, 1995). Likewise, projective tests may be useful for youth with trouble verbalizing their concerns about school. Other measures may also be used to assess youth with school refusal behavior, including sociometric ratings, role-play tests, and thought listing and think-aloud procedures.

INTEGRATING ASSESSMENT INFORMATION AND ASSIGNING PRESCRIPTIVE TREATMENT

Once all relevant information from multiple sources and methods has been solicited for a particular case of school refusal behavior, this material should be synthesized to derive primary treatment targets and the function of a child's school refusal behavior. A good starting place is the final mean ratings from the SRAS. The functional profile can be plotted, and then information from any observation that fits–confirms or does not fit–confirm this profile may be noted.

If there is relatively good fit or confirmation, information from the interviews may be evaluated; this includes diagnostic information as well as family member reports and descriptions of a child's behavior in the morning and during the day (e.g., crying–avoidant, manipulative, runs out of school). In particular, one should see if these diagnoses and descriptions align with the allegedly most influential and least influential functions. For example, a child identified as refusing school primarily for attention may show oppositional defiant disorder and cling to his mother's leg in the morning but is less likely to show social anxiety disorder and refusal to talk to peers at school. Following interview information, data from all other sources should be evaluated, especially elevated total and item scores on child self-report and parent and teacher measures and patterns in psychological testing. Convergent findings across these materials, as well as discordant pieces of information, should be recorded.

In evaluating assessment materials, patterns of behavior that coalesce around a certain function should be sought; note patterns that generally fit the functional profiles described in chapter 4. In many cases, some overall pattern emerges. Sometimes this pattern is fairly general—for example, the child is certainly refusing school because of something aversive there, but it is not clear whether this involves some social situation or some other stimulus. Other times—in fact, in most cases—a clearer picture emerges; for example, when the child is certainly refusing school for tangible reinforcement outside of school.

School refusal behavior maintained by negative reinforcement tends to have a less clear pattern, and thus require more detective work, than school refusal behavior maintained by attention and tangible reinforcement. Cases of school refusal behavior that require the most detective work, however, involve those maintained by multiple functions. In these cases, one should separately log evidence for and against each functional condition. A dimensional profile of the relatively stronger and weaker functions can then be plotted. In the final section of this chapter a multiple-function case is presented.

The scenarios just described assume good convergence in findings, but discrepancies may emerge across assessment materials with respect to the function of school refusal behavior. These discrepancies can result from several factors, two of which are described here. One involves intrarater discrepancies, when one party's reports seem to differ across measures. For example, a parent may report in an interview that her child refuses school because of anxiety but indicate on the SRAS that her child clearly refuses school only for attention. Or a child may say that his social interactions are problematic in school, but observation indicates a good quality and quantity of relationships. In these cases, further and more detailed assessment is needed to clarify discrepancies. For example, it could be the mother is unsure about her child's nervousness or the child is unclear about what constitutes an adequate social relationship.

A more common source of assessment discrepancy occurs between raters. For example, parents may claim that their teenager refuses school simply to have more fun outside of school, but the teenager claims that substantial anxiety prevents his attendance. Several possible explanations exist for this scenario. First, two functions may be truly motivating the youth's school refusal behavior, and both need to be addressed. Second, one party may have falsely stipulated a certain function to achieve some agenda. For example, the parents in this scenario may be trying to deflect blame or alleviate guilt by labeling the adolescent as lazy and unambitious. Or, the adolescent may be falsely claiming anxiety to play on parental concerns and extend the rewarding status quo as long as possible.

A third possibility, and a likely one, is that one party is simply uninformed about another's behavior. Some parents, for example, have little idea why their child is missing school and can supply only general hypotheses. This applies to many younger children as well. In these cases, clinical judgment may be necessary to determine the reliability of reports. Additional independent information (e.g., further clinician observation, teacher reports) may also be needed to help decide which functional pattern primarily maintains a child's school refusal behavior. In some cases a preponderance of evidence toward a certain primary function must suffice.

Following the derivation of the primary functions of school refusal behavior, the assignment of prescriptive treatment may be made with consent. *Prescriptive treatment* is defined here as an individualized treatment protocol based on a child's primary functions of school refusal behavior. As mentioned in chapter 4, specific treatments have been developed for children of each functional condition, and these treatments are outlined in greater depth in chapters 6–9. Youth who refuse school for multiple reasons are, within this functional model, administered a combination of prescriptive treatments.

A SAMPLE CASE OF ASSESSMENT AND ASSIGNING TREATMENT

Tyler was a 12-year-old boy referred by his parents and a school counselor to a specialized clinic for youth with school refusal behavior. He was referred in early November of the academic year following 12 full absences and 9 partial absences from school, the latter of which resulted from Tyler's skipping certain classes during the day. In addition, he had numerous problems getting to school in the morning and was sometimes late for homeroom. His attendance was especially problematic during the first 2 weeks of school in early September, had then improved slightly through mid-October, but had grown considerably worse during the past 3 weeks. In fact, during the past 10 school days, Tyler had completely missed 5 full days, skipped at least one class on 4 other days, and was late to school four times.

During the initial interview, Tyler was sullen and often fidgeted and sighed but was otherwise cooperative and respectful. He said he did not like school and wanted home schooling instead. In particular, he disliked the crowds, different classes, and harder homework assignments that went with his promotion to a new middle school and seventh grade. Tyler said school was "a terrible place" and "there's no way I'm going back." His interview (ADIS–C) ratings of fear during school were low to moderate (0–4), but he specifically complained of having to do recent oral presentations during English class. He also complained that he could not see his neighborhood friends at school because they were on a different class schedule than he. Tyler reported no other behavior problems or difficulties with his parents.

During the initial interview with Tyler's parents, Mr. and Mrs. T., it was clear they were frustrated and tense about the current situation. They indicated that Tyler's school refusal behavior in the morning was considerable; he would regularly refuse to get out of bed, dawdle, and resist being driven to school despite repeated proddings. Worse, Tyler would sometimes leave the school campus without supervision. Both parents were reportedly exhausted by their worry and Tyler's constant defiance, especially in light of the fact that they had one other school-aged child and a baby who needed frequent attention.

Mr. and Mrs. T. were unsure as to why Tyler was refusing school but said he had had similar problems before in the first, second, and sixth grades. During the last two episodes, Tyler refused to go to school for extended periods of time but eventually capitulated when his parents, facing legal action, physically brought him to school. That option, however, was reportedly no longer available because Mr. and Mrs. T. had no desire to force Tyler to school. Both parents felt they had a good relationship with their son, wanted to maintain that, and did not want to "cause any long-term damage." They acknowledged few other misbehaviors outside of absenteeism but did report that Tyler was shy in general and anxious about performing in front of others at school. Finally, Mr. and Mrs. T. said they were seriously considering home schooling at Tyler's request but wanted the opinion of a therapist first.

Each party was asked to complete several questionnaires. Tyler's scores on measures of fear and general anxiety were in the normal range, although he did rate "giving an oral report," "looking foolish," "being teased," "being called on by teacher," "failing a test," and "having to stay after school" high on the FSSC–R. In addition, an elevated but not clinical score (16) was evident on the CDI, and several items were strongly endorsed on the SASC–R: "I worry about being teased," "I worry about what other kids think of me," and "I feel that kids are making fun of me." His functional profile from the SRAS–C was 2.50–4.00–2.25–4.75.

Mr. and Mrs. T. jointly completed the CBCL and FES and completed separate versions of the SRAS–P. CBCL data indicated no elevated broad- or narrow-band factor, although some elevation on anxious–depressed and aggressive behavior was evident. FES data revealed an elevated conflict score, which was interesting given that all parties had specifically stated in the interview that family conflict was low. The functional profiles of Mr. and

Mrs. T., respectively, were 2.50–3.75–3.75–2.00 and 1.00–5.00–5.00–1.75. With Tyler's SRAS scores, this produced an overall functional profile of 2.00–4.25–3.67–2.83.

The therapist also conducted a general observation of the family's routine during a school morning. As expected, Tyler took a long time to rise from bed and dawdled constantly from 6:45 a.m. to 7:55 a.m. It is interesting that considerable yelling took place between the parents and Tyler (even in front of the therapist), especially as Tyler tried to watch television instead of preparing for school. The conflict escalated but then dropped significantly as Mr. and Mrs. T. tended to the younger children and ignored Tyler. Tyler then locked himself in his room until his father left for work, after which time he emerged and spent time with his mother, helping her care for the baby. Despite some gentle pleadings on Mrs. T.'s part to induce Tyler's school attendance, he successfully stayed home from school the rest of the day.

Contact with two of Tyler's teachers indicated that he was a fair student who was in danger of failing his classes because of his recent nonattendance and subsequent failure to complete tests and assignments. Both agreed that Tyler was a quiet and well-behaved person but one who was clearly nervous when in front of others. For example, the English teacher said Tyler had given one poor oral presentation so far; he was clearly nervous as his voice shook and because some of his classmates snickered. In addition, the math teacher said Tyler had declined several times to complete problems on the blackboard. It is interesting that both teachers also noted Tyler's sometimes annoying tendency to speak with them about nonacademic topics before and after class.

In synthesizing these assessment materials, the therapist initially scanned the overall functional profile from the SRAS (i.e., 2.00–4.25–3.67–2.83). This profile clearly indicated that Tyler was refusing school to escape aversive social or evaluative situations at school (Function 2). This did seem consistent with (a) Tyler's depressive symptoms and item elevations on the FSSC–R and SASC–R, (b) interview reports that Tyler was nervous about performing in front of others, (c) his desire to be with more friends at school, and (d) his propensity to skip classes that demanded the most performance before others (i.e., English, math, and physical education).

The therapist also noted, however, some discordant information from this functional profile. For example, (a) Tyler's conflict with his parents was indeed severe (despite initial reports that it was not); (b) he frequently refused to go to school on days when little or no performance before others was expected of him; and (c) he had not refused to go to school at all during late September and early October, even though there was no major change in his requirements at school. In other words, there was little to explain his sudden burst of school refusal behavior in the past 3 weeks.

To reconcile these discrepancies, the therapist closely re-examined each individual SRAS profile and reinterviewed Tyler and his parents. On Tyler's functional profile (i.e., 2.50–4.00–2.25–4.75), for example, he indicated that the leading reason he was refusing school was for tangible reinforcement outside of school (Function 4). During the reinterview, Tyler said he liked to stay home and watch television, play video games, sleep late, and ride his bicycle throughout the neighborhood. Mrs. T. acknowledged this as well and said that she could do little to keep Tyler in the house. It is interesting, however, that both Mr. and Mrs. T. had not rated Function 4 as particularly strong—instead, both rated attention seeking (Function 3) as prominent as escape from aversive social or evaluative situations (Function 2)—recall that their functional profiles were 2.50–3.75–3.75–2.00 and 1.00–5.00–5.00–1.75, respectively. During the reinterview, both parties mentioned how much Tyler wanted home schooling, how much he would follow them from room to room, and how much he sought reassurance from them regarding any upcoming event (e.g., doctor visit). This seemed consistent with Tyler's teacher reports that he constantly sought their attention before and after class.

After reevaluating the assessment material, the therapist concluded that Tyler was refusing school for a combination of three functions: escape from aversive social or evaluative situations, attention, and tangible reinforcement outside of school. It was possible that Tyler's initial anxiety about going to school in September had been met with parental support and even some acquiescence as Tyler successfully stayed home from school at that time. As in prior years, however, as the school pressured Mr. and Mrs. T. to take some action, Tyler was forced by his parents to return to school. As Tyler's anxiety and defiance about attending school eventually re-emerged and worsened, however, Mr. and Mrs. T. felt "worn down" and increasingly acquiesced to Tyler's demands to stay home. Tyler eventually came to enjoy the many amenities of staying home (e.g., television, bicycling), although his parents obviously felt as well that Tyler sought greater attention from them.

During a subsequent consultation with the family, the therapist recommended a three-pronged treatment approach based on the three functions that seemed to maintain Tyler's school refusal behavior. This approach consisted of (a) anxiety management to control Tyler's discomfort when performing in front of others and a class schedule change to integrate him with more of his neighborhood friends at school; (b) parent training in contingency management to attend to appropriate behaviors, ignore inappropriate behaviors, and establish a regular morning routine with consequences for dawdling; and (c) familial contingency contracting to increase incentives for Tyler's school attendance and eliminate positive reinforcers during the day should Tyler remain home.

SUMMARY

The assessment of a child with school refusal behavior should involve multiple sources of information to glean information about the form and function of behavior as well as the best treatment option. Indeed, Tyler's case illustrates the importance of attending to all sources of information and deductively piecing together evidence that supports or refutes each particular function. In doing so, a detailed scan of individual functional profiles, items, observational data, interview reports, and other information may be necessary. After this process, appropriate treatment can then be assigned. The different treatment packages that correspond with functions of school refusal behavior are described in chapters 6–9.

II

FUNCTIONALLY BASED
TREATMENT

6

YOUTH WHO AVOID STIMULI THAT PROVOKE GENERAL NEGATIVE AFFECTIVITY

Angelina is a 7-year-old girl who cries on weekday mornings. Although she attends school most days, she often has stomachaches and headaches when there. She also displays occasional morning diarrhea and nausea. Angelina is quiet and withdrawn at school and has problems going to and from class. Lately, she has been asking her parents to learn more about home schooling.

In this chapter, primary treatment strategies are reviewed for youth who refuse school to avoid stimuli that provoke negative affectivity (SPNA). Recall that this functional condition is analogous to what is traditionally thought of as anxiety-based school refusal behavior or school phobia; however, the functional condition implies a broader connotation (i.e., negative reinforcement by means of avoidance of fear, anxiety, depression, dread, somatic complaints, etc.). A brief overview is presented here of pharmacological and cognitive–behavioral treatments to address anxiety-based school refusal behavior. Following this discussion, a description is made of prescriptive treatment components for youth who refuse school to avoid SPNA. A case example is also provided.

TREATMENTS FOR YOUTH WITH ANXIETY-BASED SCHOOL REFUSAL BEHAVIOR

Pharmacotherapy

Several early investigators used or suggested pharmacotherapy, mainly antidepressants and anxiolytics, to treat youth with anxiety-based school refusal behavior (Abe, 1975; D'Amato, 1962; Frances & Petti, 1984; Frommer, 1967; Kraft, Ardali, Duffy, Hart, & Pearce, 1965; Nice, 1968). In addition, some have recommended such medication for youth with panic attacks and school refusal behavior (e.g., Ballenger, Carek, Steele, &

Cornish-McTighe, 1989; Black & Robbins, 1990; Garland & Smith, 1990; Lepola, Leinonen, & Koponen, 1996; Tiihonen, Lepola, & Kuikka, 1997). Halperidol has also been used for youth with Tourette's syndrome and school refusal behavior (Mikkelsen, Detlor, & Cohen, 1981).

Larger scale pharmacotherapy studies focusing on children with school refusal behavior have also been reported. Gittelman-Klein and Klein (1971) found that imipramine (25 mg–200 mg/day) helped improve school attendance in 13 of 16 youth (81.3%) with anxiety-based school refusal behavior. However, R. G. Klein, Koplewicz, and Kanner (1992) found, among children with separation anxiety disorder and school refusal behavior, that imipramine and a placebo were equally effective. In addition, Berney et al. (1981) placed children with "neurotic" school refusal behavior on a regimen of clomipramine (40 mg–75 mg/day). Mean improvement among three anxiety-based dependent measures was 63.1%.

Bernstein, Garfinkel, and Borchardt (1990) initially examined the effects of the anxiolytic alprazolam (0.75 mg–4.0 mg/day) or imipramine on 15 youth with anxiety-based school refusal behavior. Two thirds improved moderately to markedly. They further studied another 16 youth who also received alprazolam or imipramine. In this second study, improvement along two anxiety-based dependent measures was 50.0%. Bernstein et al. (2000) also found that imipramine (3 mg/kg/day) with cognitive–behavioral treatment was superior to a placebo for increasing school attendance and decreasing depression over an 8-week period. However, a mean of only 70% attendance was obtained in the active treatment group. Antidepressant medication has also been found to reduce school-related anxiety and related problems in other studies addressing disparate populations (e.g., Gammon & Brown, 1993). However, actual rates of school attendance do not always improve (e.g., Emslie et al., 1997).

In a review of pharmacotherapy studies for anxious children, Kearney and Silverman (1998) pointed out that many used secondary treatment strategies that may have enhanced the children's school attendance. These secondary strategies included firm parental attitudes about attendance, school–social worker contact with the family, a family member bringing the child to school, multimodal treatment and psychotherapy, and school-based support. These strategies may have heavily influenced the children's return to school, so the effects of pharmacotherapy for this population remain controversial. Medication is probably most appropriate, however, when a child's anxiety level is extremely high, substantial comorbidity (e.g., depression, obsessive–compulsive disorder) is involved, or a child is unresponsive to psychosocial treatment (N. J. King, Ollendick, & Tonge, 1995; Simeon & Wiggins, 1995; Tonge, 1998). However, parents of youth who refuse school tend to prefer pharmacotherapy least among available treatment options (Gullone & King, 1991), and potentially severe side effects must be considered (Werry & Aman, 1999).

Cognitive–Behavioral

Effective psychosocial treatment for youth with anxiety disorders has been demonstrated in several outcome studies. Kendall and colleagues (Kendall, 1994; Kendall, Flannery-Schroeder, et al., 1997), for example, have shown that cognitive–behavioral treatment is largely effective for children and adolescents with general, social, or separation anxiety. In addition, Silverman and colleagues (Eisen & Silverman, 1998; Silverman, Kurtines, Ginsburg, Weems, Lumpkin, & Carmichael, 1999; Silverman, Kurtines, Ginsburg, Weems, Rabian, & Serafini, 1999) have successfully used prescriptive, individual, and group cognitive–behavior therapy to treat youth with general or social anxiety. Cognitive elements of these therapies have generally involved (a) recognizing anxious feelings and somatic reactions to anxiety, (b) clarifying unrealistic or negative expectations or anxious cognitions in anxiety-provoking situations, (c) developing a coping plan by enhancing coping self-talk and coping actions, and (d) evaluating performance and administering self-reinforcement (Kendall, Flannery-Schroeder, et al., 1997; Kendall, Panichelli-Mindel, Sugarman, & Callahan, 1997). Behavioral elements generally involve imaginal and in vivo exposure, modeling, role play, relaxation training, contingent social reinforcement, and practice (Silverman, Kurtines, Ginsburg, Weems, Lumpkin, & Carmichael, 1999; Silverman, Kurtines, Ginsburg, Weems, Rabian, & Serafini, 1999).

For youth with school refusal behavior, systematic desensitization and related procedures have been often used to treat those with school-based fears (e.g., Blagg, 1987; Chapel, 1967; Croghan, 1981; Garvey & Hegrenes, 1966; Lazarus, 1960; Lazarus & Abramovitz, 1962; Lazarus, Davison, & Polefka, 1965; Luiselli, 1978; McNamara, 1988; Mehta & Praveenlal, 1987; P. M. Miller, 1972; O'Reilly, 1971; R. E. Smith & Sharpe, 1970). These studies typically involve analyses of one or a few cases. Since the mid-1980s, however, researchers have examined larger groups to evaluate cognitive–behavioral treatment, including desensitization, for youth with anxiety-based school refusal behavior.

Blagg and Yule (1984), for example, examined 66 youth with school phobia–refusal defined according to Berg, Nichols, and Pritchard's (1969) criteria. Youth were assigned to one of three treatment groups: behavioral, inpatient, and home schooling–psychotherapy. The mean numbers of treatment weeks for these groups were 2.5, 72.1, and 45.3, respectively. Behavioral treatment consisted of clarifying the child's problem; discussing child, parent, and teacher worries; parent training; in vivo flooding; and follow-up. Results revealed that significantly more youth in the behavioral group (93.3%) returned to school compared with the inpatient (37.5%) and home schooling–psychotherapy (10.0%) groups. These gains were largely maintained at 1-year follow-up. Blagg and Yule concluded that behavior therapy produced "rapid and successful outcomes" (p. 127) for most of the cases.

N. J. King et al. (1998; see also N. King, Tonge, Heyne, & Ollendick, 2000) randomly assigned 34 children (mean age: 11.0 years) with school refusal to two groups: wait-list control or cognitive–behavioral treatment. School refusal was defined with Berg et al.'s (1969) criteria, so only children with "severe emotional upset" were included. Various levels of severity were present, as 29.4% of the youth were completely absent from school, 50.0% were partially absent, and 20.6% attended school with anxious and resistive behavior. The youth met criteria primarily for separation anxiety, adjustment, and overanxious disorder as well as simple and social phobia. Youth were assigned to the wait list control group or the cognitive–behavioral group for 4 weeks (n = 17 in each group). Those in the wait list control group received no intervention. Cognitive–behavioral child and parent treatment over six sessions mirrored Kendall, Flannery-Schroeder, et al.'s (1997) approach. Specifically, treatment consisted of the following elements:

- treatment rationale, individual goal setting, and building rapport
- identifying anxious situations and the child's responses to anxiety
- coping skills training for addressing anxious situations
- relaxation training
- recognizing anxiety-producing–reducing self-talk in anxious situations
- assertiveness training, self-evaluation, and self-reward
- exposure and desensitization
- parent and teacher training in behavior management skills
- discussions of progress and troubleshooting.

The results indicated that youth in the cognitive–behavioral treatment group, compared with those in the wait list control group, improved significantly more with respect to school attendance, fear, anxiety, depression, general internalizing behavior, and global clinician ratings. These gains were maintained at 3-month follow-up. King et al. concluded that "[cognitive–behavioral treatment] is efficacious in the treatment of school-refusing children" (p. 401) and that several factors are important in this process. These factors included a swift return to school and involvement of the child and parents during treatment.

In a similar study, Last, Hansen, and Franco (1998) randomly assigned 56 youth with school phobia to one of two groups: cognitive–behavioral treatment (mean age: 11.7 years) and attention-placebo control (mean age: 12.4 years). Youth were accepted for the study if they had anxiety-based school refusal and at least 10% class absenteeism for 1 month prior to the study. Duration of the sample's school refusal behavior ranged from 2 weeks to 260 weeks. Primary diagnoses of the sample included separation anxiety; avoidant, overanxious, and panic disorder; and simple or social phobia.

Youth were assigned to cognitive–behavioral treatment or attention-placebo control for 12 weeks, with one session per week. The cognitive–behavioral treatment group received "graduated in vivo exposure and coping self-statement training." In vivo exposure involved reintroducing the child to school in a gradual, stepwise fashion. Related components involved the development of a fear–avoidance hierarchy, homework assignments, and regular telephone contact with the family. Cognitive self-statement training was also used before and during exposure sessions; here, youth identified problematic thoughts in anxiety-provoking situations and replaced these thoughts with more "adaptive, coping self-statements" (p. 405). The attention-placebo control group received educational-support therapy that allowed youth to discuss their concerns about school and answer posed questions about their situations. Daily diaries were also used, but no formal cognitive–behavioral treatment was introduced.

The results indicated that both groups improved substantially over time with respect to percentage of school attendance, global improvement ratings, fear, anxiety, depression, and posttreatment diagnosis. These results were largely maintained at 4-week follow-up and the following school year. Last et al. (1998) concluded that there were "no differences between the cognitive–behavioral, exposure-based treatment and the educational-support treatment" (p. 410) and that children with school refusal of a longer duration showed the most improvement. The authors further noted that "it may be that the treatment of school refusal is prescriptive, with different children responding differently to alternative types of treatment" (p. 411).

Regarding this prescriptive treatment approach, Kearney and Silverman (1990, 1999) have successfully treated several cases of youth refusing school to avoid SPNA. In particular, we have found that a prescriptive treatment approach is effective for improving attendance and for reducing distress in this population. Data from the School Refusal Assessment Scale (Kearney & Silverman, 1993), in conjunction with other measures, were used to assign prescriptive treatment. Components of this functional treatment approach are described below.

Other

Other treatments have also been proposed for anxiety-based school refusal behavior, including detailed recommendations for school officials and counselors based largely on school consultation, educational interventions, and the principles described in this book and elsewhere (see R. E. Brown, Copeland, & Hall, 1974; A. Fowler, 1978; Gresham & Nagle, 1981; S. R. Harris, 1980; Kolko, Ayllon, & Torrence, 1987; LeUnes & Siemsglusz, 1977; McAnanly, 1986; Sugar & Schrank, 1979; Wade, 1979; Want, 1983; Wataru, 1990; Weinberger, Leventhal, & Beckman, 1973). Other strategies to address this population have been advocated as well, including home-based education (Knox, 1989), peer support and counseling groups (Contessa & Paccione-Dyszlewski, 1981; Diamond, 1985), and hypnosis (Lawlor, 1976).

Inpatient or residential treatment has also been used to successfully address youth with school refusal behavior, including anxiety-based problems. For example, Berg and Fielding (1978) treated two groups of youth ($N = 32$) with school phobia for 3 or 6 months in an inpatient hospital unit. Treatment consisted of supportive and milieu therapy, social skills training, family therapy, and attendance at a school on the unit. At 1-year follow-up, however, only 17 (53.1%) were rated as well or much improved. Other examples of day, inpatient, or residential treatment and program descriptions are also available (see Barker, 1968; Beitchman, 1981; Berg, 1985a; Church & Edwards, 1984; Weiss & Cain, 1964). In general, these programs represent treatments of last resort for this population and may be best suited to youth with very severe or chronic school refusal behavior and those with extreme and pervasive comorbid symptomatology.

TREATMENT FOR YOUTH WHO REFUSE SCHOOL TO AVOID SPNA

Treatment components for children who refuse school to avoid SPNA essentially include psychoeducation, building a negative affectivity–avoidance hierarchy, somatic control exercises, imaginal and in vivo desensitization, and self-reinforcement.

Psychoeducation

Psychoeducation involves helping youth understand the nature of feelings (e.g., somatic complaints), negative and irrational thoughts, and behaviors (e.g., avoidance) that comprise anxiety. Psychoeducation is important in that it promotes better self-monitoring and allows for better identification of the parameters of a child's problem (e.g., separate logbook sections can be made for somatic problems, thoughts, and behaviors when at or near school). In addition, education about anxiety and negative affectivity promotes therapy techniques by providing a detailed rationale for their use to a child. Specifically, different experiences (e.g., physical symptoms, aversive thoughts, avoidance) can be linked to certain treatment techniques (e.g., relaxation, self-reinforcement, exposure).

Psychoeducation also includes the interaction of anxiety components within a child. Among children who refuse school, unpleasant feelings often trigger catastrophic thoughts and subsequent avoidance and other maladaptive behaviors. However, other children report simpler (e.g., thoughts to behaviors) or alternative patterns (e.g., thoughts to feelings to behaviors). To outline the specific interaction among a child's feelings, thoughts, and behaviors, different scenarios in which a child is most distressed are discussed. Likely scenarios include the night before school, getting ready for school in the morning, approaching the school building, entering a classroom, and making transitions from place to place at school. From a child's descriptions, a detailed sequence may be obtained of how his or her anxiety components interact to trigger distress and avoidance.

Finally, psychoeducation involves conveying the concept of gradual re-exposure to school. Although a long-term goal is to resume full-time school attendance, the process involves a step-by-step approach. Closer and closer proximity to the classroom is required at a pace set largely by the therapist but in conjunction with reports from the child, parents, and school officials.

Building a Negative Affectivity–Avoidance Hierarchy

Following psychoeducation, at least one hierarchy of 5–10 items and situations is developed; these represent treatment targets to be addressed over time. The hierarchy is often derived from formal assessment information, the psychoeducation process, or interview information, or some combination of these. The hierarchy is graded from low- to high-anxiety-provoking items. A common way of sorting these situations is to solicit child ratings of negative affectivity (or distress) and avoidance for each situation. To do so, one may use a fear thermometer (see chapter 5) or distress–avoidance ratings on a 0–10 scale. A sample hierarchy is shown in Table 6.1.

This hierarchy likely changes or is reconfigured multiple times during treatment. Some children require several hierarchies during treatment to address all stressful situations, and others progress rapidly through lower but not higher rungs of the hierarchy. Many youth, for example, have little

TABLE 6.1
Sample Hierarchy of Anxiety-Provoking Situations

Hierarchy item	Distress rating	Avoidance rating
Staying in class all day without talking to parents	9	9
Staying in class all day after 11:00 a.m. without parents	8	7
Staying in the library alone most of the school day	7	4
Staying in class all day after 1:30 p.m. without parents	6	7
Walking into class	6	6
Going only to lunch at school without parents	5	5
Riding the school bus by oneself	4	5
Waiting for parent to arrive for pick-up after school	3	4
Going to school to get homework when no one is there	2	2
Getting ready for school in the morning	1	1

trouble preparing for school but refuse to enter the building or classroom once there. As such, subdividing the hierarchy into smaller steps (e.g., with respect to time in school or distance to classroom) is often necessary.

Somatic Control Exercises

For youth who refuse school to avoid SPNA and aversive physical symptoms, somatic control exercises such as relaxation training and deep diaphragmatic breathing may be useful. A tension-release model of relaxation is commonly used for this population. In this procedure, which lasts 20–30 minutes, youth are taught to tense and release different muscle groups, including hands and arms, face and jaw, stomach, legs and feet, and other problematic areas (T. H. Ollendick & Cerny, 1981). This technique, in addition to calming the child, helps him or her come to understand, with help from the therapist, the difference between physical sensations of muscle tension and distress and those of relaxation and calmness.

Deep diaphragmatic breathing may also be used to prolong the effects of relaxation. A child breathes slowly though his or her nose and deeply into the diaphragm. During this procedure, it may be wise to show the child where the diaphragm is located and have him or her feel it with his or her hands. When exhaling, the child breathes out slowly through the mouth, counting slowly if helpful. For younger children, this is facilitated by having them imagine a balloon or tire expand as they breathe in and slowly contract as they breathe out.

Desensitization

Desensitization is usually an indispensable treatment component for children refusing school to avoid SPNA. Integral to this process is exposure or re-exposure to the school setting under graduated and relaxed conditions. Imaginal desensitization may be used initially but is almost always followed by real-life or in vivo desensitization. Homework assignments and practice are necessary as well. Desensitization begins with a detailed explanation for the child. In particular, the technique may be compared with some skill (e.g., bicycling) that was initially anxiety provoking but that the child now does well. The child is reminded of the aversive physical feelings, thoughts, and behaviors initially associated with learning the skill. Then, with practice, he or she was able to master the skill. This process is compared with the skill of controlling negative affectivity: Initially, the process may be somewhat anxiety provoking and painful but, with exposure-based practice, the child should master his or her distress and overcome school avoidance.

Imaginal

Imaginal desensitization involves practice in thinking about troubling situations to facilitate later in vivo exposure. In this process, a school-related scene that provokes negative affectivity is presented to the child. Descriptions of lower and then higher rungs on the negative affectivity hierarchy are presented. Descriptions include sights, sounds, smells, places, thoughts, and feelings that provoke or comprise a child's negative affectivity. Potential catastrophes are also described. The scene is realistic, closely attuned to the child's concerns and school setting, and specific. In many cases, embellishment is needed to match the potential horrors dreamed up by the child but sometimes left unspoken:

> You are in the school building near the front office as other people are milling around. You have to go to your classroom, but you haven't been there for about 2 weeks. Someone in the front office says that you better get to class, and that immediately makes your heart race and your stomach feel tight. You start to walk down one of the two halls you have to travel to get to class. You see other kids and adults looking at you, and think they must know how you're feeling! The tension must be so obvious! You continue to walk down the first hallway and turn into the second hallway, which leads to your classroom. Your heart is beating even faster and your stomach feels like it's going to crumble in your body. As you near the classroom, you start to worry that you'll be the last one there! What if everyone stares at you as you enter the classroom? What if the teacher gives you a dirty look? What if your classmates want to know where you've been? What if you get sent to the principal for being late? All of these thoughts race through your mind as you get closer to the door and as your heart is pounding and your stomach feels like it will explode. You reach for the handle of the door and pull back as your anxiety becomes almost unbearable. You look through the small window in the door and see everyone looking

back at you. Oh, no! They're all there and waiting for me, you think. You reach again for the door handle and walk in. As you do, you vomit and everyone starts screaming. You ask for help, but all the kids and the teacher get away from you as fast as possible.

During the description, the child raises his or her hand whenever negative affectivity becomes moderate to severe or uncomfortable. For a very young child, he or she would not raise his or her hand when feeling fine but would do so when feeling "really bad" or "very upset." For a young child, a fear thermometer or similar device may be used; here, uncomfortable distress may be defined as a level of 3 or greater on a 0–8 scale. For an older child or adolescent, a broader 0–100 Subjective Units of Distress Disturbance scale (Wolpe, 1969) may be used; here, a rating of 40 or greater would define uncomfortable distress. Use whatever measure the child prefers or understands best.

Relaxation, correct breathing, or pleasurable scenes are introduced whenever the child reports uncomfortable levels of distress. As anxiety abates, the scene is reintroduced. Over time, the child is asked to tolerate slightly greater levels of discomfort before signaling (e.g., 60 on a 0–100 scale). Relaxation is always the final step. The imaginal desensitization procedure is audiotaped for the child to practice at home.

If a child did not raise his or her hand during the imaginal exposure, he or she may not have understood what was expected of him or her, and the procedure must be simplified or clarified. In addition, the imagined scenario may not have been aversive enough to provoke negative affectivity. Further discussion with the child and a new, more anxiety-provoking scenario may be needed. Finally, the scenario may have produced anxiety but the child was barely able to handle it. Further discussion with the child may reveal the need for a slightly more embellished scenario with more severe consequences.

After imaginal desensitization, the therapist, parents, and child discuss the procedure. In particular, the child describes the course of his or her anxiety during the exposure, and this may be graphed. The child should describe why his or her anxiety declined (i.e., with repeated exposures, anxiety declines). Imaginal desensitization generally lasts one to two sessions, but it may be extended, shortened, or even skipped, depending on the severity of a case. All of the hierarchy scenarios are practiced until each is nonaversive. Ideally, anxiety at the end of imaginal exposure should be near zero, thus setting the stage for in vivo desensitization.

In Vivo

Imaginal and in vivo desensitization involve similar procedures, although the latter involves real-life anxiety-provoking experiences intermixed with relaxation. As with imaginal exposure, in vivo desensitization begins with lower rungs on the negative affectivity hierarchy. As exposure occurs, somatic control exercises are introduced so the child can manage his or her aversive physical symptoms. The child can signal when he or she feels uncomfortable, and the in vivo exposure can temporarily stop as relaxation or better breathing ensue. As the child learns to tolerate a given situation, more challenging steps are taken. Gradual in vivo desensitization should help reduce the child's negative affectivity, give him or her practice in coping with difficult unpredictable situations, and teach him or her to gather information about his or her own coping resources and skills when tolerating and controlling arousal.

The most common type of exposure, of course, is gradual exposure to the school building itself, particularly for children who have been out of school for a long time. For other children, the following sets of gradual exposures are common:

- increasing the amount of time riding alone in a school bus
- increasingly entering a classroom setting by oneself
- approaching a specific object or situation
- being in a classroom without parents for longer periods of time
- being in a classroom without calling parents for longer periods of time
- being in a classroom without going to the nurse or other part of the school building (e.g., library) for longer periods of time
- interoceptive exposures to internal panic sensations, such as accelerated heart rate, dizziness, and hyperventilation, among others
- for children who worry about untoward consequences in school, exposure to increasingly unpredictable or fluctuating circumstances at school (best for children who are overly perfectionistic or preoccupied).

Over time, more difficult in vivo scenarios are constructed for the child. Some of these can take place in session (e.g., separation from parents), but the most pertinent exposures take place between sessions (with or without the therapist) as the child nears school. Advanced exposures also involve approach toward aversive stimuli without safety signals. A *safety signal* is any object or person on which a child relies to feel less anxious in a given situation. Common safety signals of children who refuse school include parents, cellular telephones to contact parents, a particular friend, repeated questioning or reassurance seeking, carrying many school materials, and checking the weather. Ongoing in vivo exposures involve increased approach to school and gradual elimination of safety signals.

After in vivo exposures, graphs may be used to provide feedback on performance. In most cases, anxiety increases at the beginning of an exposure and then declines. Other patterns (e.g., rising or fast declines in anxiety) may indicate that exposures must be altered. This may include, for example, extended exposures with somatic control exercises, addressing problematic thoughts, designing easier exposures, and increasing parental help.

Self-Reinforcement

Throughout this prescriptive treatment package, children are encouraged to praise themselves for effort and success during somatic control and exposure-based practices. Over the course of therapy, child self-praise should be encouraged by many people (e.g., parents, teachers). The goals here are to have children take pride in their accomplishments, enhance persistence at homework and exposure assignments, and maintain treatment progress.

Maintaining a School Schedule

During this and all functionally based treatments, a child and family should maintain a regular morning schedule. Youth who have been out of school for some time may have gotten accustomed to sleeping late, eating and dressing later in the day, and having too much fun on school days. Treatment is usually facilitated by having youth adhere to a strict morning routine that includes times for rising from bed and preparing for school. This helps ease the in vivo exposures that take place and reminds family members of the eventual goal of treatment (i.e., a return to full-time school attendance without distress). Procedures to address these morning concerns are outlined in chapter 8 and involve rewards for maintaining a regular daily schedule and punishments for dawdling, noncompliance, or related school refusal behaviors.

A CASE EXAMPLE

Eric was an 8-year-old boy referred to an outpatient mental health clinic for recent problems attending school. The assessment took place in early March of the school year and followed a telephone call from Eric's school counselor that he had missed the last 3 weeks of third grade. The call also revealed that Eric had just been transferred from another elementary school. In his new school, Eric had spent only 2 partial days in his classroom. Otherwise, he would curl up in the lobby and cry or run from the school building.

The initial assessment session was attended by Eric, his mother, and his grandmother. Eric was interviewed first and appeared subdued and somewhat confused as to why he was at the clinic. Eric was asked what general problems he was having, but he shrugged his shoulders and remained quiet. When asked about school, Eric became tearful and lowered his head, stating softly that he did not like school and that the teacher was "mean" to him. When asked to give specific examples of this meanness, however, Eric was unable to produce any. In addition, Eric did not endorse any other specific situations at school (e.g., fire alarm, being with classmates) that were uncomfortable. When asked about other topics, such as friends or family, Eric's mood improved considerably. With respect to school, however, he said he had no desire to go back and wanted his mother to pursue home schooling. He also complained of stomach pain when he got near the school building.

Eric's mother reported that her son had had intermittent problems attending school in the past, especially during kindergarten and first grade. These problems had largely subsided and did not recur for the remainder of the school year. This year, however, had been marked by substantial changes in Eric's home life. He began school with little difficulty but was forced to leave when his parents divorced and his mother relocated to an apartment building in another school zone. In addition, Eric's grandmother had moved in to help lower expenses. On transfer to his new school, Eric would "seize up" on the way there and cry as he was led into the school building. His mother tried different ways of getting him to class (e.g., talking, cajoling, dragging), but Eric was able to attend only twice. On both occasions, Eric bolted from class and ran down the street. On the last occasion, he was missing for several hours and eventually found hiding behind a neighbor's house. On other days, Eric would sit in a corner of the lobby and cry. No attempts from school officials to bring Eric into his classroom were successful.

Interview and questionnaire data revealed that Eric was indeed refusing school to avoid general negative affectivity and stomach pain while there. In addition, no specific fear-inducing stimuli were identified, Eric did not appear to have any social anxiety, he did not run home for attention after leaving school, and he was not pursuing tangible reinforcement outside of school. The therapist and Eric's mother and grandmother agreed on a treatment program to help alleviate Eric's stomach pain (medical reasons had already been ruled out) and ease his transition back into his regular classroom setting. This originally consisted of all of the functionally based treatment components described in this chapter, but exigent circumstances forced several modifications of the plan.

One exigent circumstance involved Eric's refusal to enter the clinic for the first treatment session. Instead, Eric sat in the car as his mother and grandmother came inside. The therapist went to the car to try to convince Eric to participate, but he remained quiet and would not move. Instead of postponing the session, however, the therapist decided to proceed with Eric's mother and grandmother. A hierarchy of situations was developed to which Eric would gradually approach. These situations included walking to the school door, being in the school lobby, walking to class, being in class for 1 hour, being in class for 2 hours, being in class all morning, and being in class all day. The therapist then went back to the car to ask Eric to supply ratings for each of these situations. The boy was initially silent but eventually gave ratings on a 0–10 scale of 5, 7, and 9 for the first three items and ratings of 10 for the remaining (all classroom attendance) items. He was asked to come into the clinic to answer some additional questions and ultimately did so. The therapist took this opportunity to educate Eric about the nature of his anxiety and to introduce diaphragmatic breathing, which Eric mastered with little effort.

The therapist also conveyed that a long-term goal would be to resume school attendance but at a slow pace and one set with Eric. This induced crying, however, and Eric went back to the car. In addition, this episode prompted Eric's mother to miss the next two treatment sessions as she considered home schooling. After several extended discussions with the therapist over a 2-week period, she agreed to give outpatient therapy another try. However, she insisted that Eric's teacher be changed (she was convinced that the teacher was the source of Eric's anxiety). After a conversation with the school counselor, Eric's classroom was switched. In addition, Eric's morning routine was reinstituted.

Given the urgency of the situation and Eric's mother's fragile confidence in the therapy plan, gradual in vivo exposure began immediately. Eric was asked what he could realistically do, and he said "go to the school door." Eric was asked to go to the school door for 3 days and practice his breathing, after which he could go home and be rewarded by his mother and grandmother. He successfully did so—a substantial accomplishment, because it got Eric "on board" the treatment plan, and he was able to approach school for at least a limited amount of time. Over the next week, Eric was eventually able to stand in the lobby with his grandmother for up to 3 hours. Unfortunately, one of the school officials tried to take Eric into his classroom, which provoked Eric to flee the school building; he was missing for several hours. By telephone that night, the therapist apologized to Eric for the mistake and told him he would ensure that all school officials were aware of his re-entry plan. Eric agreed to try again in a few days and, over a 2-week period, was able to attend the library or counselor's office for the entire day. In addition, he met his new teacher and some of his classmates in the library, and he seemed pleased.

Eric was then asked to spend a small amount of time in his classroom. The first 2 days, Eric spent 2 hours in class before being allowed to spend the rest of the day in the library. He then spent most of the morning in class, but fled the school building one day when his teacher asked him to go to lunch with the rest of the class. Eric was eventually found by his mother who, fortunately, brought Eric back to school for the remaining half-hour of the day (which he spent in the principal's office). That night, the therapist contacted the family to address this slip. It was agreed that, should Eric flee again, the school police would be contacted to bring Eric back to school and that he would lose certain privileges at night and on weekends. The therapist also told Eric that leaving the school building was unacceptable but that he could request a respite at the library when needed. Over the next few days, Eric attended class in the morning and the library in the afternoon.

The remaining part of therapy was designed to help Eric with transitions in school (e.g., from class to lunch or from class to specialized class). Many children of this functional group have trouble initiating change to another setting, so extra practice or exposure regarding these must be built into the therapy regimen. Eric was instructed to perform these transitions twice the first week, four times (but not Monday) the second week, and each day the third week. By the end of this period, Eric was attending school full time with little distress or stomach pain. The rest of the school year was also mostly nonproblematic, although Eric's mother reported some difficulty following extended breaks. She was advised to maintain the exposure-based program and to have Eric meet his new teacher and explore his new classroom prior to the start of the next school year.

SUMMARY

Functionally based treatment for children with anxiety-based school refusal behavior focuses on methods to increase knowledge about anxiety and increase control in anxiety-provoking situations. Although effective, important others in the child's environment are often needed to increase treatment compliance and enhance a child's exposures. In addition, the urgency of a situation may dictate a faster progression to in vivo exposure (Hargett & Webster, 1996), as described in Eric's case.

7

YOUTH WHO ESCAPE AVERSIVE
SOCIAL OR EVALUATIVE SITUATIONS

Chad is a 13-year-old boy who is somewhat shy and overweight. He is relatively withdrawn in class and seems to shun interactions with others. Lately, he has been missing certain classes, especially those that involve some performance before others (e.g., choir, English, physical education). Chad's teachers also seem concerned about the time he wishes to spend with them.

In this chapter, primary treatment strategies are reviewed for youth who refuse school to escape aversive social or evaluative situations. The profile of this functional condition is often similar to youth who refuse school to avoid stimuli that provoke negative affectivity (see chapters 4 and 6). As such, some overlap in functionally based treatment (e.g., exposure) occurs as well. However, intervention for youth who refuse school to escape aversive social or evaluative situations more specifically targets social anxiety and social skills. Both social anxiety and skills deficits are prevalent in this functional condition, so both must often be addressed extensively before, or with, a child's school refusal behavior. Brief overviews are presented here of treatment for youth with social anxiety, social skills deficits, or both. More specific functionally based treatment components are then described for youth who refuse school to escape aversive social or evaluative situations. A case example is also provided.

YOUTH WITH SOCIAL ANXIETY

Contemporary treatment of youth with social anxiety parallels to some extent the psychosocial and psychopharmacological procedures discussed early in chapter 6. Indeed, in many studies reviewed in chapter 6, children with social anxiety were included. Other researchers, however, have developed and tested protocols specific to youth with social anxiety. Albano and colleagues (Albano & Barlow, 1996; Albano, Detweiler, & Logsdon-Conradsen, 1999), for example, described a 16-session protocol that includes psychoeducation, modeling and role-playing, shaping and social reinforcement, cognitive restructuring, role reversal and perspective taking, exposure, homework assignments, and relapse prevention training. Preliminary support for this protocol was derived from the successful treatment of five young adolescents with generalized social phobia (Albano, Marten, Holt, Heimberg, & Barlow, 1995). The general goals of this therapeutic package are to help youth identify triggers to their social anxiety, fully understand the nature of social anxiety, manage excessive social anxiety, and cope with normal levels of social anxiety (Albano & Barlow, 1996).

Components of Albano and Barlow's (1996) cognitive–behavioral protocol have been used successfully to treat various youth with anxiety in social situations (e.g., Esveldt-Dawson, Wisner, Unis, Matson, & Kazdin, 1982; Evers & Schwarz, 1973; Franco, Christoff, Crimmins, & Kelly, 1983; Harris & Brown, 1982; Kandal, Ayllon, & Rosenbaum, 1977; Keller & Carlson, 1974; Matson, 1981; O'Connor, 1972). The most common components include exposure, modeling, and some form of cognitive therapy. These components have been used as well to treat youth with fears in evaluative situations such as tests or public speaking (e.g., Cradock, Cotler, & Jason, 1978; Fox & Houston, 1981; Grindler, 1988; T. Johnson, Tyler, Thompson, & Jones, 1971; Leal, Baxter, Martin, & Marx, 1981; Little & Jackson, 1974; Mann, 1972; Raskind & Nagle, 1980; Ribordy, Tracy, & Bernotas, 1981; van der Ploeg-Stapert & van der Ploeg, 1986; Wilson & Rotter, 1986). Although less complex than the overarching Albano and Barlow (1996) protocol, these studies address the severity of social–evaluative anxiety along different response systems, and youth were helped to participate more in required and desirable social or evaluative activities.

YOUTH WITH PROBLEMATIC SOCIAL SKILLS

Contemporary treatment of youth with problematic social skills also involves mostly behavioral and cognitive components. Behavioral social skills training usually includes instructions, coaching, modeling, role-play or behavior rehearsal, practice in session and in real life situations, feedback, and social and other reinforcement. These components have been used successfully to improve a variety of social behaviors in youth, including key ones such as starting and maintaining appropriate conversations. Cognitive approaches have also been used to improve social skills in children and include, among other strategies, training in social problem solving, anger management, social perception and decoding skills, communication skills, and empathy (Cartledge & Milburn, 1995; McFayden-Ketchum & Dodge, 1998). Affective approaches, such as teaching youth about facial expressions, body language, and the verbal content of others, as well as more general family- and school-based interventions, have also been used. An integration of these approaches has been proposed as well (McFayden-Ketchum & Dodge, 1998).

Functionally based treatment for youth who refuse school to escape aversive social or evaluative situations is oriented primarily toward reducing anxiety in those situations. However, some researchers claim that social maladjustment and lack of intact peer relationships predict poor treatment outcome in youth with school refusal behavior (e.g., Berg, 1980; Last & Francis, 1988). Therefore, training to address deficient social skills may be necessary before focusing on a child's school refusal behavior. In other cases, however, social skills instruction can be integrated into several of the treatment components described here, especially cognitive restructuring and behavioral exposures with modeling and role-play. Concurrent treatment of a child's deficient social skills and school refusal behavior may thus occur.

YOUTH WHO REFUSE SCHOOL TO ESCAPE AVERSIVE SOCIAL–EVALUATIVE SITUATIONS

Several treatment components comprise functionally based treatment for children who refuse school to escape aversive social or evaluative situations. These components essentially include psychoeducation, building a social–evaluative anxiety hierarchy, cognitive restructuring, and behavioral exposures.

Psychoeducation

Psychoeducation regarding the nature of social or evaluative anxiety is similar to that described in chapter 6. Youth are taught about the components of anxiety (i.e., feelings, thoughts, behaviors) as well as their interaction. Because youth in this functional condition tend to be older children and adolescents, substantial detail may be gleaned as well about their thoughts, feelings, and behaviors in anxiety-provoking social or evaluative situations. This enhances cognitive therapy (discussed later in this chapter) as well. To help determine anxious reactions in a certain youth, he or she can examine social scenes (e.g., a group of teenagers talking) from magazines or advertisements and state what thoughts, feelings, and behaviors apply to each person in the scene. Blank thought bubbles above socially oriented drawings can be used as well (Kendall, Chansky, et al., 1992).

As a youth describes what is happening in a scene, the therapist derives information about the client's pattern of social or evaluative anxiety, his or her interpretation of events and cognitive distortions, and anxiety-provoking stimuli. These should be clearly pointed out to the youth. In addition, the therapist may use the scene to describe how someone might calm him- or herself or how social–evaluative anxiety declines over time. The youth's current strategies for coping with aversive social–evaluative situations or calming him- or herself may be explored during this process as well. Finally, youth are made aware of the normative nature of social–evaluative anxiety, that this anxiety usually fades as a person grows more accustomed to a situation, and the final goals of treatment (i.e., to reduce school refusal behavior and to increase adequate functioning in troublesome social or evaluative situations).

Building a Social–Evaluative Anxiety–Avoidance Hierarchy

From information gathered during assessment and psychoeducation, a therapist and youth can identify what specific social–evaluative situations at school are most problematic. These 5–10 situations are the primary treatment targets, and the hierarchy is graded so a youth can progress from relatively easier social–evaluative situations to more difficult ones during treatment. Specifically, the hierarchy may be sorted along child and adult ratings of distress and avoidance on a 0–10 or other scale. Table 7.1 contains a sample social–evaluative hierarchy and includes some common areas of focus in youth of this functional condition.

Note that some children may progress quickly at first and then more slowly as school attendance becomes increasingly required. In addition, subdivisions of the hierarchy or multiple hierarchies may be necessary during treatment. The hierarchy should also be geared toward increased school attendance during treatment, so items should be linked to behavioral exposures (discussed subsequently). The pace of this reintegration is set largely by the therapist but in conjunction with reports from the child, parents, school officials, and relevant others. In the meantime, for youth missing

TABLE 7.1
Sample Social–Evaluative Hierarchy

Hierarchy item	Distress rating	Avoidance rating
Speaking in front of the entire class	10	9
Starting a conversation with someone not well known	8	8
Going to gym class	7	5
Eating lunch in the cafeteria without friends there	7	3
Asking or answering a question in class	6	7
Taking a test	6	6
Asking a teacher for help	5	2
Listening to others not well known	4	5
Walking in the hallways at school	4	4
Singing in choir/playing an instrument	2	1

large amounts of school, regular morning routines and times should be set for rising from bed, preparing as if going to school, and conducting other daily activities (see chapter 8). In this way, later reintegration to school is facilitated.

Cognitive Restructuring

Many youth who refuse school to escape aversive social or evaluative situations are plagued by cognitive distortions in key interactive situations at school. For example, many catastrophize about their appearance, potential negative events, or beliefs that others have about them. These youth continually focus on negative thoughts and beliefs at the expense of a realistic examination of a given situation, an accurate assessment of the resources one has to manage the situation, a problem-solving focus, and an ability to think adaptively (i.e., healthy thinking; Kendall, Chansky, et al., 1992). As a youth's social or evaluative anxiety worsens in a given situation it may inhibit healthy thinking, overwhelm the youth, and lead to avoidance. Addressing negative thought patterns and teaching youth to engage in healthy thinking are thus high priorities in this functional treatment package.

Cognitive therapy must be tailored to a child's developmental abilities. In general, more concrete work needs to be done with children, although more complex, adultlike therapy may proceed with adolescents. For younger children, researchers have developed various acronym-oriented procedures to help them identify negative thoughts, focus elsewhere, and reward themselves for doing so. For example, Kendall, Chansky, et al. (1992) outlined the FEAR acronym:

F: Feeling frightened? (Recognizing physical symptoms of anxiety)
E: Expecting bad things to happen? (recognizing self-talk and what one worries will happen)
A. Actions and attitudes that will help (problem-solving behaviors and coping statements one can use in anxiety-provoking situations)
R: Results and rewards (self-evaluation and reward).

In addition, Silverman and Kurtines (1996) outlined the STOP acronym:

S: Are you feeling Scared or anxious?
T: What are your scary or anxious Thoughts?
O: What Other coping thoughts and behaviors can you think of?
P: Praise yourself for using these steps and Plan for next time.

These acronyms are used to help children rehearse the steps necessary for coping with negative thoughts or focusing more intently on positive, adaptive thoughts. More specifically, the goals are to have children recognize problematic thoughts, implement a solution-based process to address them, and evaluate their plan and reward themselves for doing so. These goals are met initially in session and then more independently by the child in natural settings, such as school.

For older children and adolescents, more complex cognitive therapy may be used as appropriate. Along the Beckian (Beck, Rush, Shaw, & Emery, 1979) approach, youth are taught to identify automatic thoughts or those distortions that focus a person on what is most dangerous or potentially upsetting about a given situation. Common distortions in youth with school refusal behavior include all-or-none thinking, catastrophizing, overgeneralizing, negative labeling, using *can'ts* or *shoulds*, mind reading, fortune telling, and canceling positives. Youth are instructed as to the nature of these and other distortions relevant to them.

Initial

The initial focus of cognitive restructuring for children and adolescents is to increase awareness of the primary triggers that lead to anxious reactions (i.e., the *F* or *S* steps from FEAR and STOP). Regarding socially anxious situations, the most pertinent triggers are often negative, distorted thoughts. To clarify these triggers, younger children can draw pictures of general events and situations that make them anxious, and older children and adolescents can maintain a daily log of general anxiety-provoking social–evaluative situations. Youth should list unsettling somatic, cognitive, and behavioral actions that coexist with these situations. The use of charts and analogue situations, such as in-session tests or encounters with strangers, may also help identify these triggers. A discussion is then held to see how a youth anticipates negative events and what thoughts, images, and other problems occur during anxiety-provoking events.

In a related fashion, a therapist must explore in depth the specific thought patterns a youth has in situations from the hierarchy (i.e., the *E* and *T* steps from FEAR and STOP). These automatic thoughts often reflect consequences that could, but probably will not, occur. Items on the earlier hierarchy—for example, common negative thoughts—might include "What if other kids start snickering at me?," "What if I look like an idiot?," or "What if I faint?"

Advanced

After the initial cognitive restructuring phases, each problematic thought is methodically analyzed and modified. In particular, each party searches for more adaptive, helpful, accurate, or realistic thoughts that are pertinent to a situation (i.e., the *A* and *O* steps from FEAR and STOP). More formal cognitive therapy procedures may commence for older children and adolescents, and a full explication of these procedures is available elsewhere (e.g., Beck et al., 1979; Beck, Emery, & Greenberg, 1985). A key goal here is to have a youth habitually examine and challenge each automatic or problematic thought. One way of doing so is to teach him or her to examine all the evidence for a given thought and dispute negative thoughts with rational and realistic thinking. The following questions, or *dispute handles*, may be used to do so (Kearney & Albano, 2000). Dispute handles are used for problematic social–evaluative situations using the FEAR–STOP procedure in children and during formal cognitive therapy for adolescents.

- Am I 100% sure that this will happen?
- Can I really know what that person thinks of me?
- What's the worst thing that can really happen?
- Have I ever been in a situation like this before, and was it really that bad?
- How many times has this terrible thing actually happened?
- So what if the situation doesn't go perfectly?
- Am I the only person who has ever had to deal with this situation?

Cognitive procedures are usually incorporated into many different role-plays or behavioral exposures to give children more opportunities to evaluate and change their thoughts and to demonstrate their ability to handle anxious situations. As therapy progresses, children should use cognitive restructuring techniques more independently to uncover irrational or negative thoughts (the *F/S* and *E/T* steps) and change them to more realistic and adaptive coping statements (the *A/O* step and use of dispute handles). Self-praise and other rewards for doing so are also established (i.e., the *R* and *P* steps from FEAR and STOP).

Behavioral Exposures

Behavioral exposures are usually coupled with cognitive restructuring to provoke anxiety reactions, provide opportunities to practice cognitive procedures, increase school attendance, and help youth enter and master different anxiety-provoking situations. A focus on similar situations to which a child habituated and mastered in the past is thus important here (see chapter 6). Youth may also be asked to compare their anxious experiences (e.g., conversations at school) with similar situations that are not anxiety provoking (e.g., conversations at a mall). These examples provide evidence that a child is capable of mastering nerve-wracking situations, including ones about to be designed.

A typical behavioral exposure involves the re-creation of some social or evaluative scene from the hierarchy. Some exposures can be initially simulated in session (e.g., tests, conversations, presentations before others), but exposures specific to a school setting (e.g., talking to the teacher in front of the class) will have to be conducted there. These latter exposures are sometimes referred to as "show that I can" (STIC) tasks (Kendall, Chansky, et al., 1992). Specific goals for each exposure must be established beforehand. These goals should involve well-defined behaviors (e.g., maintain eye contact, increase time walking down a hallway) that are observable and within a child's reach.

During an exposure session, anxiety is monitored by the child. This is done to evaluate progress and provide feedback to the child afterward. For younger children, a fear thermometer on a 0–8 scale (see chapters 5 and 6) may be used; for older children and adolescents, broader Subjective Units of Distress/Disturbance Scale (Wolpe, 1969) ratings on a 0–100 scale may be feasible. These ratings are optimally taken every minute during an 8- to 10-minute exposure; some exposures may be longer and so ratings may be more spread out. The goal, however, is to secure enough data points to illustrate a youth's pattern of anxiety during the exposure.

Slower paced exposures are desirable for young children, those with comorbid problems (e.g., learning disabilities), and those with very high levels of anxiety. More protracted exposures allow these children greater opportunities to practice cognitive and exposure skills and to habituate to anxiety-provoking events. Children may also require some assistance with exposures from friends or parents, especially during initial exposures and difficult ones later in treatment. Assistance may also be more necessary for younger clients, those with more severe social–evaluative anxiety, those who need some nudging to practice the exposures, and those whose parents can readily establish social–evaluative scenarios in different settings. Therapists must ensure, however, that people assisting a child during exposure do not prevent him or her from fully managing or experiencing a situation. In addition, the child should note how any assistant (or model) appropriately addressed or coped with an anxiety-provoking situation. Finally, the child should attempt at least some independent management of the situation and praise him- or herself for engaging in the exposure.

Initial

Initial behavioral exposures involve lower level items on a youth's social–evaluative anxiety hierarchy. Such exposure usually involves role-playing in session and may be combined with modeling procedures as appropriate (e.g., for conditions noted above or for teaching social skills). The exposure should be somewhat anxiety provoking and allow a youth to practice cognitive procedures. Over time, the youth should be able to endure greater amounts of distress and discover that his or her anxiety will abate as he or she stays in a situation. Examples of exposures from the earlier hierarchy follow here:

- Speaking in front of the entire class: reading in front of a sample audience in session who seems disinterested or deliberately snickers or otherwise acts inappropriately, reading a report with words that are difficult to pronounce (so the child necessarily makes mistakes), reading a difficult report in a short time period, reading the report to an actual class at school.
- Starting or having a conversation: physically placing oneself close to peers who are talking, starting a conversation with someone in session and at school, calling a classmate about homework, joining a group of kids who are already playing, saying "no" when necessary.
- Going to gym class: attending gym class for increasing periods of time, approaching peers during gym class, appropriately responding to teasing.
- Eating somewhere without friends: eating with strangers in the office setting, eating alone in a food court or restaurant, increased time eating without friends in the school cafeteria, sitting next to peers in the school cafeteria, starting or joining a conversation with peers in the school cafeteria.
- Asking or answering a question in class: asking a question in session and in class, asking someone to stop doing something annoying, answering at least one question per class (to be set up with teacher cooperation).
- Taking a test: preparing for a test, anticipating a test, sample surprise tests in session, having to take multiple-choice and essay tests in session and in school.
- Walking in the hallways at school: walking through large, crowded corridors in non-school buildings; increasing the amount of time in school hallways; making eye contact with at least five people in a hallway.
- Singing in choir/playing an instrument: performing a recital in front of others in session, preparing for a performance, increased time performing in front of others, performing in a formal recital.

After the exposure a discussion is held about the level of anxiety faced by the youth and his or her cognitive and somatic triggers to anxiety. To facilitate this discussion, the child's social–evaluative anxiety ratings may be graphed to analyze various patterns of habituation or nonhabituation (see chapter 6). A discussion is also held about whether and how many of the exposure goals were met, and the number of goals met can be charted over time to evaluate progress. In cases where few goals were met, the child can still be shown that the consequences were not as catastrophic as he or she initially believed (if this is true). The child may also be asked to view his or her performance from the perspective of others and asked how he or she would rate others in a similar situation (e.g., another child having trouble pronouncing a word during an oral report). In addition, alternative possibilities for others' behavior (e.g., rudeness) should be explored.

Debriefing allows a child to further process his or her anxiety and behavior. In particular, discussions are held about high levels of anxiety and whether these interfered with the goals of the exposure. The youth's methods of changing cognitive distortions throughout the exposure are discussed as well. A key aspect of debriefing is to give the youth feedback about his or her behavior. If the exposure was relatively unsuccessful, then feedback is given on what the child could have done differently or better. A revision of the hierarchy to include smaller steps may also be necessary. If the exposure was relatively successful, and the youth's anxiety waned as he or she endured the entire situation, then the youth receives additional feedback that ongoing practice, endurance, and a focus on the situation at hand lead naturally to lower anxiety.

Subsequent

Subsequent exposures during treatment involve middle and higher items from the youth's social–evaluative anxiety hierarchy. More challenging and anxiety-provoking situations are thus addressed, and outcomes are usually more variable than before. As each exposure is designed and carried out, youth should continue to identify anxiety-provoking thoughts and other triggers and challenge distortions as appropriate. Modeling and role-play may also continue as necessary. Successful exposures should, of course, be liberally rewarded by the therapist, parents, child, and others. In addition, the child should focus on the positive feeling of completing difficult exposures and implementing anxiety management skills.

As behavioral exposures become more difficult, any difficulties in carrying out homework assignments (i.e., avoidance or escape) are reviewed. To overcome problems, a revision of the hierarchy and a re-emphasis on cognitive restructuring (e.g., review of dispute handles), modeling and role-play, contingency management (see chapter 8), or other treatment procedures may have to be considered. As greater tolerance is developed for longer and more anxiety-provoking social–evaluative situations, however, more time in school should ensue. For youth who are completely or almost completely out of school, this would initially involve part-time attendance during easier times of the day (e.g., 1 hour at the end of the school day). In addition, youth with more severe school refusal behavior may initially require a parent or someone else to accompany them to school to help carry out the exposures. Therapy sessions may also be scheduled at school as appropriate.

A CASE EXAMPLE

Jana was a 14-year-old female student referred to an outpatient mental health clinic for recent problems attending school. The assessment took place in mid-November of the school year and followed a telephone call from Jana's counselor that she had missed about 60% of school days so far. In addition, the counselor stated that Jana seemed withdrawn in class and not overly interactive with her peers. The counselor speculated that Jana was depressed but the counselor had interacted with Jana only three times since the beginning of the school year.

The initial assessment session was attended by Jana and her mother. Jana reported that her entry into high school had been difficult, as she was suddenly swamped by a brand-new set of classes and teachers. Apparently, her high school was quite different from her middle school, as the former had few windows and more of an enclosed feel. In addition, Jana complained about the amount and difficulty of the schoolwork and documented her past academic struggles (she had typically been a "C" student). Most of all, however, Jana was upset with the way others were treating her at school. In particular, she did not like the noise level of her classmates and she often felt alienated from the already well-formed cliques at the school. She was gradually becoming more withdrawn and was leaving school during the day to come home. Usually, Jana would skip her afternoon classes, which consisted of physical education, English, and choir. All of these classes involved some level of performance (i.e., athletics, speaking, singing) before others, or tasks that Jana reportedly had great difficulty completing. She had been increasingly asking her mother to allow her to drop out of school and start work.

Jana's mother was insistent that Jana remain in school but was equally insistent that school officials were to blame for her daughter's predicament. In particular, she complained that the school unfairly recorded her daughter as "absent" when she attended at least half a day, that the school failed to inform her promptly of her daughter's absenteeism, and that the teachers were unnecessarily loading Jana with overly difficult homework. Jana's mother stopped short, however, of advocating a change of school for her daughter (her high school was within easy walking distance of home). She also said that Jana did seem more withdrawn, speaking to her friends less and sleeping more than usual.

Interview and questionnaire data indicated that Jana was refusing school primarily to escape aversive social or evaluative situations while there. This applied not only to her afternoon classes but also to lunchtime in the cafeteria, which was noisy and crowded and where it was difficult to find a place to sit. In essence, then, Jana was having trouble attending school from 11:30 a.m. to the end of the day, especially when she was expected to engage in some performance-based task. In addition, assessment data revealed subclinical depression and some learning problems, although the latter were thought to be secondary to her absenteeism and lack of motivation to complete assigned work.

Jana's depression worsened after this session, possibly because of discussions about eventually returning to school full time. She refused to come to the next two appointments and began talking openly about killing herself. Jana's mother was advised to call the hospital crisis unit, which came to Jana's home to assess her. Her situation was not deemed life threatening, however, and she was not admitted to the hospital. Still, her mother took time off work to supervise her daughter closely during the next few days. The therapist also contacted Jana and urged her to resume therapy. She was assured that school attendance would not progress at a pace too difficult for her and that all options would be pursued. In addition, the therapist explained that the therapeutic procedures might reduce not only her social–evaluative anxiety at school but also her sadness in general. Jana agreed to come to the next session, and did so, but had now missed 4 straight weeks of school because of holidays and parental acquiescence.

In the first treatment session the therapist explored Jana's cycle of anxiety and depression at school and developed a hierarchy of situations that Jana could eventually approach. Jana reported few physical symptoms at school, although she did feel "knots" in her stomach when having to speak before others. Instead, Jana's thoughts seemed to trigger her anxiety and desire to escape aversive social and evaluative situations. In particular, Jana was convinced that others would disparage her for her performance. She was concerned that her overweight status would be a source of ridicule in physical education class, that her "shaky voice" would bring derision in English class, and that she would be forced to sing a solo in choir. Jana was also convinced that her peers were actively rejecting her, as few approached her to solicit her attention or friendship. Jana was shown how her thoughts led directly to anxiety and avoidance and how changing those thoughts to more positive, coping ones would need to be emphasized. Jana understood and accepted this rationale. Jana's hierarchy of social–evaluative situations generally consisted of returning to school in the morning, attending morning classes and lunch, attending afternoon classes without any expectation for performance (e.g., no oral presentations in English), and attending afternoon classes with some expectation for performance.

Jana's mother also understood and accepted the rationale for this therapy plan but continued to criticize school officials for their insensitivity to her daughter's condition and threats to refer the family to juvenile court for educational neglect. The therapist, recognizing that the mother's frustration with the school could lead to further acquiescence and lack of motivation on Jana's part, struck a deal with her: Jana's mother would vigorously encourage Jana to complete her therapeutic homework assignments in exchange for a meeting with school officials to be attended by the therapist. At that meeting, the therapist was able to convince school officials to delay the referral to juvenile court and allow Jana to receive full credit for make-up work until the end of February. The latter process was designed to keep Jana motivated to attend school and be able to pass the school year. In addition, school officials agreed to have the school attendance officer contact Jana's mother immediately if Jana skipped class during the day. They refused to change their policy, however, of marking Jana absent for the day if any class were missed. In addition, it was made clear that any further regression in her behavior would prompt the juvenile court referral.

Jana was informed of this and agreed to go back to school in the morning. Surprisingly, she also attended lunchtime at school before walking home (she was allowed to do so). The therapist continued to examine her mood and anxiety level by means of daily logbooks and frequent telephone conversations during the week, and Jana agreed at this point to attend therapy twice per week. During the second week of this renewed therapy process, Jana was asked to pick which class to add next. She chose choir, a fortunate choice because it meant that Jana would have to remain in the school building for the entire day. She attended two study hall periods between lunch and choir and was not required to sing any solos. In addition, the therapist asked Jana to choose an extracurricular activity to give her an opportunity to build friendships and emphasized trying an exercise class so that she would have more energy and feel more fit. Jana agreed to do so. In addition, a nighttime and weekend homework schedule was designed so that Jana could make up her work in time to get full credit. Extra tutoring was also made available to her.

The therapist also engaged in intense cognitive work with Jana, exploring her worry about being ridiculed before others. Dispute handles were used, particularly those regarding the worst possibilities that could happen and what if they did happen. Jana came to realize that the worst possibility would be a subtle feeling of embarrassment, and she talked about methods of coping with such embarrassment (e.g., continuing with a task, laughing along with her peers). In addition, Jana came to realize that, by avoiding others, there was little likelihood that others would approach her or appreciate her warmth and other positive qualities. Some of her therapeutic homework assignments included initiating interactions with others during morning and exercise classes, and Jana was able to make some friends rather quickly. Her schedule was also rearranged so that she could share lunchtime with her new friends.

Over time, Jana completed most, although not all, of her make-up work. It eventually became clear that Jana would likely pass the school year, although just barely. She added English class and, following some in-session practice, was able to complete her oral presentations. One area that remained highly problematic, however, was physical education class. Jana completely refused to attend that class, and another meeting with school officials was necessary to allow Jana to go to study hall during that time (to meet with a tutor and complete schoolwork) and retake physical education over the summer. Overall, however, her mood and social anxiety had improved to such an extent that she was attending school on a regular basis. In addition, regular parent–school official meetings were set up to reduce friction and misunderstandings and increase awareness of Jana's status. In many cases of school refusal behavior, resolving the rift between parents and school officials is critical to successful resolution.

SUMMARY

Functionally based treatment for youth who refuse school to escape aversive social or evaluative situations focuses on psychoeducation, hierarchy development, cognitive restructuring, and behavioral exposures to reduce anxiety and build mastery in these situations. In many cases in this functional condition, comorbid conditions, such as depression or academic difficulty, also apply, so such procedures could be generalized to address these problems as well (see Jana's case example).

8

YOUTH WHO REFUSE SCHOOL
FOR ATTENTION

Jenna is a 5-year-old girl who throws temper tantrums almost every morning before school. She also clings to her mother, locks herself in the bathroom, and occasionally hits her siblings in an attempt to stay home from school. When at school, Jenna is sometimes disruptive, and school officials have been sending her home lately as a result.

In this chapter, primary treatment strategies are reviewed for youth who refuse school for attention. Unlike the first treatment sets discussed in chapters 6–7, which are focused more on the child, functionally based treatment for attention-seeking children is focused more on parents and parent training. In many of these families the child dictates to parents when he or she will go to school or is controlling in nature when seeking attention. The general goal of treatment is thus to reverse this situation so parents are more firmly in control of the child and his or her school attendance.

Some general principles of parent training are reviewed here first. A discussion of separation anxiety is subsequently presented because this condition is frequently associated with children who refuse school for attention. However, attention-seeking school refusal behavior is meant to imply a broader connotation (e.g., manipulation of parents, externalizing behaviors). Finally, prescriptive treatment components from a functional model are presented, along with a case example.

AN OVERVIEW OF PARENT TRAINING

The essence of parent training is to change whatever parental or familial dynamics contribute to a child's misbehavior. In addition, a key goal of parent training is to give parents the skills necessary to successfully resolve present and future misbehaviors and conflicts. Briesmeister and Schaefer (1998) noted that various methods have been used to teach parents these skills, including, among others, education, modeling, rehearsal, feedback, and structured homework assignments. Specific parent training models have also been designed (e.g., Child Relationship Enhancement Therapy; Guerney & Guerney, 1989; Parent–Child Interaction Therapy; Eyberg & Boggs, 1998). Parent training has several alluring features, including improvement of parenting skills and the parent–child relationship, increased parental monitoring and involvement in a child's life, maintenance of therapy attendance and compliance, increased generalization of skills, and application to various situations and different types of families (Briesmeister & Schaefer, 1998).

Parent training is effective for teaching parents to modify many different child misbehaviors and is especially useful for addressing children who refuse school for attention. This is so because these children are quite attuned to caregiver attention and often want to spend a great deal of time with their parents. In addition, because many parents of this functional condition have a history of acquiescence to their child's behavior, because many of these families are enmeshed, and because many of these children are young, parent training is probably the most sensible and viable approach for reinstituting parent control and improving appropriate parent–child communication. Various aspects of contingency management and shaping have been used to successfully address school refusal behavior in youth (e.g., Ayllon, Smith, & Rogers, 1970; J. Cooper, 1973; Doleys & Williams, 1977; Hersen, 1970; Meyer, Hagopian, & Paclawskyj, 1999; Rines, 1973; Tahmisian & McReynolds, 1971).

CHILDREN WITH SEPARATION ANXIETY

Separation anxiety tends to be more prevalent among children who refuse school for attention compared with children of other functional conditions. The treatment of youth with separation anxiety remains in a state of development, and most studies focus on case reports or single-participant research designs (Thyer & Sowers-Hoag, 1988). Early studies concentrated on some variant of exposure-based desensitization that gradually increased the time of separation and distance between a parent and child. More contemporary studies add treatment components to desensitization, with good results (Hagopian & Slifer, 1993; Kendall, 1994; R. G. Klein, Koplewicz, & Kanner, 1992; Montenegro, 1968; T. H. Ollendick, Hagopian, & Huntzinger, 1991). These added components include pharmacotherapy, self-statement modification, positive and self-reinforcement, problem-solving training, psychoeducation, and relaxation training. Other treatments for separation anxiety include cognitive self-instruction (Mansdorf & Lukens, 1987), drawings (LeRoy & Derdeyn, 1976), differential reinforcement of other behavior, and stimulus fading (Neisworth, Madle, & Goeke, 1975).

For many children who refuse school for attention, addressing true separation anxiety-based concerns is essential. However, our knowledge of separation anxiety disorder (SAD) remains in a state of evolution, and it is possible that some cases of separation "anxiety" actually reflect controlling, manipulative, or attention-seeking behavior on the child's part. I (Kearney, 1997), for example, reported on 24 youth with school refusal behavior who also met criteria for SAD. Of the *Diagnostic and Statistical Manual of Mental Disorders* (4th ed.; *DSM–IV*; American Psychiatric Association, 1994) criteria and related symptoms that make up SAD, parents in the sample primarily endorsed more externalizing ones. These included, for example, exaggerated somatic complaints (75%), tantrums on separation (71%), school refusal behavior (69%), sleep refusal (63%), and avoidance of being left alone–clinging (56%). It is interesting that internalizing problems, such as worry about parental harm (44%), worry about child harm (31%), and nightmares about separation (13%), were seen in only a minority of the sample. In addition, these children scored in the normal range on various measures of fear and general anxiety. Recall from chapter 4 as well that parents of this functional condition often say their children demand much attention. Other authors have also criticized the traditional separation anxiety construct in children with school refusal behavior (e.g., Knox, 1989; Pilkington & Piersel, 1991).

The concept of separation anxiety may comprise three subtypes: children who are truly anxious on separation from caregivers, children who are more broadly seeking attention from caregivers, and children who are both anxious and seeking attention. For the first subtype, procedures described in chapter 6 would be helpful. For children whose school refusal behavior is primarily attention based, procedures described in this chapter would likely be most helpful. For children refusing school for a combination of reasons, more than one prescriptive treatment set will likely be necessary.

Kearney and Silverman (1990, 1999) have reported on several cases of children who were successfully treated for separation anxiety and attention-based school refusal behavior. Chorpita, Albano, Heimberg, and Barlow (1996) also treated a 10-year-old girl with separation anxiety and attention-based school refusal behavior by teaching parents to attend to appropriate behavior and ignore inappropriate behavior. Role-play was primarily used for this purpose. Results from a multiple-baseline design across behaviors revealed substantial decreases in somatic complaints, anger and tantrums, and tears. Specific components for children who refuse school for attention are further described next.

Functionally based prescriptive treatment for youth who refuse school for attention is designed to place parents more in control of their child and his or her school attendance. Treatment components to accomplish this include restructuring parent commands, ignoring simple inappropriate behaviors, establishing fixed routines, developing negative and positive consequences for child behavior, forced school attendance under certain conditions, and ameliorating excessive reassurance seeking.

Restructuring Parent Commands

In many families of children who refuse school for attention, a key first step is to restructure parental commands given in the morning and other times. Such commands are often vague or deteriorate into long negotiation sessions with the child. A main goal of treatment is to transform these extended discussions into short parent commands and simple child responses. Initially, parents express what they typically, and exactly, command of their child during the day. This may be done by means of interview and recollection, or it may be done more proactively using a logbook in which commands are recorded after they are issued. This applies especially to commands regarding school refusal behavior and the morning routine.

This information is analyzed carefully to identify key errors that parents might be making when giving commands. Errors include commands that are questionlike, vague, incomplete, interrupted, overly difficult or long, or eventually completed by someone else (Forehand & McMahon, 1981; Kearney & Albano, 2000). During treatment it is important to continually monitor these commands and provide constructive feedback about problematic patterns. Modeling and role-play may be used to help parents structure and implement appropriate commands. Over time, parents should also develop a good understanding of what comprises good and less adequate commands.

In particular, parents should be exact about what is required of a child and when a task is to be completed. Emphasize simple commands that the child is capable of doing and that nothing should compete with the child's attention during the command. In addition, parents should eliminate criticism, sarcasm, and lecturing and should adopt a neutral tone. No one should complete the command for the child, but parents should engage in a task (e.g., morning preparation) with the child following the command. Appropriate rewards and punishments should also follow compliance and noncompliance, respectively, to commands.

Parents should be active during this restructuring process, responding to feedback, speaking frequently with one other, revising their commands as necessary, monitoring any factor (e.g., lack of firm tone) that detracts from the effectiveness of commands, and physically prompting the child's compliance as necessary. Many children deliberately worsen their misbehavior to force parents to abandon the therapy process, so parents may need to learn to work through noncompliance, such as refusal to get out of bed or to get dressed. For example, parents may have to physically dress a child who is having a tantrum and carry him or her downstairs. Although difficult, this conveys to a child that misbehavior will not be tolerated and that parents will take a firm stand against school refusal behavior.

Ignoring Simple Inappropriate Behaviors

Parents must also ignore a child's inappropriate behaviors. Some parents fall in the trap of attending to a child primarily when he or she misbehaves and leaving the child alone when he or she is behaving appropriately (e.g., playing quietly). Inappropriate attention may involve lecturing or yelling, negotiating or trying to calm the child, or physical force. Give parents an example of child misbehavior (e.g., crying) and ask how they have responded, or would respond, to it verbally and physically. If necessary, teach parents to engage in methods to downplay simple inappropriate behaviors, including ignoring the child, averting eye contact, using time out, working through misbehaviors, attending more closely to siblings, and conversing with others. More serious misbehaviors (e.g., severe tantrums), however, may require more serious consequences.

Ignoring often applies most to the exaggerated physical complaints (e.g., headaches, nausea, stomachaches) that are common to attention-seeking children. Assuming a true medical condition has been ruled out, parents should ignore such complaints. Parents may be asked to require school attendance unless the child has a fever or some obvious physical condition (e.g., vomiting, lice, diarrhea, congestion). If the child is legitimately sick and stays home, little verbal or physical attention should be given, and the child should stay in bed all day without privileges. In this situation and others where a child legitimately stays home from school (e.g., funeral), he or she is informed that the home stay will be short and that school attendance will resume as soon as possible.

Establishing Fixed Routines

Restructuring chaotic morning, daytime, and evening routines is often necessary as well to address a child's attention-based school refusal behavior. This restructuring helps streamline morning preparations for school and work, establish house rules, and allow parents to adequately respond to rule violations and child noncompliance with commands. Initially, parents supply a detailed description of their daily routines. This is especially pertinent to the morning routine before school, and a description should involve events that occur every 10 minutes (e.g., from 6:30 a.m. to 9:00 a.m.). Discussions may be held as well about the absence of a routine, day-to-day changes in the routine, separate routines for parents and children, and future alterations in the routine. Attend especially to times when the child rises from bed, washes and gets dressed, eats breakfast, does extraneous activities (e.g., playing), makes final preparations for school, and leaves home. As the daily routines are discussed, including those for the afternoon and evening, see how parents respond to their child's misbehavior in time-limited situations and modify these responses as necessary. Also, note parental acquiescence and the child's activities if home from school during the day.

When the routines have been fully examined, the morning routine is restructured first; set times for all basic morning activities are designed. The routine must be flexible, to give the family ample time to prepare for school and work and to address any misbehaviors, including dawdling, on the child's part. However, the routine should also be structured enough to allow for a smooth transition to school. Ask clients to have the child rise from bed about 90–120 minutes prior to the start of school. In addition, permit the child to be in bed no longer than 10 minutes after waking. This is designed to promote industriousness in the morning and prevent the temptation to fall back asleep. The rest of the morning routine can then be established:

6:30 a.m.	Wake the child (the child is required to be out of bed by 6:40 a.m.).
6:40–7:00 a.m.	Child uses the bathroom and washes as necessary.
7:00–7:15 a.m.	Child dresses and accessorizes as necessary.
7:15–7:35 a.m.	Child eats breakfast and discusses his or her day with parents.
7:35–7:50 a.m.	Child makes final preparations for school (e.g., gathers books, jacket, lunch).
7:50–8:15 a.m.	Child goes to school with parents or rides the bus.
8:30 a.m.	Child enters school and classroom.

This routine is established and practiced, even if the child is not yet attending school. Having the child accustomed to getting up and getting ready facilitates future school attendance by minimizing morning misbehaviors such as excessive sleepiness and verbal complaints. During treatment, the morning routine is structured and restructured as necessary, although it should eventually be quite predictable and comfortable for all family members. Also parents should respond to how a child adheres to the routine. If a child adheres to the morning routine without difficulty, then verbal praise should be given in the morning and evening. If the child strays significantly from the routine, or shows serious misbehaviors, such as tantrums, then parents may work through the misbehaviors or administer punishments that morning (e.g., reprimand) or at night (e.g., grounding, loss of privileges; see later sections on consequences).

During each morning, struggles with the child and his or her behavior are to be expected. Therefore, parents should not be overly concerned that their child is late for school. If the process of getting the child to school lasts until 9:30, 11:00, or even 2:00, the message is still conveyed to the child that school attendance is mandatory and will be pursued even after school starts in the morning. Obviously, however, this must be coordinated with school personnel. Later in treatment, a child should attend school immediately following the morning routine. For children already attending school after morning behavior problems, attendance should continue. For children just starting to return to school, initial attendance may be part time, required in some alternative setting at school (e.g., library), or both. For children still refusing school completely for attention, forced school attendance (discussed later) may be considered.

Daytime Routines and Consequences

Daytime routines and consequences may need to be established if a child is still not in school and forced school attendance is not yet an option. If parents are not home during the day, child care may be arranged, or parents can bring their child to work, assign him or her boring tasks, or have him or her sit with little attention from others. An alternative is for the child to go to a friend or relative who can do the same thing. If a parent can supervise the child when he or she is home from school, then attention toward the child during normal school hours (e.g., 9:00 a.m.–3:00 p.m.) should be extremely limited. The child should sit alone, complete boring chores alone, or finish homework sent from school. The goals here are to limit attention from others when a child should be in school, have the child expend some effort for his or her disruption to the family, and maintain academic performance to ease later reintegration into school. During the day, parents should still prod the child to attend school, even if attendance is for a short time. Parents may, for example, issue the command to go to school each hour and administer appropriate rewards and punishments as necessary.

Evening Routines and Consequences

Parents should also structure evening routines (e.g., dinner, homework, bedtime) for a child who refused to attend school. This may also involve some limitation (e.g., grounding, suspension of sporting events) of the child's social activities if he or she was inappropriately home from school that day.

The child optimally should spend time with parents completing homework obtained from the teacher. If this is too rewarding for the child, then other "tutors" may be used. Any evening punishments for school refusal behavior are administered before dinner, after dinner, or both. A common rule of thumb is to double the amount of time for punishment that the child spent refusing school that morning. A 15-minute tantrum, for example, might result in a 30-minute sentence of having to sit on the stairs and talk to no one. For children with extensive school refusal behavior, a large "debt" of time may be owed to parents and can be "paid" at night and on weekends or by means of extra chores. Rewards for school attendance are administered as well; for example, parents could spend extra time with and give extra attention to the child. A key to evening consequences is that the child understands that attendance is taken seriously, even after school hours.

Punishments for School Refusal Behavior

Parents must establish punishments for their child's noncompliance and school refusal behavior. Parents initially list what methods of punishment, if any, they have tried in the past to provide consequences for or control their child's misbehavior. Examples include grounding, other restrictions of privileges, lectures, fines, loss of valued items, and spankings. Parents also rate each punishment with respect to its alleged effectiveness and identify which punishments are still used. In addition, assess for consistency in punishment, severity of child misbehavior that is punished, differences in punishment between parents, parent attitudes about the effectiveness of punishment, and parents' willingness to consider new rules and consequences for their children.

Five specific school refusal behaviors are usually targeted for punishment. These are ranked from most to least problematic; in attention-seeking children, common targets include refusal to move, crying or screaming, aggression, and excessive reassurance seeking (discussed later). Initially, a specific punishment is designed and applied to two of the lower severity behaviors (e.g., crying, screaming). This is done so parents can practice administering punishments with less effort and a higher likelihood of success. Punishments must be practical, fit a family's resources and value system, and be able to be given both in the morning and in the evening. Examples include ignoring the child and working through misbehavior without verbal attention. Stronger, more tangible punishments may also be necessary. Punishments are given for specific school refusal behaviors as well as noncompliance with commands during the morning routine.

Continually review how parents implement punishments for various school refusal behaviors. In addition, watch for circumstances that damage the effectiveness of punishments, especially inconsistent administration by parents. If the punishments were unsuccessful, rework them, or have parents practice new methods of administration. If the punishments were successful, gradually extend them to increasingly more severe school refusal behaviors. Give feedback to parents about which consequences are and are not effective.

Rewards for School Attendance

Rewards should also be designed for children's compliance and attendance. Assess what rewards, if any, parents used in the past to reinforce their child's appropriate behavior. Rewards should be ranked in order of their effectiveness, and parents should identify those currently used. Common examples include praise or attention, play or reading time with parents, food, money, toys, and privileges. Assess whether rewards differ across children, parent attitudes and resources regarding rewards, and willingness to consider new types of rewards.

Rewards are implemented in conjunction with punishments and are linked to the absence of certain school refusal behaviors. This would initially involve, for example, rewarding the absence of two lower severity misbehaviors (e.g., no crying or screaming). The best rewards for this group are usually attention based and involve some joint parent–child activity. However, more tangible reinforcers may be necessary and appropriate. Children are foretold of all consequences and reminded that it is initially their choice whether to attend school and receive punishments or rewards. Parents should also repeat this to children at home to reinforce their assertiveness and control of the home situation.

PROBLEMS IN ESTABLISHING PARENT COMMANDS, ROUTINES, AND CONSEQUENCES

Several problems may interfere with the procedures described thus far, and these should be addressed quickly. Some parents acquiesce to a child's misbehavior; apply commands, routines, or consequences inconsistently; argue about what to do; leave the situation for the other parent to handle; or do some combination of these. In these cases additional training may be needed, or changes may be explored in parental work schedules or a child's method of getting to school to ease a parent's burden. In addition, parents must know that maintaining a united front is essential. Some parents also find it difficult to ignore their child's misbehavior, especially exaggerated physical complaints. This is sometimes due to guilt or fear of harm to the child. Here, a full discussion should be held on the true effect of treatment on the child, differences between parental firmness and overprotectiveness, original goals of treatment, and other interfering factors.

Some parents are also prone to find some reason to keep a child home from school. Common reasons surround an exaggerated fear of harm to the child, perceived illness, alleged problems with the child's teacher and other school officials, or even problems with the therapist. Often, these parents induce school refusal behavior in their child (i.e., school withdrawal; see chapter 1). If a child is ready to go to school but is impeded by a parent, a broader treatment approach that targets the parent's insecurity, psychopathology, or other problem should be pursued. Developing a strong therapist–parent relationship is often crucial for this population and may be a high priority in early treatment.

Forced School Attendance

Forced school attendance was popularized by Kennedy (1965), who reported a 100% success rate for children with first-episode school refusal behavior. Kennedy's "rapid treatment procedure" consisted of establishing good therapist–school official relations, having parents downplay or ignore somatic complaints, and requiring the "child to go to school (by) any force necessary" (pp. 287, 288). Fathers were encouraged to take their child to school, and the help of school officials was enlisted to keep the child there. Unfortunately, mothers in this treatment program were allowed to stand in the hall. This may have served as a reinforcer for attention-seeking children or as a safety signal to reduce negative affectivity. In addition, the lack of a control group meant that many of these children might have gone back to school on their own anyway (i.e., spontaneous remission), a point that Kennedy conceded. Despite these issues, aspects of forced school attendance remain a useful treatment option in some, but not all, cases of school refusal behavior.

Forced school attendance may be viewed as a flooding procedure for children with anxiety-based school refusal behavior and should be used with great caution. Forced school attendance may also be useful for children who doggedly refuse school for attention, but again, the procedure must be used with caution and only under certain circumstances. Forced school attendance should be used only if (a) the child is refusing school most of the time, (b) the child is refusing school only for attention (i.e., has little distress or anxiety), (c) parents are willing to take the child to school and deposit him or her with school officials who escort the child to class and closely supervise his or her attendance, (d) two parents or one parent and another adult can take the child to school (and then leave), (e) the child understands what will happen if he or she refuses school, and (f) the child is under age 11 years (Kearney & Albano, 2000).

Forced school attendance can initially be raised with parents as a potential treatment option, and the logistics of the procedure can be discussed. Normally, forced school attendance is a later option that may be used if other procedures are in place but not working sufficiently, if the situation calls for it, or both. However, if a child's return to school is urgently necessary, forced school attendance may be used earlier. A discussion with parents is needed to fully assess their energy and resources to engage in this procedure as well as any guilt or hesitation. Dithering about the process may be harmful, because this can be exploited by the child and make future attendance even more difficult to achieve. Emphasize alternative procedures if parents are wavering or if other obstacles are present.

Forced school attendance is a relatively straightforward process. Parents help prepare their child for school in the morning—physically, if necessary— and then issue a command to the child to go to the car to be taken to school. If the child refuses, then parents issue a short and clear warning (e.g., "Go to the car now, or I will take you there"). If the child still refuses, then parents physically carry him or her to the car; generally one parent (or another adult) drives as one parent sits with the child to prevent dangerous misbehavior (e.g., jumping from the car). Obviously, this process is not to be linked with any abusive behavior. Parents should ignore inappropriate behaviors, work through tantrums and other misbehaviors, and maintain a neutral demeanor and tone in statements to their child. At school, parents repeat the command to enter the school building and provide a warning if necessary. If the child still refuses, then parents physically take the child inside, and school officials may help as appropriate. In many cases, attention-seeking children end their misbehavior once in school. However, to prevent the child from running away or from engaging in misbehaviors to be sent home from school, he or she should be closely supervised by school officials.

Forced school attendance may be stopped midway in the process if the child becomes genuinely overanxious, if the process becomes unbearable for parents, if school officials become unsupportive, or if unseen and formidable obstacles occur. However, stopping this procedure midway threatens treatment progress, because the child's resolve to refuse school is reinforced. In addition, exceptionally strong-willed children often resist this procedure for long periods of time to try to induce parental acquiescence. Forced school attendance must therefore be used with great care, under the right circumstances, and with good follow through.

Excessive Reassurance-Seeking Behavior

Many children who refuse school for attention also engage in excessive reassurance-seeking behavior (this may also be evident in other children who refuse school, however; see chapter 6). This usually involves asking the same question, or some form of it, over and over. Common topics for questions include home schooling, changing something related to school (e.g., teacher, class schedule), deals to stay home or to end therapy, somatic complaints, contact with parents (e.g., pick-up time), and schoolwork. However, reassurance seeking also may come in the form of children who (a) go to school but frequently call their parents during the day or (b) become disruptive in school to be sent home.

For children who constantly ask the same question over and over, parents should answer the question once. On receiving the question again, parents should remind the child that he or she knows the answer to the question. All other attempts should be ignored. When the child later acts appropriately or asks another question, parents can administer praise and other reinforcement. For young children, this type of excessive reassurance-seeking may be defined as asking the same question more than once in an hour. This time can be gradually increased during the course of treatment (e.g., once every 2 hours).

For children who go to school but constantly call their parents during the day, cooperation with school officials is needed to limit calls to 1–2 per day. In addition, calls should be made contingent on the child's appropriate behavior in school and suit the parents' work schedules. Excess calls should be met with punishment that night. For children who are disruptive in school to be sent home (or have parents called), therapists and school officials should establish rewards and punishments for the child's in-class behavior. For example, a card system could be used to reward appropriate behavior and include warnings and increasingly severe penalties for misbehavior. The worst penalty, however, must still involve the child's attendance at school in some form (e.g., sitting in the principal's office). For older children and adolescents, daily report cards, token economies, detention, and other methods may be used.

A CASE EXAMPLE

Rudy was a 6-year-old boy referred to an outpatient mental health clinic for recent problems attending school. The assessment took place in mid-October of the school year and followed a call from the principal about Rudy's high rate of tardiness over the past several weeks and absences the past few days. In addition, the principal stated that Rudy's 8-year-old sister Randi came late to school most days. However, it was Rudy's behavior that concerned her most. In particular, Rudy would come late to class, sulk, and repeatedly ask his teacher to send him home. In addition, he had tried to leave the school building once on his own.

The initial assessment session was attended by Rudy's parents; Rudy; Randi; and the family's other child, 3-year-old Sierra. Immediately, the waiting room was quite chaotic, as the children essentially had their way around the room and picked things up with little feedback from the parents. Rudy was interviewed first and said that he "didn't like school" and would rather be home with his mother. Extensive discussions about school revealed that he was relatively unconcerned about anything there and, in fact, liked most aspects of school. He repeatedly stated, however, that he would rather be home and wanted his mother to help him with his schoolwork. Rudy especially enjoyed reading time with his mother and seemed to believe that reading time could simply be extended to his schoolwork during the day at home. He also wished to help his mother with Sierra at home. An interview with Randi revealed less of a desire to seek attention from her parents, although she was constantly late for school because of Rudy's dawdling and crying in the morning.

The interview with Rudy's parents clearly revealed significant tension between the two, with the father openly stating that this his son's problem was a simple issue of discipline and that Rudy's mother should be "tougher" in dealing with the children. Rudy's mother responded that it was too difficult for her to deal with all three children in the morning without additional help from her husband. Rudy's father fumed at this and was defensive and quiet for most of the remaining time. Rudy's mother reported that her son would frequently dawdle in the morning before school, throw temper tantrums, cry, and lock himself in the bathroom to avoid school. None of these problems was evident on the weekends or holidays. As a result, Rudy and Randi were late to school almost every day, and Rudy had actually missed 5 of the last 9 days of school.

A separate telephone conversation with Rudy's mother the next day further revealed a history of marital problems and abusive behavior on the part of Rudy's father. In particular, he had been physically abusive toward her in the past and had spent some time in jail for domestic violence. Although matters had been calm in recent weeks, the father's difficulties at work and Rudy's problems had reignited his temper, and she seemed to think he was at risk for further violence. The therapist assessed for child abuse (this had never been a problem), provided crisis referrals to Rudy's mother, and rehearsed an escape plan for her should it be necessary. In addition, the therapist was supportive and discussed the cycle of domestic violence and encouraged her and her husband to attend the next therapy session. After one postponement, the family returned to the clinic.

At this next session, the therapist spent most of the time with Rudy's father. In particular, the therapist raised concerns about family violence and gently assessed for signs that such violence could recur soon (e.g., substance use, access to weapons, anger management skill). Rudy's father confirmed that he had been under enormous stress at work and that he had to work long hours to keep his job. This meant leaving early in the morning and not being able to help his wife. The therapist set up a no-violence contract with Rudy's father and explained that the therapy process would, she hoped, allow the family to have a smoother transition in the morning and less stress overall. Rudy's father said that he understood but that he would no longer be attending the therapy sessions. He did agree, however, to speak to the therapist by telephone each week. He then left.

Rudy's mother was informed of the no-violence contract, and the rehearsal and other contingency plans for violence were covered anew. Given the unavailability of Rudy's father in the morning, she was asked if any other adults could help her during the morning routine. Fortunately, Rudy's grandmother was available, and she was asked to attend the next therapy session (in other cases, extensive time must be spent identifying and building social supports). In the meantime, Rudy's mother was instructed to bring her son to school at whatever time he happened to be ready that day. He was not to miss any school because his misbehavior. Success on this front was only sporadic, however.

At the next therapy session, the therapist met extensively with Rudy's mother and grandmother (in this functional condition, the first formal treatment session is usually quite long). In general, it was agreed that Rudy's grandmother would tend to Sierra and Randi during the morning given that their behaviors were not overly problematic. This would free up Rudy's mother to concentrate almost solely on Rudy. The therapist worked to establish a set morning routine for each of the children, especially Rudy. As described earlier in the chapter, specific times were set for waking and rising from bed, washing and dressing, eating, brushing teeth, making final preparations for school, leaving the house, and going to school. It was agreed that Rudy's grandmother would drive Randi to school and that Rudy's mother would drive Rudy to school. In addition, consequences were established such that, for any number of minutes Rudy was late, he would lose that much time reading with his mother that night.

Over the next few days, Rudy's behavior became considerably worse, requiring the therapist to maintain daily contact with Rudy's mother and, sometimes, his father. This was done to provide support and encouragement and refine the treatment procedures to outlast Rudy's extinction burst. At the time of the next treatment session, Rudy's morning misbehavior had not improved, but he was attending school each day, albeit late. The therapist discovered at this session that Rudy's mother was continuing to talk to her son in the morning and cajoling him to attend school. In essence, she worried about the effects of therapy on her son and was concerned that this approach, coupled with his explosive father, might be harming Rudy in some way. The therapist explained that the structure and consequences were necessary to control Rudy's own explosive behavior and prevent problems in the long run, and Rudy's mother agreed to try further and reduce her attention to inappropriate behaviors in the morning. Specific work was also done to restructure the commands Rudy's mother gave to her son.

Over the next 2 weeks, Rudy's behavior did not improve. Part of this was explained by the fact that Rudy had an extended Thanksgiving break from school and had trouble returning afterward (such is the case for many children of this functional condition). However, Rudy's mother did reinstitute the treatment procedures after the break and saw rapid progress. Rudy had come to see that reading time at night with his mother was specifically and consistently tied to his morning misbehaviors. By Christmas break, the main problem in the morning was simple dawdling.

Unfortunately, a series of holiday arguments led Rudy's father to move out of the house and Rudy's mother to file for divorce. Coupled with the long holiday break, Rudy often cried in the morning before school and refused to go. Therapy at this point primarily involved referral for divorce counseling for Rudy's mother and extensive conversations with Rudy about the ongoing changes in his life, anger management, and the need to continue to attend school. Over time, Rudy was able to adjust and attend school with mild to moderate problems, although the family was forced to relocate and terminated therapy.

SUMMARY

Treatment for children who refuse school for attention involves a careful development or restructuring of parent commands, family routines, and consequences. A crucial element of this treatment approach is to have a full discussion with parents about all relevant and possible scenarios that may occur during the mornings. Parents must be fully prepared to respond to any misbehavior shown by the child. Therefore, discuss all the likely morning scenarios and develop a detailed response plan for each. Also, the development of a united parental front that effectively and consistently responds to a child's school refusal behavior is most critical to families of this functional condition.

9

YOUTH WHO REFUSE SCHOOL FOR TANGIBLE REINFORCEMENT OUTSIDE OF SCHOOL

Yancy is a 17-year-old boy who has missed the last 42 of 61 days of school. He has a history of school refusal behavior but this year has been missing more days than usual. Yancy reports no desire to attend school, says it is "boring," and prefers to sleep late or hang out with his friends during the day. He has had two job interviews and soon plans to start work and drop out of school.

In this chapter, primary treatment strategies are reviewed for youth who refuse school for tangible reinforcement outside of school. This is perhaps the most common reason why youth miss school (Stickney & Miltenberger, 1998). Unlike the treatment sets discussed in chapters 6–8, which focused more on either a child or parents, functionally based intervention for youth refusing school for tangible reinforcement is focused on a variety of family members. Because antagonism and poor problem-solving skills are common to many families in this functional condition, the general treatment goal is to enhance a family's ability to resolve conflict and appropriately address a child's school refusal behavior. In this chapter traditional treatments for youth with truancy and some general principles of family therapy and contracting are reviewed first. Discussions of functionally based prescriptive treatments and a case example are presented subsequently.

TREATMENTS FOR TRUANCY IN YOUTH

Although speculative at this point, many similarities likely exist between youth with so-called truancy and youth who refuse school for tangible reinforcement outside of school. For example, many in each group are adolescents who are neither anxious nor have any desire to remain home.

In addition, many in each group enjoy fun activities outside of school during school hours.

Treatments for so-called truant adolescents have been myriad. Child-based strategies have aimed to alter attitudes about school or self-esteem by means of cognitive work or to improve academic performance by means of supportive instruction (Grala & McCauley, 1976; D. Miller, 1986). Day treatment has also been implemented (e.g., Matzner et al., 1998). Parent- and school-based strategies have included contingency management and contracting (see Family Therapy and Contracting for Youth section, next), token economy, verbal praise and tangible rewards, increased support and monitoring of a student's attendance, denial of admission following tardiness and expulsion following absences, social reinforcement of parents, and multi-modal intervention (Bell, Rosen, & Dynlacht, 1994; Berg, 1985b; Nevetsky, 1991; Rogers, 1980; Schloss, Kane, & Miller, 1981; Schultz, 1987; Truox, 1985). These generally non-anxiety-based treatments often aim to increase incentives for youth to attend school and reduce incentives or provide punishments for youth (and their parents) who refuse school (Atkeson & Forehand, 1978). This premise is also the basis of family-oriented treatment of youth who refuse school for tangible reinforcement.

Although this book concentrates on treatment for individual youth, systemic programs to reduce truancy have also been implemented by many school districts. These programs include systematic monitoring and recording of absences, parent–teacher alliances, consistent penalties for repeat offenders, and interventions for youth with school refusal behavior (Duckworth, 1988). Other key aspects include increased attendance staff, attendance assemblies, student involvement in extracurricular activities, publicizing students with good attendance, rearranging student schedules, improved teacher attendance, and exemption from final examinations for good grades, among others (D. Miller, 1986; Stine, 1990; Tuck & Shimburi, 1988). To reduce or eradicate school refusal behavior in the future, systemic and clinical intervention strategies will be necessary.

FAMILY THERAPY AND CONTRACTING FOR YOUTH

The general goal of family-based intervention is to change problematic interactions or dynamics that allegedly trigger misbehaviors in children. Many different approaches to family therapy have been developed, including structural, strategic, transgenerational, experiential, and behavioral approaches (J. H. Brown & Christensen, 1986). Each approach shares basic assumptions, including (a) a view of behavior as generally nonpathological and environmentally driven and (b) an emphasis on treating family systems and relationships over individual members (Griffin, 1993). Family therapy in different forms has been reportedly effective for addressing various cases of school refusal behavior (Baideme, Kern, & Taffel-Cohen, 1979; Bryce & Baird, 1986; Crumley, 1974; Hsia, 1984; Malmquist, 1965; Messer, 1964; Sherman & Formanek, 1985; Stewart, Valentine, & Amundson, 1991; Wetchler, 1986). However, no large-scale studies of traditional family therapy for this population are available.

Within a functionally based treatment approach for youth who refuse school for tangible reinforcement, behavioral family therapy is emphasized. Specifically, modeling and role-play are emphasized to improve the negotiation, problem-solving, and communication skills in these often-conflictive families. A core component of this approach, behavioral or contingency contracting, is a structured arbitration process whereby a therapist helps family members design formal definitions of and solutions to a given problem. Written contracts between relevant parties (e.g., adolescent and parents) are then drawn to formalize and reify this problem-solving process. The basic components of a contract include privileges and responsibilities; a timeline; and rewards and punishments for fulfilling or failing to fulfill, respectively, one's obligations in the contract. Each component is, of course, negotiated and eventually agreed to by all relevant family members (e.g., adolescent and parents).

Contracts are especially useful for youth who refuse school for tangible reinforcement. Within a contract, specific incentives for school attendance and disincentives for school absence can be formulated; these incentives and disincentives can match those often sought by youth and their parents. Contracts have been used successfully for youth who refuse school and who have related problems (Bizzis & Bradley-Johnson, 1981; Brooks, 1974; Cantrell, Cantrell, Huddleston, & Woolridge, 1969; Cretekos, 1977; MacDonald, Gallimore, & MacDonald, 1970; Stuart, 1971; Stuart & Lott, 1972; Vaal, 1973). Contracts are often coupled with communication skills training to enhance the negotiation process (Kifer, Lewis, Green, & Phillips, 1974). These components within a functionally based prescriptive treatment model of school refusal behavior are described next.

TREATMENT FOR YOUTH WHO REFUSE SCHOOL FOR TANGIBLE REINFORCEMENT OUTSIDE OF SCHOOL

Components of functionally based treatment for children who refuse school for tangible reinforcement include contracts, escorting the child to school, communication skills training, and peer refusal skills training.

Contracts

Family Meetings

The first step in building a contract is to negotiate its provisions among family members. Because conflict is inherent to many families in this functional condition, initial and substantive contract negotiations often take place under therapist supervision. This allows the therapist to provide immediate, corrective feedback and further assess what family dynamics need to be addressed. However, contracts, other therapy procedures, new problems, and changes to the therapy process can also be discussed generally at home. The idea here is to give the family an opportunity to practice regular and thoughtful discussions of problems and their solutions. Initially, this may involve about one to two 15-minute sessions per week.

During these home-based meetings, all members should have equal time to speak. Discussion is initially limited to simple statements about contracts and complaints or problems, and members should avoid lectures, tangential statements, hurtful comments, distractions, excessive questions, and interruptions. All family members should attend the meeting and be praised for doing so. Highly problematic meetings can be rescheduled or suspended until the next therapy session.

The therapist monitors attendance and problems following these home meetings. Reviewing audiotapes of the meetings or lists of problems may be helpful in doing so, and complex issues should be addressed in session. At some point, families may start practicing the negotiation, contracting, communication, and other skills to be described. Family members can also be given hypothetical problems to solve at home; this allows a therapist to assess a family's problem-solving skills as well as any obstacles. Eventually, families should understand how to negotiate problem solutions independently and communicate effectively. In some cases, however, family therapy following the resolution of school refusal behavior is also necessary to address broader conflict or deeper concerns.

Negotiating and Designing Contracts in Session

For the school refusal behavior population, in-session negotiation and design of contracts usually requires a linear and methodical approach. This approach typically involves initial, basic agreements that have nothing to do with school refusal behavior and later, complex agreements that include more diverse issues. This stepwise progression is described here.

The first contract. Negotiating and designing the first contract with a family is often a delicate process that requires diplomatic skill on a therapist's part and separation of youth and parents. To introduce a family to this process, the first contract may involve a simple and easily defined problem that has nothing to do with school refusal behavior. Instead, the first contract should focus family members on appropriate problem solving at a basic level. If the family has problems with this elementary contract, then more intense intervention or practice is necessary. If the family succeeds, however, then evidence is made available that members can indeed solve problems without acrimony. For more urgent cases, school attendance contracts may be cautiously designed at this point.

The first contract often involves one relatively minor household problem, such as a particular chore that is not being completed regularly. All relevant family members (e.g., youth and parents) should agree that the problem is genuine and appropriate to solve. Simplicity is key here; convoluted or volatile problems should be avoided. As the therapist shuttles back and forth among youth and parents, each defines the behavior problem. The therapist can enhance this process by suggesting definitions that are not blaming or counterproductive.

After this definition process, each family member describes as many potential solutions to the problem as possible. After the generation of 5–10 proposed solutions, family members rank the solutions in order of practicality, specificity, and potential agreeableness to everyone. The therapist then works, sometimes by means of nudging, to develop an acceptable solution with family members. An emphasis on good-faith negotiations and compromise should be made, and no party should be forced to agree to anything to which he or she strongly objects.

Rewards and punishments for fulfilling or not fulfilling one's role in the contract, respectively, must also be designed. Rewards and punishments must be fair, pertinent, strong, and acceptable to all parties. The first contract should be relatively straightforward, simple, and last no longer than 2–3 days. Loopholes should be closed, and exact definitions should be made regarding timelines, each family member's responsibilities, required tasks, criteria for task completion, rewards and punishments, and other pertinent variables.

After the first contract is constructed, all relevant family members carefully read it and, on approval, sign it. Renegotiation may ensue, if necessary, until everyone is satisfied. The contract is then displayed in some open area of the home where it is read and initialed daily by the child and parents. If the negotiation process was relatively successful, remind family members that it is possible for them to appropriately solve problems without conflict. It is hoped that this initial contracting process will serve as a model for other contracts to be designed.

The first school attendance contract. The first school attendance contract usually involves some precursor to full attendance (e.g., morning preparation) without necessarily requiring much, or any, time in school. In many cases the child has been out of school for some time and a return to full-time attendance is not yet feasible. Requiring set routines to lay the groundwork for eventual school attendance may thus be desirable at this point. In addition, the first school attendance contract may involve additional home-based chores that the child can do in exchange for certain rewards. This allows the child to stay busy during the day and gain practice at receiving rewards and complying with contracts. These chores can be linked to school attendance in subsequent contracts. Procedures for negotiating, designing, and implementing the first school attendance contract remain the same as before. The contract should last no longer than 3–5 days, and specific morning preparation times and other pertinent variables should be thoroughly defined and agreed on. Rewards and punishments for completing or not completing the contract must be designed as well. A sample contract appears near the case example at the end of the chapter.

A school attendance contract is appropriate only if the family has successfully completed simpler contracts and is not plagued by severe conflict or difficulty with the complexity of this contract. In addition, this contract is especially useful for adolescents with moderate to severe school refusal behavior. For youth whose attendance is not problematic but whose morning behaviors are, a contract that focuses on morning preparation behaviors may be sufficient. A set of initial school attendance contracts may also be designed over several sessions as necessary in accordance with the family's progress.

The second school attendance contract. Should the family continue to progress well, the second school attendance contract (or set of contracts) may be negotiated and designed. The best form of this contract links the child's school attendance with a powerful reward and household tasks. Such rewards include money, extensions of curfew, time with friends, release from certain responsibilities, shopping, video games and movies, and car rides to school, among others. Specifically, the child is required to attend school for some period of time in exchange for the privilege of completing tasks at home for money or other reward. As such, the child is not directly paid or rewarded for a task—going to school—that he or she should be doing anyway. This contract must comply with the family's value system and resources, of course, and painstaking attention to detail and closure of loopholes is usually necessary.

Full-time school attendance does not necessarily have to be pursued at this point. Indeed, the first contract requiring actual school attendance is often the one most difficult for a child to keep, especially for a child who has been out of school for a long time. As such, it may be necessary to start with a few classes or time periods (e.g., lunch) that are easiest for the child to attend. However, many adolescents are able to attend school for only part of the contracted time or try to become better at hiding their nonattendance. In these situations it may be necessary to backtrack to simpler contracts or to supervise the child better at school.

Subsequent school attendance contracts. Subsequent school attendance contracts focus on greater amounts of attendance, more complex arrangements involving other family members or misbehaviors, and extended timelines. In addition, communication skills and peer refusal skills training, discussed later, can be integrated into contract negotiations. In doing so, family members spend increasingly more time together in session to design contracts and practice appropriate and adaptive interactions (e.g., listening, paraphrasing, constructively conversing).

By the later stages of treatment, family members should effectively define problems and design appropriate contracts with rewards and punishments. If a family continues to have problems doing so, it may be necessary to return to simpler and more time-limited contracts. To assess whether a family can adequately design a contract, supply the family members with hypothetical and vague problems. Family members would then be required to form a good definition of the problem and develop a contract using appropriate communication and negotiating skills. Contracting may also be extended to other areas of concern as appropriate.

As a family finalizes treatment, a therapist can also help members form a list of behavior problem definitions and contracts to address any likely future problems (e.g., school attendance, curfew, chores). Reminding the family of the basic themes regarding contract success would also be helpful. These themes include simplicity, specificity, addressing one issue at a time, full family participation and agreement, strong rewards and punishments, limited timeline, and daily monitoring by all family members.

Problems With Contracts

Several problems may arise during contract implementation, especially continued association with peers who promote attractive activities outside of school, excessive sleepiness in the morning, and frustration with the contract. To address the first problem, more powerful incentives and punishments can be added to the contract, police intervention may be sought, or the child may be escorted from class to class during the day (see Escorting Youth to School and Classes). With respect to excessive sleepiness, this can be due to a long-term lack of routines in the morning, a sleep disorder, dawdling, or faking. To address these problems, additional intervention (e.g., for a sleep disorder) may be necessary. Otherwise, establishing routines (see chapter 8), contract provisions that target sleeping and rising, and innovative ways to get the child out of bed are recommended.

For families that are frustrated with the contracting process, therapist support, balance in the contract process, and days set aside for no contracts or worries about school attendance may have to be accented. In addition, some strategy for helping a child complete unfinished schoolwork is often necessary in cases of extended absence. These strategies may be incorporated into contracts and potentially include tutoring or afterschool programs, supervised homework time, daily and weekly progress reports, rearrangements of class schedules, and frequent parent–teacher meetings. Adequate academic competence is often a key to maintaining a child's interest in school. In other, more severe situations, it may be necessary to rely on different problem-solving strategies or other family therapy approaches. In cases where a youth is manipulating the contracting process for his or her own gain without any intention of returning to school, treatment goals must be further clarified, alternative academic programs should be explored, or optional treatments should be considered.

Escorting Youth to School and Classes

Contracts are quite useful for expediting school attendance but, in many cases, adolescents have trouble fulfilling their obligations and therefore do not receive any rewards. This is often due to peer pressure and close proximity to fun activities outside of school. In these cases, having someone escort the adolescent to school, to and from each class, or both may be necessary. School officials may not be available for this task, so it may fall to parents or other adults (e.g., friend, grandparent) to do so. Although inordinately time consuming and potentially exhausting for the escort, successful use of this procedure allows an adolescent to receive rewards for school attendance. This procedure is often mentioned at the start of therapy as a possible option if contracts falter. Adolescents often pay closer attention to a contract with the impending threat of an escort, and they often adhere better to a contract when parents actually attend school with them. Obviously, the specter of social embarrassment is at play here. This procedure may also be used earlier in treatment should some urgency exist in getting a child back to school.

If a child has been escorted to school and classes, contract rewards for attendance should still be given. Plans should also be made (e.g., contact school police) in case the child runs away or eludes the escort during the day and misses school. In this case, appropriate punishments from the contract should also be administered. In addition, some plan should be designed so the escort (prompt) is gradually faded from school and school officials provide daily reports of the child's attendance. The goal is to ensure and make the child aware that his or her attendance is almost always being monitored.

Communication Skills Training

Communication skills training is often used to enhance the contracting process by addressing problematic interactions that prevent successful contract negotiation and implementation. As such, it may be unnecessary in families without such problems. A full explication of communication skills training is beyond the scope of this chapter, but a summary of stages is presented here for families of children who refuse school.

Initially, communication skills training for this population focuses on basic interaction problems, such as interruptions, poor listening, silence, refusal to participate, and arguing. Specifically, one family member makes a statement or forms a question for another member, who listens and repeats or paraphrases what the first person said. Therapist-involved instructions, modeling, role-play, feedback, and reframing are often necessary to facilitate this process. Initially, family members practice paraphrasing in session; as treatment progresses, family members can practice this skill during extended conversations at home.

The next stage targets more extended, nonacrimonious conversations. A therapist can establish certain rules for such conversations, including avoidance of insulting or sarcastic statements, inappropriate suggestions or volume, and poor eye contact and articulation, among others. Initial conversations are short, limited to two family members, and closely monitored by the therapist. In severe cases, the therapist may play the role of one family member (or even two) as other family members model the conversation. Following each conversation, the therapist describes positive and negative features of the interaction. A key goal is to accurately identify and define problems and allow family members to vent negative emotions appropriately.

More advanced communication skills training targets actual and longer discussions between two family members and then among multiple members. Eventually, appropriate communication should also be taking place at home, become more positive and spontaneous, and be integrated into the contracting process. For severe cases, extended practice at a simpler level; establishing basic, positive conversations; and incorporating these conversations to some extent into a problem-solving process may be a realistic and adequate set of goals. As mentioned earlier, other family dynamics may also have to be addressed using alternative or more intense family therapy methods.

Peer Refusal Skills Training

Peer pressure is a common reason why many adolescents continue to miss school, even when powerful contract incentives for attendance are available. Peer refusal skills training is most useful for adolescents who intend to stay in school but otherwise succumb to pressure from others to leave prematurely. The training is obviously less useful for those who need no encouragement to leave school. Peer refusal skills training can be implemented in conjunction with communication skills training because of the similarity in goals (e.g., talking to another person more constructively) and methods (e.g., modeling and role-play).

Initially, a youth describes in detail what others are saying or doing to entice his or her school nonattendance. Following this process, the therapist and youth design different statements to firmly but appropriately refuse offers to leave school. This is done by means of modeling and role-play. In addition, strategies are developed (e.g., changing class schedules) for avoiding certain "tempting" peers at school. Eventually, the youth should have a workable strategy for appropriately responding to peer pressures to leave school without suffering social ridicule or rejection. This strategy is then implemented and evaluated often by the youth and therapist. Peer refusal skills may also be broadened to address related problems, such as drug refusal. A common problem in this training is a youth's refusal to implement it out of indifference or social anxiety. For indifference, alternative treatments may need to be emphasized (e.g., escorting to school). For social anxiety, cognitive restructuring (see chapter 7) may be needed to address unrealistic thoughts one has about refusing offers to leave school.

A CASE EXAMPLE

Carla was a 16-year-old girl referred to an outpatient mental health clinic for long-term problems attending school. The assessment took place in late January of the school year and followed a telephone call from Carla's father. He indicated that his daughter had missed most days of 11th grade this year and that the school had referred her case to the juvenile court system. He did not know exactly how many days Carla had missed but guessed around 80%. In addition, she had not been in school since before Thanksgiving.

The initial assessment session was attended by Carla and her father (two other, younger siblings lived in the house but were home with a babysitter). Carla reported that she had a lot of difficulty getting up in the morning and that school held no attraction for her. On most days, she would get out of bed about 10:00 a.m., watch television, eat, and then "hang out with my friends" for the rest of the day. Carla expressed little desire to go back to school but did recognize the long-term benefits of an education. She said she wanted to be enrolled in home schooling and that she would not return to her high school. Part of this was due to her anxiety about being behind in her schoolwork and having to face teachers and others who "will ask me a million questions about where I've been."

Carla's father reported that his daughter had a long history of school refusal behavior, beginning in the middle grades. Specifically, she began to cut classes in seventh grade following her parents' divorce and the subsequent diminished supervision regarding her homework and attendance. She had barely passed the seventh and eighth grades and had general but less severe difficulties in the ninth and 10th grades (missing about 15%–20% of days in each grade). This year, however, had been marked by several key changes in the home. Carla's father was considering remarriage, her younger sister had begun middle school, and her younger brother had been in a car accident and had to stay home for several weeks. As a result, Carla's father was less able to supervise her attendance, and her absenteeism grew out of control rather quickly. He stated that he did not know what to do with Carla now, as she was too old to be forced to school and he had to work during the day. Tension between Carla and her father was rising substantially as well. A friend had suggested medicating Carla, and Carla's father had taken her to a psychiatrist to be placed on an antidepressant. This had not seemed to affect her behavior, however.

Building on Carla's insight about the need for an education, the therapist outlined a plan to Carla and her father about resuming her attendance in her high school. Specifically, the plan would entail a series of contracts in which incentives for Carla's attendance would be designed in addition to disincentives for failure to attend school. An initial contract would involve something other than school attendance, and both parties chose a specific chore that Carla was supposed to do (i.e., feed the dog). It was agreed that Carla would feed the dog each day in exchange for a set amount of money. Failure to feed the dog would result in loss of pay and having to complete another chore chosen by Carla's father. The contract was drawn, and both parties agreed to it by signing it. The therapist also held extended discussions with Carla's principal and school counselor about the therapy program, although they refused to delay her referral to the juvenile court system, citing state law.

During the second therapy session both parties reported that the contract had gone smoothly. Both Carla and her father were praised and reminded that larger problems could also be solved in such a way. A second contract was designed to target Carla's morning routine. Both parties agreed to adhere to a regular morning routine with set times for waking and rising, washing and dressing, eating, and preparing for school as if going. Carla was also required to walk to school but was allowed to turn back if she chose. The primary incentive was time with friends during the evening; the primary disincentive was grounding. In addition, Carla's nighttime schedule was adjusted so that she would go to bed at a specific time each night and would not drink any caffeine for at least 3 hours prior to sleep.

During the next therapy session both parties reported great difficulty with the contract. In essence, Carla was not getting out of bed in the morning and was seeing her friends during the day anyway. The contract was adjusted so that Carla would attend work with her father if she did not get up on time, and this seemed to motivate her to adhere better to the morning routine. Within 1 additional week, she was getting up in the morning with some, but less, difficulty than before.

Given the urgency of Carla's situation (her first court date had now been scheduled), the therapist moved on to the next contract stage: school attendance. Both parties agreed to a contract that required Carla to attend school for one-half day in exchange for the opportunity to complete certain chores at home for payment. At the next therapy session, Carla reported attending school with little difficulty. She indicated that, to her surprise, she enjoyed school more than she thought she would and that the projects being worked on in class were quite interesting. When asked to discuss what she did in class, she mentioned specific science and health projects, compositions, and math assignments. She was also asked if she could extend the contract to a full-day attendance schedule, and she agreed. Her report the following week indicated little difficulty attending the entire day, and her father was quite pleased with her progress. Carla went into detail about her afternoon class assignments, including songs in choir, sporting activities in physical education, and computer programs in an explorations class.

At this point, Carla mentioned ending the therapy process. Her remark, coupled with her long history of school refusal behavior and suspicion about her lack of homework, led the therapist to contact the school attendance officer. Sure enough, there was no record of Carla's attendance at all during the past weeks. When confronted with this, Carla smirked, and her father began to berate her. The therapist defused the situation and began looking for reasons why Carla had refused school. She simply shrugged her shoulders. Carla's father agreed to take time off work to escort Carla to school over the next few days, but she was able to slip her father's supervision and leave the school campus twice. On one occasion, she did not return home until late at night.

Following some postponements after this debacle, the therapist was able to convince Carla and her father to try another approach. Instead of full-time school attendance, which might be pointless anyway given the lateness of the academic year (it was now the end of March), Carla was encouraged to enroll in a part-time program. Specifically, she was eligible for an alternative high school program that allowed students to complete credits at different hours of the day and evening and stay in a study laboratory where schoolwork would be completed (thus eliminating reliance on homework). Students were required, however, to attend summer school to make up for lost time. In addition, the program provided door-to-door transportation. In essence, Carla could attend school from 1:00 to 4:00 p.m. each day and still be able to socialize.

A contract was established (see Exhibit 9.1, from Stuart's, 1971, model) so that Carla would participate in this program through the remainder of

EXHIBIT 9.1
Carla's School Attendance Contract

Privileges	Responsibilities
General	
In exchange for decreased family tension and a resolution to school refusal behavior, all family members agree to	try as hard as possible to maintain this contract and fully participate in therapy.
Specific	
In exchange for the privilege of being paid $20 (on Friday night) to vacuum and dust the family room and feed the dog each day between now and the next therapy session, Carla agrees to	attend the alternative high school program from 1:00 to 4:00 p.m. **each day** between now and the next therapy session.
Should Carla not complete this responsibility	she will be required to complete the household chores without being paid.
In exchange for the privilege of visiting with friends in the afternoon and evening, Carla agrees to	attend the alternative high school program from 1:00 to 4:00 p.m. each school day between now and the next therapy session **and** complete her morning routine on time **and** read books in the morning.
Should Carla not complete this responsibility,	she will be grounded for that day and lose television and computer privileges for that day.

Carla and her father agree to uphold the conditions of this contract and to read and initial the contract each day.

Signatures of Carla and her father:

_____ Date: _____

_____ Date: _____

the spring and summer. Success in doing so would still be rewarded by the opportunity to complete chores for pay, and grounding remained a primary disincentive. In addition, the therapist and, eventually, Carla's father contacted the school each day to check whether Carla had actually attended. This approach was mostly successful, although Carla reportedly balked later at having to attend summer school and did miss several Mondays and Fridays at her alternative school. In chronic cases such as these, success is often defined by limited steps forward.

SUMMARY

The overall goals of treatment for children who refuse school for tangible reinforcement outside of school are to reduce family conflict, provide a family with a problem-solving strategy, and reduce school refusal behavior. As such, themes of negotiation, communication, and structured problem-solving processes are emphasized. Treatment in this functional condition is likely to be longer and more intricate than treatments for children of other functional conditions. This is due to a higher likelihood of comorbid conditions, longer school refusal behavior, and familial dysfunction. In addition, success in this functional condition is less likely to be defined by full-time attendance (Evans, 2000), as evidenced in the case of Carla.

10

EXTREME CASES, PREVENTION, AND RELAPSE

Caprio is a 17-year-old boy who has missed the past 15 weeks of school. He has a long history of nonattendance, and extensive therapeutic and academic interventions to help keep him in school last year were barely successful. He feels fatigued and bored at school, is failing his classes, has been arrested twice for stealing and vandalism, and is considering leaving school and pursuing work.

In this chapter, an initial discussion is made about addressing extreme cases of school refusal behavior, like Caprio's. In addition, strategies are presented for preventing school refusal behavior before it starts or recurs. These strategies are divided into (a) overall approaches to prevent school refusal behavior and school dropout among groups of youth and (b) clinical approaches to prevent slips and relapses of school refusal behavior among individual youth.

EXTREME CASES OF SCHOOL REFUSAL BEHAVIOR

Extreme cases of school refusal behavior refer to youth who have (a) missed school for a highly extended time (e.g., 2+ years), (b) many comorbid conditions (e.g., depression, substance abuse), (c) very severe symptoms (e.g., excessive anxiety), (d) strong resistance to treatment, or (e) some combination of these. These scenarios may apply to any of the functional conditions of school refusal behavior, although many are seen in youth who refuse school for tangible reinforcement.

Youth who have been out of school for extended periods of time (i.e., chronic school refusal behavior) are much less likely to return to full-time school attendance than youth with acute school refusal behavior. To address these cases, the therapist will likely focus on alternative educational plans (see the case example in chapter 9), such as part-time schooling, night schooling, credit by examination, independent study, and vocational counseling and placement programs. Some melding of work and school might be advisable as well, especially if economic lures are enticing a youth to quit school. In other cases, information about equivalency diplomas and other compensatory strategies might be helpful. Information from school districts is crucial here.

Extreme cases of school refusal behavior might also involve several comorbid conditions, as it is not unusual for absenteeism to be intermixed with delinquency, substance abuse, depression, low grades, and other problems. In these cases a combination of prescriptive treatments for school refusal behavior must be added to a grander treatment plan that targets all of these problems in multiple settings. Attendance at school is often a good first step in this direction, however, because it tends to enhance supervision of the child (who has less opportunity to get into trouble), academic and social competence (which is shown to buffer against mental disorder) and, in a rudimentary sense, compliance. In other cases, treatment of a more severe comorbid condition should be implemented before school refusal behavior is addressed.

Severe school refusal behaviors also characterize some cases in this population. A common example is very high levels of anxiety that prevent any approach to school. In these cases, factors about the school that legitimately induce anxiety (e.g., gangs, victimization) must be taken into account, and changes in classes, schools, or other environmental variables may be necessary. If these factors are not present, then medication to reduce anxiety and increase approach may be considered (see chapter 6 for commonly used medications). However, severe tantrums, running away from school or home, aggressive responses, self-mutilation and suicide attempt, and other extreme behaviors also mark some cases of school refusal behavior. In these situations, extra attention must be paid to the safety of the child and others, and detailed plans (e.g., contacting the school or general police, pursuing inpatient treatment) must be formed to address the misbehaviors.

Finally, cases of extreme school refusal behavior might also be marked by strong resistance to treatment. This usually refers to a child who refuses to attend school under any circumstance. Common behaviors include refusal to move, talk, get out of bed in the morning, or attend therapy. In other cases, treatment resistance is marked by lack of motivation or a noncaring attitude about consequences. Many youth, for example, have made up their minds to outlast their parents and are successful at doing so. Some of these children eventually reach the legal age of dropping out of school and try to do so.

The best remedy for treatment-resistant cases is persistence on the part of therapists, parents, friends, and school and legal officials. Treatments described in this book, for example, must sometimes last for weeks or months to work. Obviously, this is quite taxing for family members, who cannot always maintain the energy needed for these procedures. Building or accessing a social support network (including truant officers) is often critical here so that different people can take turns getting a child up in the morning, supervising his or her daily activities, following through on consequences, and bringing him or her to school. Legal intervention may also be necessary and appropriate in some cases, and innovation (e.g., part-time instruction, making noise in the child's bedroom in the morning) should be incorporated into the treatment plan. In addition, a thorough examination of distal factors at home, school, or elsewhere (see chapter 2 and Factors Predictive of School Refusal Behavior and Dropout section, next) should be pursued to see what is preventing school attendance. Many youth rebel, for example, against unfair rules or policies at school, and redressing these factors may help induce attendance. Family therapy is also a must in many of these cases.

Extreme cases of school refusal behavior generally require extensive time and effort, but successful resolution is possible. Ideally, of course, such behavior should be prevented before it starts, and strategies for doing so are discussed next. Factors that have been found to predict school refusal behavior and dropout, and which may serve as targets for prevention programs, are first outlined.

FACTORS PREDICTIVE OF SCHOOL REFUSAL BEHAVIOR AND DROPOUT

Many researchers have examined and identified some of the primary warning signs or predictors of school refusal behavior and dropout in youth (e.g., Barth, 1984; Corville-Smith, Ryan, Adams, & Dalicandro, 1998; Gingras & Careaga, 1989; Janosz, LeBlanc, Boulerice, & Tremblay, 1997; Jenkins, 1995; Kortering & Blackorby, 1992; Levine, 1984; McWhirter, McWhirter, McWhirter, & McWhirter, 1998; Mills, Dunham, & Alpert, 1988). These predictors may be grouped into community, school, parent–family, social, personal, and academic success issues (McWhirter et al., 1998).

Community issues refers here to global factors that trigger or lay the groundwork for extensive school refusal behavior or dropout in various schools or neighborhoods. Community factors linked to school refusal behavior and dropout include

- gang-related activity or strong interracial tensions
- lack of neighborhood support and facilities to address school refusal behavior and dropout, and lack of community support for such facilities
- substantial economic lures (e.g., plentiful jobs that do not require high school education, opportunities for drug sales).

School issues refers here to variables of the school environment or personnel that trigger or lay the groundwork for school refusal behavior or dropout in youth. School factors linked to school refusal behavior and dropout include

- curricula that are irrelevant to student needs
- decreased homework and teaching time
- ethnic–racial dissonance
- frequent changes of a student's school or service placement or school transitions
- frequent teacher absences, inadequate documentation of a child's absences, and long-term ignorance of a student's attendance record
- inappropriate retention or promotion of a student
- inappropriate school placement (e.g., for a child with learning disability)
- inconsistent enforcement of rules regarding absenteeism
- low expectations for student achievement, lack of praise for achievement, and lack of educational goals for students
- school violence, class disruptions, and corporal punishment
- teacher incompetence
- unwillingness to work with a family or therapist to help return a student to school
- use of suspensions and expulsions to discipline students with school refusal behavior.

Parent–family issues refers here to home-based variables that trigger or lay the groundwork for school refusal behavior or dropout in youth. Parent–family issues linked to school refusal behavior and dropout include

- family transitions (e.g., divorce, illness, unemployment, moving)
- few study aids at home and lack of social or material support
- infrequent parental supervision or low expectations for the child
- lack of parental knowledge or interest regarding absenteeism
- maltreatment of the child
- minority or non-English-speaking parents
- poor parental motivation to address the child's initial school refusal behavior
- poor parent–school official communication
- problematic family dynamics (see chapters 4–5) and ineffective parenting skills
- school dropout among relatives
- single-parent or large families (i.e., 5+ children)
- stressful home life and financial problems.

Social issues refers here to problematic interactions with peers and significant others that trigger or lay the groundwork for school refusal behavior or dropout in youth. Social issues linked to school refusal behavior and dropout include

- being 2 years older or more than one's school peer group
- close identification with peers who engage in delinquent or drug use behavior outside of school
- lack of social skills and severe social or evaluative anxiety
- numerous friends who have dropped out of school
- poor relations with authority figures
- poor student participation in school-related extracurricular activities.

Personal student issues refers here to variables specific to the child that trigger or lay the groundwork for school refusal behavior or dropout in youth. Personal student issues linked to school refusal behavior and dropout include

- above- or below-average intelligence
- anxious–depressive features, emotional trauma, or lack of motivation
- attention seeking or pursuit of tangible rewards outside of school
- cognitive misattributions (e.g., belief that all peers view oneself as inferior)
- emphasis on immediate gratification and lack of a long-term life strategy
- extensive work hours outside of school
- fear of competition
- frequent absences and classroom disruption and other school misbehavior
- intolerance of structured activities or dissatisfaction with or lack of enjoyment of school
- perceived discontinuity between one's current classes and later life experiences
- poor health or self-esteem, feelings of unpopularity
- poor school commitment (i.e., valuing educational goals) and previous dropout
- student alienation from school and nondeviant lifestyles.

Finally, *academic success issues* refers here to personal student variables most closely related to scholastic performance that trigger or lay the groundwork for school refusal behavior or dropout in youth. Academic success issues linked to school refusal behavior and dropout include

- general discrepancies between a student's ability and performance and specific discrepancies between a student's grade level and reading level
- history of poor grades
- lack of basic academic skills
- poor proficiency in English and arithmetic
- retention in one or more grades.

Although listed separately here, these issues clearly interact to provoke school refusal behavior, dropout, or both. As such, overall prevention strategies for this population must be generally multidisciplinary and complex in nature. Following are some overall strategies that have been implemented to prevent school refusal behavior and dropout.

OVERALL STRATEGIES TO PREVENT SCHOOL REFUSAL BEHAVIOR AND DROPOUT

Kearney and Hugelshofer (2000), in a summary of systemic prevention programs for school refusal behavior and dropout, grouped these into community-, school-, and parent–family-based strategies. These are briefly described here.

Community-Based Systemic Prevention Strategies

Community-based prevention programs for school refusal behavior and dropout generally involve the cooperation of different professionals among different systems (e.g., mental health, legal, school). In addition, these efforts tend to focus on high-risk students and families with many of the risk factors listed above (Berg, 1985b). Common components of these programs include individual and group therapies; diagnostic screening and health services; drug education; alternative classroom instruction and tutoring; home visits and parent–teacher conferences; ethnic identity programs; and community service, cultural, recreational, and scouting activities. Although some community-based prevention strategies have shown promise for improving school attendance and related problems (e.g., W. S. Davidson & Robinson, 1975; Jones, 1992), others have not (Denno & Clelland, 1986; Roundtree, Grenier, & Hoffman, 1993).

School-Based Systemic Prevention Strategies

School-based prevention programs for school refusal behavior and dropout involve either sweeping strategies or more direct approaches. Components of more sweeping strategies include early, intense intervention with at-risk children; teacher home visits and progress reports; parent support groups; and restructuring the role of the homeroom teacher to provide more student guidance and support and parent–teacher contact. These strategies have also involved restructuring the school environment to establish more meaningful curricula, smaller learning settings, and stronger peer support across classes. Some sweeping school-based programs have led to reductions in school refusal behavior and dropout (Berrueta-Clement, Schweinhart, Barnett, Epstein, & Weikart, 1984; Felner et al., 1993; Pearson & Banerji, 1993), although others have not (Reyes & Hedeker, 1993).

Specific school-based prevention strategies have focused on peers or youth advocates and support–therapy regimens. For example, Noonan and Thibeault (1974) successfully used popular peers as reinforcing agents for youth with problematic school attendance. These peers contacted students who were not in school a particular day, asked about the reason for nonattendance, and encouraged attendance the next day. Attendance at school was also praised. Youth advocates in the form of teachers, social workers, and guidance counselors have also been used successfully to help adolescents transition from a correctional institution to school and maintain enrollment there (Higgins, 1978). Effective advocates tend to be assertive, persistent, good communicators, and knowledgeable of relevant school activities and job opportunities for students.

School-based support–therapy regimens have also been used to successfully reduce school refusal behavior and dropout. Components of these regimens include increased monitoring of schoolwork and attendance; feedback to parents and students; token economy; academic support; formation and review of firm school rules and procedures; increased recreational and community-service opportunities; cognitive therapy; increased social awareness; modeling and role-play; and training in communication, social, and problem-solving skills (Bry & George, 1980; Gottfredson, 1983; I. G. Sarason & Sarason, 1981; Sinclair, Christenson, Evelo, & Hurley, 1998). Training teachers to provide appropriate discipline, manage their own and student stress, improve classroom learning and motivation, and address other important predictors of school refusal behavior and dropout have also been proposed (Echterling, 1989; Mills et al., 1988). Mentoring with family skills training and other procedures has been advocated as well (Blechman, 1992).

Parent–Family-Based Systemic Prevention Strategies

Many of the parent–family-based procedures discussed in this book (see chapters 8 and 9), albeit on a grander scale, may also be used to help prevent school refusal behavior and dropout. Important components to do so would likely include improved monitoring of a child's overall behavior and school attendance, contingency management and contracts, communication skills training, and various forms of family therapy, among others (Kearney & Hugelshofer, 2000). For children with separation anxiety, increasing daily parent–child distancing and peer socialization and activities has also been recommended (Scott, Cully, & Weissberg, 1995). Finally, parent–family-based procedures to reduce attrition in therapy are crucial (Fraser, Hawkins, & Howard, 1988) for preventing further episodes of school refusal behavior.

CLINICAL STRATEGIES TO PREVENT RELAPSE IN INDIVIDUAL CASES

Clinical strategies to prevent relapse at the individual case level are also extremely important for families of youth with previous school refusal behavior. A child's recidivism to such behavior is often demoralizing to family members, who may then acquiesce and allow the situation to fester. As such, the child's school refusal behavior may become even more serious and resistant to treatment than before. The aim of the next section is to define relapse and slips and outline strategies to prevent such backsliding.

RELAPSE AND SLIPS

Formal relapse is a complete or near-complete return to functioning that existed prior to therapy. Formal relapse in the school refusal behavior population would thus include problems such as missing large amounts of school, extreme distress about school and subsequent avoidance, and substantial misbehaviors for attention or tangible rewards. However, relapse could also involve ancillary problems that were addressed in therapy, such as family conflict, that now threaten the child's ability or desire to attend school. Formal relapse is generally marked by significant interference in a child and family's daily routine and ability to function.

Formal relapse is not unusual, but it is not nearly as common as slips, which usually involve smaller problems or minor backsliding (Brownell, Marlatt, Lichtenstein, & Wilson, 1986). Slips in the school refusal behavior population might involve missing 1 or 2 school days or classes, a brief period of distress, and moderate acting-out behaviors to stay home from school. Slips are generally marked by minor interference in a child and family's daily routine and ability to function. By themselves, slips are not too serious and are common after breaks from school. Ongoing slips, however, could evolve into formal relapse and should thus be addressed immediately.

Addressing Slips

In most cases families and children can address slips by revisiting and repracticing key aspects of prescriptive treatment. These aspects would most likely involve exposure, somatic control exercises, cognitive restructuring, increased social interaction, parenting strategies, contracts and related family interventions, and peer refusal skills training. However, any treatment element that promoted recovery should be re-emphasized (e.g., escorting the child to school, daily monitoring of attendance). If necessary, reminders can be listed for families at the end of treatment. This list can indicate what to do in a given situation (e.g., when a child runs away from school or engages in excessive reassurance seeking) or when slips occur.

Family members are often dismayed when slips occur and mistakenly believe that therapy was for naught. In addition, they often believe that some incompetence on their part or others caused the resurgence of problems. Typically, however, slips arise when children and families become complacent about, and ease back from, treatment procedures. This is especially so after long breaks or if the child has been going to school regularly for some time. Refocusing the family members on resuming treatment efforts and seeing the situation as an opportunity to practice their new skills is essential here. In addition, for families and children at particular risk for slips, regular telephone contact with family members should be maintained for some time after formal treatment. This allows for support, encouragement, feedback, and enhanced monitoring of any changes at school or home that might threaten treatment progress.

Addressing Relapse

Frequent, unaddressed slips may lead to relapse. At relapse, renewed consultation with a therapist is recommended in addition to new assessment, a booster treatment session, or a new set of treatment sessions, as necessary. A common mistake made by parents is to wait to address relapse. For example, some families successfully resolve their child's school refusal behavior during autumn months but witness relapse in the spring. Parents may then get discouraged and wait until the following school year to address the problem again. With possible summer vacation, however, the child may be out of school for several months.

The best strategy here is to reintegrate the child into school and finish uncompleted schoolwork as soon as possible. This may involve, for example, reinstituting treatment and pursuing summer classes. In addition to getting the child back in school, this strategy reinforces the notion that school refusal behavior can be addressed whatever time of year it occurs. Family members should also be given support and informed that relapse does happen, particularly in severe cases of school refusal behavior. Persistence in addressing the problem is often as necessary as active treatment to achieve long-term success.

Prevention

Preventing slips and relapse before they even happen is, of course, the most desirable option. Several methods to do so for this population have been delineated (Kearney & Albano, 2000) and are described separately here.

Photograph and Videotape Reminders

One method of relapse prevention involves formal reminders of a child's success in returning to school and using strategies to manage negative affectivity. These reminders could involve photographs of the child during exposure exercises, attendance at class, or performance during a task that was previously unattainable or highly difficult (e.g., interacting with others, walking into the classroom, riding the school bus). Children can also write captions for each picture that include positive and adaptive descriptions of their thoughts, feelings, and behaviors. These photographs can be placed in a scrapbook with other notable awards or achievements, and the pictures and captions can be referred to in later times of stress, slips, or potential relapse.

Reminders of success and stress management and other skills may also involve a videotape commercial (Kendall, Chansky, et al., 1992). Here, a child is videotaped while describing his or her success and methods to overcome negative affectivity or school refusal behavior. The child is represented as an expert in overcoming certain difficulties, and the tape serves as a reminder of what he or she must do to address such difficulties in the future. In the commercial, the child describes all the key components of his or her treatment (e.g., exposure, somatic control and cognitive methods, self-reinforcement) and how to go about them. In addition, he or she reviews his or her education about anxiety–negative affectivity, including the response systems (thoughts, feelings, behaviors) and their personal interaction pattern. Children and parents are encouraged to play this videotape periodically to reinforce the child's skills, especially during future stressors such as tests or the start of school.

Photographs and videotapes are typically compiled at the end of formal treatment when a child's success and skills have peaked. Most commonly, they are used for children with anxiety-based school refusal behavior, but they may also apply sometimes to youth who refuse school for positive reinforcement. For an adolescent who has been out of school for some time, for example, such reminders could reinforce parental support and enhance self-esteem and empowerment.

Structured Routines and Activities

When a child is legitimately off school for some time, because of vacation or other extended breaks, families tend to relax treatment procedures and skills developed in therapy. This is prime breeding ground for slips and relapse, but certain procedures can help prevent these. One procedure involves keeping a child on a regular morning and daytime schedule during holidays and other days off. In particular, youth should keep to a regular schedule for going to bed, getting up in the morning, and getting dressed and preparing for the day. Therefore, when school does start again, the transition is not so jolting. This procedure is obviously less feasible during long summer breaks, but starting a routine about 3 weeks before resuming school is reasonable. This may be linked as well to gradual restrictions on curfew and other positive reinforcers a child has enjoyed during the summer but cannot once school starts.

Children and adolescents may also participate in various activities during extended breaks to practice skills learned in therapy and help prevent slips and relapse. Camps, sports, reading programs, and other youth-based activities, for example, are especially useful for practicing and refining anxiety management skills, particularly exposure. These situations also allow for more socialization, increased physical distance from parents, and opportunities to address new and different situations more independently.

Booster Sessions

For youth with previous school refusal behavior who are about to enter a new or very stressful situation (e.g., new school, examination period), booster sessions may be used to review and enhance therapy skills and allow a child to discuss anticipated problems. Booster sessions, whether done individually or in a group format, are typically structured, brief, and tailored to a student's needs. These sessions are most useful for youth who are about to enter a new school building (e.g., middle, high school). Many youth have difficulty making this transition and coping with vastly different social and academic scenarios.

Booster sessions may also be linked to a tour of a child's new school setting a few days before school starts. In particular, youth should be apprised of locations for their classrooms; common meeting areas, such as cafeteria or libraries; offices; lockers; and school bus arrivals and departures. In addition, youth should be informed of, and encouraged to join, various school, sporting, and other extracurricular activities that are available. The goals here are to reduce a child's anticipatory anxiety, enhance his or her self-efficacy with respect to going to school, and prevent slips and relapse.

Monitoring School Attendance and Related Variables

The best way to prevent slips and relapse is to intensely monitor a child's school attendance and daily behavior. However, any other variable that might trigger school refusal behavior in a particular case should be watched carefully as well. Common examples include new maladaptive behaviors (e.g., substance abuse, depression); family conflict; negative parent attitudes; changes in school schedules or medical regimens; reduced motivation to attend school; and reduced participation in social, academic, and extracurricular activities.

Close collaboration among parents, teachers, guidance counselors, attendance officers, and relevant others is usually necessary to accomplish such monitoring. Daily report cards, regular parent–school official contact, and increased supervision of the child during the school day are most helpful in this regard. For youth with chronic school refusal behavior, monitoring generally needs to be longer in duration and more intense than acute cases. Contact with a therapist for several months after formal treatment is also suggested in case the need arises for feedback, additional therapy, or appropriate referrals.

SUMMARY AND FINAL COMMENTS

For many professionals, youth with school refusal behavior are among the most difficult populations to assess and treat. Such difficulty arises from the heterogeneous and often covert nature of the problem and serious disruptions to family life. In addition, the scattered nature of the historical literature on this topic has not made the job of addressing these youth any easier. In this book a functional model for defining, classifying, assessing, and treating this population was proposed and explicated. Although this model and the area of school refusal behavior remains in development, work toward a systematic approach to addressing this tumultuous population is both imperative and desirable. Toward this end, I encourage readers to contribute to this process in different venues and in different ways. I also invite comments from readers regarding aspects of this book or youth with school refusal behavior.

GLOSSARY

Acute versus chronic school refusal behavior: School refusal behavior lasting less than 1 calendar year (acute) versus more than 1 calendar year (chronic).

Attention seeking: Refusal of school for attention, praise, support or intangible rewards from parents or significant others.

Avoidance of stimuli that provoke negative affectivity: Refusal of school because of stimuli that induce combined and vaguely defined anxiety, depression, fear, worry, or somatic complaints.

Booster session: A relapse prevention treatment session designed to reinforce treatment techniques and provide a client with strategies for addressing anticipated future stressors.

Cognitive restructuring: A child-based treatment technique designed to reduce illogical or irrational thoughts and replace such thoughts with healthy, realistic thinking. Used in this population primarily for youth refusing school to escape aversive social or evaluative situations.

Communication skills training: A family-based treatment technique designed to improve methods of communication among members by reducing negative interactions and increasing positive, problem-solving interactions. Used in this population primarily for youth refusing school for tangible reinforcement outside of school and in conjunction with contracts.

Conduct disorder: According to the *Diagnostic and Statistical Manual of Mental Disorders* (4th ed. [DSM–IV]; American Psychiatric Association, 1994), "a repetitive and persistent pattern of behavior in which the basic rights of others or major age-appropriate societal norms or rules are violated" (p. 85). One symptom of conduct disorder is "often truant from school, beginning before age 13 years" (p. 90).

Contract: A family-based treatment technique designed to improve problem solving by establishing negotiated and written agreements between youth and parents or others. Used in this population primarily for youth refusing school for tangible reinforcement outside of school.

Descriptive functional analysis: A process of assessing the primary function (maintaining variable) of school refusal behavior by means of questionnaire (e.g., the School Refusal Assessment Scale). This process should be confirmed by means of experimental functional analysis that relies on behavioral observation.

Desensitization: A treatment technique to reduce anxiety by inducing relaxation and pairing such relaxation with school-related stimuli during exposure. Often done imaginally and in vivo (real life).

Dispute handles: Questions posed to clients during cognitive restructuring to help decatastrophize anxiety-provoking situations and determine exactly what the person is concerned will happen.

Escape from aversive social or evaluative situations: Refusal of school because of difficulty interacting with, or performing in front of, others.

Excessive reassurance-seeking behavior: Continual asking of the same questions (e.g., "Do I have to go to school?") or otherwise behaving to seek assurance that some situation will not be overly problematic or to be relieved from that situation.

Exposure: A treatment technique to gradually reintroduce a child to school or class. An essential element of desensitization.

Forced school attendance: A treatment technique whereby a child is brought to school physically by his or her parents or others. Used under very certain circumstances and primarily for youth who refuse school for attention.

Functional model of school refusal behavior: A system of classifying, assessing, and treating school refusal behavior on the basis of the primary motivating factor or maintaining variable for the behavior.

Functionally based prescriptive treatment: The assignment of specific treatment packages for youth who refuse school for a specific reason or function.

Negative affectivity–avoidance hierarchy: A list of 5–10 school-based stimuli that provoke aversive reactions in youth. Used in conjunction with desensitization and primarily for youth who refuse school to avoid stimuli that provoke negative affectivity.

Negative reinforcement: Reward by means of termination of an aversive stimulus. In a school refusal behavior population, this refers to youth who avoid stimuli that provoke negative affectivity or escape aversive social or evaluative situations.

Parent training: A treatment technique designed to increase parent efficacy at commands, routines, and reactions to appropriate and inappropriate behavior in their children. Used primarily in this population for youth who refuse school for attention.

Peer refusal skills training: A treatment technique designed to assist youth in refusing offers to miss school or avoid situations that tempt school refusal behavior. Used primarily for youth who refuse school for tangible reinforcement outside of school.

Positive reinforcement: Reward by means of administration of a positive stimulus. In a school refusal behavior population, this refers to youth who seek attention or tangible reinforcement outside of school.

Psychoeducation: A treatment technique designed to educate youth about the components of anxiety and their interaction. Used primarily for youth who refuse school to avoid stimuli that provoke negative affectivity or escape aversive social or evaluative situations.

Psychoneurotic truancy–school refusal: School absenteeism marked by general symptoms of anxiety, worry, compulsions, hysteria–panic, depression, or other indications of negative affectivity.

Relapse: Return to premorbid or near-premorbid level of functioning.

School absenteeism: Student absence from school for any period of time and for any legal or illegal reason.

School dropout: Permanent withdrawal or absenteeism from school prior to graduation for any reason.

School phobia: A specific form of psychoneurotic truancy–school refusal that is characterized by absenteeism with parental knowledge and due to separation anxiety or specific fears of school-related stimuli. This is often associated, correctly or incorrectly, with separation anxiety disorder or specific phobia of school.

School refusal behavior: Child-motivated refusal to attend school or difficulties remaining in classes for an entire day; the term refers to children and adolescents aged 5–17 years who are (a) completely absent from school, (b) attend but then leave school at some time during the day (i.e., skip classes), (c) attend school following severe misbehaviors in the morning (e.g., tantrums, clinging, aggression, running away, refusal to move, dawdling), (d) attend school under great duress that may precipitate pleas for future nonattendance to parents or others, or a combination of the above. This term is meant to incorporate the primary aspects of the terms *truancy*, *psychoneurotic truancy–school refusal*, and *school phobia*.

School victimization: Harm or property destruction suffered by a student at school.

School withdrawal: An act on the part of a parent or other person to encourage a child's school absenteeism or to deliberately keep a child home from school.

Self-corrective school refusal behavior: School refusal behavior that dissipates on its own within 2 weeks of onset.

Separation anxiety: Intense distress when anticipating or experiencing separation from a specific other person or people.

Separation anxiety disorder: According to the *DSM–IV*, "excessive anxiety concerning separation from the home or from those to whom the person is attached" (American Psychiatric Association, 1994, p. 110). One symptom of separation anxiety disorder is "persistent reluctance or refusal to go to school or elsewhere because of fear of separation" (p. 113).

Slip: A minor setback in treatment progress or long-term functioning.

Social–evaluative anxiety–avoidance hierarchy: A list of 5–10 school-based social–evaluative situations that provoke aversive reactions in youth. Used in conjunction with exposures and primarily for youth who refuse school to escape aversive social or evaluative situations.

Somatic control exercise: A strategy (e.g., relaxation training, breathing retraining) designed to help youth control aversive physical symptoms of anxiety. Used primarily for youth who refuse school to avoid stimuli that provoke negative affectivity.

Specific phobia (of school): According to the *DSM–IV*, "marked and persistent fear of clearly discernible, circumscribed objects or situations" (American Psychiatric Association, 1994, p. 405). A specific phobia of school indicates intense fear of some school-related stimulus.

Tangible reinforcement outside of school: Refusal of school to pursue specific rewards (e.g., time with friends, sleeping, drug use) outside of school.

Truancy: Illegal absence from school without parental knowledge and in concert with delinquent or acting-out behaviors. This is often associated, correctly or incorrectly, with conduct disorder.

REFERENCES

Abe, K. (1975). Sulpiride in depressive school phobic children. *Psychopharmacologia*, 43, 101.

Achenbach, T. M. (1991a). *Manual for the Child Behavior Checklist/4-18 and 1991 profile*. Burlington: University of Vermont, Department of Psychiatry.

Achenbach, T. M. (1991b). *Manual for the Teacher's Report Form and 1991 profile*. Burlington: University of Vermont, Department of Psychiatry.

Achenbach, T. M. (1991c). *Manual for the Youth Self-Report and 1991 profile*. Burlington: University of Vermont, Department of Psychiatry.

Achenbach, T. M., & Edelbrock, C. S. (1978). The classification of child psychopathology: A review and analysis of empirical efforts. *Psychological Bulletin*, 85, 1275–1301.

Achenbach, T. M., Howell, C., Quay, H. C., & Conners, C. K. (1991). National survey of problems and competencies among four- to sixteen-year-olds. *Monographs of the Society of Research in Child Development*, 56(3, Serial No. 225).

Achenbach, T. M., & McConaughy, S. H. (1997). *Empirically based assessment of child and adolescent psychopathology: Practical applications*. Thousand Oaks, CA: Sage.

Adams, P. L., McDonald, N. F., & Huey, W. P. (1966). School phobia and bisexual conflict: A report of 21 cases. *American Journal of Psychiatry*, 123, 541–547.

Agras, S. (1959). The relationship of school phobia to childhood depression. *American Journal of Psychiatry*, 116, 533–536.

Albano, A. M., & Barlow, D. H. (1996). Breaking the vicious cycle: Cognitive–behavioral group treatment for socially anxious youth. In E. D. Hibbs & P. S. Jensen (Eds.), *Psychosocial treatments for child and adolescent disorders: Empirically* based *strategies for clinical practice* (pp. 43–62). Washington, DC: American Psychological Association.

Albano, A. M., Chorpita, B. F., & Barlow, D. H. (1996). Childhood anxiety disorders. In E. J. Mash & R. A. Barkley (Eds.), *Child psychopathology* (pp. 196–241). New York: Guilford Press.

Albano, A. M., Detweiler, M. F., & Logsdon-Conradsen, S. (1999). Cognitive–behavioral interventions with socially phobic children. In S. W. Russ & T. H. Ollendick (Eds.), *Handbook of psychotherapies with children and families* (pp. 255–280). New York: Kluwer Academic/Plenum Press.

Albano, A. M., Marten, P. A., Holt, C. S., Heimberg, R. G., & Barlow, D. H. (1995). Cognitive–behavioral group treatment for social phobia in adolescents: A preliminary study. *Journal of Nervous and Mental Disease, 183,* 649–656.

American Psychiatric Association. (1980). *Diagnostic and statistical manual of mental disorders* (3rd ed.). Washington, DC: Author.

American Psychiatric Association. (1987). *Diagnostic and statistical manual of mental disorders* (3rd ed. rev.). Washington, DC: Author.

American Psychiatric Association. (1994). *Diagnostic and statistical manual of mental disorders* (4th ed.). Washington, DC: Author.

Anderson, J. C., Williams, S., McGee, R., & Silva, P. A. (1987). DSM–III disorders in pre-adolescent children. *Archives of General Psychiatry, 44,* 69–76.

Angold, A., & Costello, E. J. (2000). The Child and Adolescent Psychiatric Assessment (CAPA). *Journal of the American Academy of Child and Adolescent Psychiatry, 39,* 39–48.

Asher, S. J. (1988). The effects of child sexual abuse: A review of the issues and evidence. In L. E. A. Walker (Ed.), *Handbook on sexual abuse of children* (pp. 3–18). New York: Springer.

Atkeson, B. M., & Forehand, R. (1978). Parents as behavior change agents with school-related problems. *Education and Urban Society, 10,* 521–538.

Atkinson, L. (1986). Depression in school phobia. *British Journal of Psychiatry, 148,* 335–336.

Atkinson, L., Quarrington, B., Cyr, J. J., & Atkinson, F. V. (1989). Differential classification in school refusal. *British Journal of Psychiatry, 155,* 191–195.

Ayllon, T., Smith, D., & Rogers, M. (1970). Behavioral management of school phobia. *Journal of Behavior Therapy and Experimental Psychiatry, 1,* 125–138.

Baideme, S. M., Kern, R. M., & Taffel-Cohen, S. (1979). The use of Adlerian family therapy in a case of school phobia. *Journal of Individual Psychology, 35,* 58–69.

Baker, H., & Wills, U. (1978). School phobia: Classification and treatment. *British Journal of Psychiatry, 132,* 492–499.

Baker, H., & Wills, U. (1979). School phobic children at work. *British Journal of Psychiatry, 135,* 561–564.

Ballenger, J. C., Carek, D. J., Steele, J. J., & Cornish-McTighe, D. (1989). Three cases of panic disorder with agoraphobia in children. *American Journal of Psychiatry, 146,* 922–924.

Barker, P. (1968). The in-patient treatment of school refusal. *British Journal of Medical Psychology, 41,* 381–387.

Barkley, R. A. (1996). Attention-deficit/hyperactivity disorder. In E. J. Mash & R. A. Barkley (Eds.), *Child psychopathology* (pp. 63–112). New York: Guilford Press.

Barlow, D. H. (1988). *Anxiety and its disorders: The nature and treatment of anxiety and panic.* New York: Guilford Press.

Barrios, B. A., & Hartmann, D. P. (1997). Fears and anxieties. In E. J. Mash & L. G. Terdal (Eds.), *Assessment of childhood disorders* (3rd. ed., pp. 230–327). New York: Guilford Press.

Barth, R. P. (1984). Reducing nonattendance in elementary schools. *Social Work in Education, 6,* 151–166.

Beck, A. T., Brown, G., Epstein, N., & Steer, R. A. (1988). An inventory for measuring clinical anxiety: Psychometric properties. *Journal of Consulting and Clinical Psychology, 56,* 893–897.

Beck, A. T., Emery, G., & Greenberg, R. L. (1985). *Anxiety disorders and phobias: A cognitive perspective.* New York: Basic Books.

Beck, A. T., Rush, A. J., Shaw, B. F., & Emery, G. (1979). *Cognitive therapy of depression.* New York: Guilford Press.

Becker, E., Rankin, E., & Rickel, A. U. (1998). *High-risk sexual behavior: Interventions with vulnerable populations.* New York: Plenum Press.

Beidel, D. C., Neal, A. M., & Lederer, A. S. (1991). The feasibility and validity of a daily diary for the assessment of anxiety in children. *Behavior Therapy, 22,* 505–517.

Beidel, D. C., Turner, S. M., & Morris, T. L. (1999). Psychopathology of childhood social phobia. *Journal of the American Academy of Child and Adolescent Psychiatry, 38,* 643–650.

Beitchman, J. H. (1981). A sick father and his son: A clinical case and some therapeutic considerations. *Bulletin of the Menninger Clinic, 45,* 29–42.

Beitchman, J. H., Zucker, K. J., Hood, J. E., daCosta, G. A., & Akman, D. (1991). A review of the short-term effects of child sexual abuse. *Child Abuse and Neglect, 15,* 537–556.

Bell, A. J., Rosen, L. A., & Dynlacht, D. (1994). Truancy intervention. *Journal of Research and Development in Education, 27,* 203–211.

Bell-Dolan, D., & Brazeal, T. J. (1993). Separation anxiety disorder, overanxious disorder, and school refusal. *Child and Adolescent Psychiatric Clinics of North America, 2,* 563–580.

Benin, M., & Chong, Y. (1993). Child care concerns of employed mothers. In J. Frankel (Ed.), *The employed mother and the family context* (pp. 229–244). New York: Springer.

Berecz, J. M. (1980). Treatment of school phobia. In G. P. Sholevar (Ed.), *Emotional disorders of children and adolescents: Medical and psychological approaches to treatment* (pp. 563–587). New York: Spectrum.

Berg, I. (1970). A follow-up study of school phobic adolescents admitted to an in-patient unit. *Journal of Child Psychology and Psychiatry, 11*, 37–47.

Berg, I. (1974). A self-administered dependency questionnaire (SADQ) for use with mothers of school children. *British Journal of Psychiatry, 124*, 1–9.

Berg, I. (1976). School phobia in the children of agoraphobic women. *British Journal of Psychiatry, 128*, 86–89.

Berg, I. (1980). School refusal in early adolescence. In L. Hersov & I. Berg (Eds.), *Out of school* (pp. 231–249). New York: Wiley.

Berg, I. (1983). School non-attendance. In G. F. M. Russell & L. A. Hersov (Eds.), *Handbook of psychiatry: Vol. 4. The neuroses and personality disorders* (pp. 159–164). Cambridge, England: Cambridge University Press.

Berg, I. (1985a). Management of school refusal. *Archives of Disease in Childhood, 60*, 486–488.

Berg, I. (1985b). The management of truancy. *Journal of Child Psychology and Psychiatry, 26*, 325–331.

Berg, I. (1992). Absence from school and mental health. *British Journal of Psychiatry, 161*, 154–166.

Berg, I., Brown, I., & Hullin, R. (1988). *Off school, in court: An experimental and psychiatric investigation of severe school attendance problems.* New York: Springer-Verlag.

Berg, I., Butler, A., Franklin, J., Hayes, H., Lucas, C., & Sims, R. (1993). DSM–III–R disorders, social factors and management of school attendance problems in the normal population. *Journal of Child Psychology and Psychiatry, 34*, 1187–1203.

Berg, I., Butler, A., & Hall, G. (1976). The outcome of adolescent school phobia. *British Journal of Psychiatry, 128*, 80–85.

Berg, I., Butler, A., & McGuire, R. (1972). Birth order and family size of school-phobic adolescents. *British Journal of Psychiatry, 121*, 509–514.

Berg, I., Butler, A., & Pritchard, J. (1974). Psychiatric illness in the mothers of school-phobic adolescents. *British Journal of Psychiatry, 125*, 466–467.

Berg, I., Casswell, G., Goodwin, A., Hullin, R., McGuire, R., & Tagg, G. (1985). Classification of severe school attendance problems. *Psychological Medicine, 15*, 157–165.

Berg, I., & Collins, T. (1974). Wilfulness in school-phobic adolescents. *British Journal of Psychiatry, 125*, 468–469.

Berg, I., Collins, T., McGuire, R., & O'Melia, J. (1975). Educational attainment in adolescent school phobia. *British Journal of Psychiatry, 126*, 435–438.

Berg, I., & Fielding, D. (1978). An evaluation of hospital in-patient treatment for adolescent school phobia. *British Journal of Psychiatry, 132*, 500–505.

Berg, I., & Jackson, A. (1985). Teenage school refusers grow up: A follow-up study of 168 subjects, ten years on average after inpatient treatment. *British Journal of Psychiatry, 147*, 366–370.

Berg, I., & McGuire, R. (1971). Are school phobic adolescents overdependent? *British Journal of Psychiatry, 119*, 167–168.

Berg, I., & McGuire, R. (1974). Are mothers of school-phobic adolescents overprotective? *British Journal of Psychiatry, 124*, 10–13.

Berg, I., Nichols, K., & Pritchard, C. (1969). School phobia: Its classification and relationship to dependency. *Journal of Child Psychology and Psychiatry, 10*, 123–141.

Berney, T., Kolvin, I., Bhate, S. R., Garside, R. F., Jeans, J., Kaye, B., & Scarth, L. (1981). School phobia: A therapeutic trial with clomipramine and short-term outcomes. *British Journal of Psychiatry, 138*, 110–118.

Bernstein, G. A., & Borchardt, C. M. (1996). School refusal: Family constellation and family functioning. *Journal of Anxiety Disorders, 10*, 1–19.

Bernstein, G. A., Borchardt, C. M., Perwein, A. R., Crosby, R. D., Kushner, M. G., Thuras, P. D., & Last, C. G. (2000). Imipramine plus cognitive–behavioral therapy in the treatment of school refusal. *Journal of the American Academy of Child and Adolescent Psychiatry, 39*, 276–283.

Bernstein, G. A., Crosby, R. D., Perwien, A. R., & Borchardt, C. M. (1996). Anxiety Rating for Children—Revised: Reliability and validity. *Journal of Anxiety Disorders, 10*, 97–114.

Bernstein, G. A., & Garfinkel, B. D. (1986). School phobia: The overlap of affective and anxiety disorders. *Journal of the American Academy of Child and Adolescent Psychiatry, 25*, 235–241.

Bernstein, G. A., & Garfinkel, B. D. (1988). Pedigrees, functioning, and psychopathology in families of school phobic children. *American Journal of Psychiatry, 145*, 70–74.

Bernstein, G. A., & Garfinkel, B. D. (1992). The Visual Analog Scale of Anxiety—Revised: Psychometric properties. *Journal of Anxiety Disorders, 6*, 223–239.

Bernstein, G. A., Garfinkel, B. D., & Borchardt, C. M. (1990). Comparative studies of pharmacotherapy for school refusal. *Journal of the American Academy of Child and Adolescent Psychiatry, 29*, 773–781.

Bernstein, G. A., Massie, E. D., Thuras, P. D., Perwien, A. R., Borchardt, C. M., & Crosby, R. D. (1997). Somatic symptoms in anxious–depressed school refusers. *Journal of the American Academy of Child and Adolescent Psychiatry, 36*, 661–668.

Bernstein, G. A., Svingen, P. H., & Garfinkel, B. D. (1990). School phobia: Patterns of family functioning. *Journal of the American Academy of Child and Adolescent Psychiatry, 29*, 24–30.

Bernstein, G. A., Warren, S. L., Massie, E. D., & Thuras, P. D. (1999). Family dimensions in anxious–depressed school refusers. *Journal of Anxiety Disorders, 13*, 513–528.

Berrueta-Clement, J. R., Schweinhart, L. J., Barnett, W. S., Epstein, A. S., & Weikart, D. P. (1984). *Changed lives: The effects of the Perry Preschool Program on youths through age 19.* Ypsilanti, MI: High/Scope Press.

Berry, G. L., & Lizardi, A. (1985). The school phobic child and special services providers: Guidelines for early identification. *Special Services in the Schools, 2,* 63–72.

Berryman, E. (1959). School phobia: Management problems in private practice. *Psychological Reports, 5,* 19–25.

Biederman, J., Newcorn, J., & Sprich, S. (1991). Comorbidity of attention deficit hyperactivity disorder with conduct, depressive, anxiety, and other disorders. *American Journal of Psychiatry, 148,* 564–577.

Bizzis, J., & Bradley-Johnson, S. (1981). Increasing the school attendance of a truant adolescent. *Education and Treatment of Children, 4,* 149–155.

Black, B., & Robbins, D. R. (1990). Panic disorder in children and adolescents. *Journal of the American Academy of Child and Adolescent Psychiatry, 29,* 36–44.

Blagg, N. R. (1987). *School phobia and its treatment.* London: Croom Helm.

Blagg, N. R., & Yule, W. (1984). The behavioural treatment of school refusal: A comparative study. *Behaviour Research and Therapy, 22,* 119–127.

Blashfield, R. K., & Draguns, J. G. (1976). Toward a taxonomy of psychopathology: The purpose of psychiatric classification. *British Journal of Psychiatry, 129,* 574–583.

Blechman, E. A. (1992). Mentors for high-risk minority youth: From effective communication to bicultural competence. *Journal of Clinical Child Psychology, 21,* 160–169.

Bools, C., Foster, J., Brown, I., & Berg, I. (1990). The identification of psychiatric disorders in children who fail to attend school: A cluster analysis of a non-clinical population. *Psychological Medicine, 20,* 171–181.

Borchardt, C. M., Giesler, J., Bernstein, G. A., & Crosby, R. D. (1994). A comparison of inpatient and outpatient school refusers. *Child Psychiatry and Human Development, 24,* 255–264.

Bos, K. T., Ruijters, A. M., & Visscher, A. J. (1990). Truancy, drop-out, class repeating and their relation with school characteristics. *Educational Research, 32,* 175–185.

Bowlby, J. (1980). *Attachment and loss: Vol. 3. Loss.* New York: Basic Books.

Briesmeister, J. M., & Schaefer, C. E. (1998). *Handbook of parent training* (2nd. ed.). New York: Wiley.

Broadwin, I. T. (1932). A contribution to the study of truancy. *American Journal of Orthopsychiatry, 2,* 253–259.

Brooks, B. D. (1974). Contingency contracts with truants. *Personnel and Guidance Journal, 52,* 316–320.

Brown, J. H., & Christensen, D. N. (1986). *Family therapy: Theory and practice.* Monterey, CA: Brooks/Cole.

Brown, R. E., Copeland, R. E., & Hall, R. V. (1974). School phobia: Effects of behavior modification treatment applied by an elementary school principal. *Child Study Journal, 4,* 125–133.

Brownell, K. D., Marlatt, G. A., Lichtenstein, E., & Wilson, G. T. (1986). Understanding and preventing relapse. *American Psychologist, 41,* 765–776.

Brulle, A. R., McIntyre, T. C., & Mills, J. C. (1985). School phobia: Its educational implications. *Elementary School Guidance and Counseling, 20,* 19–28.

Bry, B. H., & George, F. E. (1980). The preventive effects of early intervention on the attendance and grades of urban adolescents. *Professional Psychology, 11,* 252–260.

Bryce, G., & Baird, D. (1986). Precipitating a crisis: Family therapy and adolescent school refusers. *Journal of Adolescence, 9,* 199–213.

Buchanan, C. M., Maccoby, E. E., & Dornbusch, S. M. (1996). *Adolescents after divorce.* Cambridge, MA: Harvard University Press.

Buitelaar, J. K., van Andel, H., Duyx, J. H. M., & van Strien, D. C. (1994). Depressive and anxiety disorders in adolescence: A follow-up study of adolescents with school refusal. *Acta Paedopsychiatrica, 56,* 249–253.

Burke, A. E., & Silverman, W. K. (1987). The prescriptive treatment of school refusal. *Clinical Psychology Review, 7,* 353–362.

Butcher, P. (1983). The treatment of childhood-rooted separation anxiety in an adult. *Journal of Behavior Therapy and Experimental Psychiatry, 14,* 61–65.

Campbell, J. D. (1955). Manic–depressive disease in children. *Journal of the American Medical Association, 158,* 154–157.

Cantrell, R. P., Cantrell, M. L., Huddleston, C. M., & Woolridge, R. L. (1969). Contingency contracting with school problems. *Journal of Applied Behavior Analysis, 2,* 215–220.

Caron, C., & Rutter, M. (1991). Comorbidity in child psychopathology: Concepts, issues, and research strategies. *Journal of Child Psychology and Psychiatry, 32,* 1063–1080.

Cartledge, G., & Milburn, J. F. (1995). *Teaching social skills to children and youth: Innovative approaches* (3rd ed.). Boston: Allyn & Bacon.

Chapel, J. L. (1967). Treatment of a case of school phobia by reciprocal inhibition. *Canadian Psychiatric Association Journal, 12,* 25–28.

Charlton, A., & Blair, V. (1989). Absence from school related to children's and parental smoking habits. *British Medical Journal, 298,* 90–92.

Chazan, M. (1962). School phobia. *British Journal of Educational Psychology, 32,* 200–217.

Cherry, A. (1992). Separation anxiety and school phobia: An intervention to revive the school bond. *Case Analysis, 3,* 3–10.

Cherry, N. (1976). Persistent job changing—Is it a problem? *Journal of Occupational Psychology, 49,* 203–221.

Chiland, C., & Young, J. G. (1990). *Why children reject school: Views from seven countries.* New Haven, CT: Yale University Press.

Chorpita, B. F., Albano, A. M., & Barlow, D. H. (1998). The structure of negative emotions in a clinical sample of children and adolescents. *Journal of Abnormal Psychology, 107,* 74–85.

Chorpita, B. F., Albano, A. M., Heimberg, R. G., & Barlow, D. H. (1996). A systematic replication of the prescriptive treatment of school refusal behavior in a single subject. *Journal of Behavior Therapy and Experimental Psychiatry, 27,* 281–290.

Chotiner, M. M., & Forrest, D. V. (1974). Adolescent school phobia: Six controlled cases studied retrospectively. *Adolescence, 9,* 467–480.

Church, J., & Edwards, B. (1984). Helping pupils who refuse school. *Special Education: Forward Trends, 11,* 28–31.

Clark, D. B., Turner, S. M., Beidel, D. C., Donovan, J. E., Kirisci, L., & Jacob, R. G. (1994). Reliability and validity of the Social Phobia and Anxiety Inventory for Adolescents. *Psychological Assessment, 6,* 135–140.

Concannon, J. (1980). Examination of school phobia. *Momentum, 11,* 42–44.

Conners, C. K. (1997). *Conners Rating Scales–Revised.* North Tonawanda, NY: Multi-Health Systems.

Contessa, M. A., & Paccione-Dyszlewski, M. R. (1981). An application of a group counseling technique with school-phobic adolescents. *Adolescence, 16,* 901–904.

Coolidge, J. C., Brodie, R. D., & Feeney, B. (1964). A ten-year follow-up study of sixty-six school-phobic children. *American Journal of Orthopsychiatry, 34,* 675–684.

Coolidge, J. C., Hahn, P. B., & Peck, A. L. (1957). School phobia: Neurotic crisis or way of life? *American Journal of Orthopsychiatry, 27,* 296–306.

Cooper, J. (1973). Application of the consultant role to parent–teacher management of school avoidance behavior. *Psychology in the Schools, 10,* 259–262.

Cooper, M. (1986). A model of persistent absenteeism. *Educational Research, 28,* 14–20.

Cooper, M. G. (1966a). School refusal. *Educational Research, 8,* 115–127.

Cooper, M. G. (1966b). School refusal: An inquiry into the part played by school and home. *Educational Research, 8,* 223–229.

Corville-Smith, J., Ryan, B. A., Adams, G. R., & Dalicandro, T. (1998). Distinguishing absentee students from regular attenders: The combined influence of personal, family, and school factors. *Journal of Youth and Adolescence, 27,* 629–640.

Cradock, C., Cotler, S., & Jason, L. A. (1978). Primary prevention: Immunization of children for speech anxiety. *Cognitive Therapy and Research, 2,* 389–396.

Creer, T. L., Renne, C. M., & Chai, H. (1982). The application of behavioral techniques to childhood asthma. In D. C. Russo & J. W. Varni (Eds.), *Behavioral pediatrics: Research and practice* (pp. 27–66). New York: Plenum Press.

Cretekos, C. J. G. (1977). Some techniques in rehabilitating the school phobic adolescent. *Adolescence, 12,* 237–246.

Croghan, L. M. (1981). Conceptualizing the critical elements in a rapid desensitization to school anxiety: A case study. *Journal of Pediatric Psychology, 6*, 165–170.

Crumley, F. E. (1974). A school phobia in a three-generation family conflict. *Journal of the American Academy of Child Psychiatry, 13*, 536–550.

Cwayna, K. (1993). *Knowing where the fountains are: Stories and stark realities of homeless youth.* Minneapolis, MN: Fairview.

Daleiden, E. L., Chorpita, B. F., Kollins, S. H., & Drabman, R. S. (1999). Factors affecting the reliability of clinical judgments about the function of children's school-refusal behavior. *Journal of Clinical Child Psychology, 28*, 396–406.

D'Amato, G. (1962). Chlordiazepoxide in the treatment of school phobia. *Diseases of the Nervous System, 23*, 292–295.

D'Amico, R. J., Haurin, R. J., & Mott, F. L. (1983). The effects of mothers' employment on adolescent and early adult outcomes of young men and women. In C. D. Hayes & S. B. Kamerman (Eds.), *Children of working parents: Experiences and outcomes* (pp. 130–219). Washington, DC: National Academy Press.

Davidson, S. (1960). School phobia as a manifestation of family disturbance: Its structure and treatment. *Journal of Child Psychology and Psychiatry, 1*, 270–287.

Davidson, W. S., & Robinson, M. J. (1975). Community psychology and behavior modification: A community based program for the prevention of delinquency. *Corrective and Social Psychiatry and Journal of Behavior Technology Methods and Therapy, 21*, 1–12.

Dayton, N. (1928). Mental deficiency and other factors that influence school attendance. *Mental Hygiene, 12*, 794–800.

Dennison, C., & Coleman, J. (1998). Teenage motherhood: Experiences and relationships. In S. Clement (Ed.), *Psychological perspectives on pregnancy and childhood* (pp. 245–263). New York: Churchill Livingstone.

Denno, D. W., & Clelland, R. C. (1986). Longitudinal evaluation of a delinquency prevention program by self-report. *Journal of Offender Counseling, Services and Rehabilitation, 10*, 59–82.

Derogatis, L. R. (1994). *SCL-90-R: Administration, scoring, and procedures manual.* Minneapolis, MN: National Computer Systems.

De Sousa, A., & De Sousa, D. A. (1980). School phobia. *Child Psychiatry Quarterly, 13*, 98–103.

Diamond, S. C. (1985). School phobic adolescents and a peer support group. *Clearinghouse, 59*, 125–126.

Doleys, D. M., & Williams, M. C. (1977). The use of natural consequences and a make-up period to eliminate school phobic behavior: A case study. *Journal of School Psychology, 15*, 44–50.

Doll, E. A. (1921). Mental types, truancy, and delinquency. *School and Society, 14*, 482–485.

Doris, J., McIntyre, A., Kelsey, C., & Lehman, E. (1971). Separation anxiety in nursery school children. *Proceedings of the Annual Convention of the American Psychological Association, 79*, 145–146.

Duckworth, K. (1988). Coping with student absenteeism. *The Practitioner, 14,* 1–14.

Duckworth, K., & deJung, J. (1989). Inhibiting class cutting among high school students. *High School Journal, 72,* 188–195.

Durand, V. M., & Crimmins, D. B. (1988). Identifying the variables maintaining self-injurious behavior. *Journal of Autism and Developmental Disorders, 18,* 99–117.

Echterling, L. G. (1989). An ark of prevention: Preventing school absenteeism after a flood. *Journal of Primary Prevention, 9,* 177–184.

Eisen, A. R., & Kearney, C. A. (1995). *Practitioner's guide to treating fear and anxiety in children and adolescents: A cognitive–behavioral approach.* Northvale, NJ: Aronson.

Eisen, A. R., & Silverman, W. K. (1998). Prescriptive treatment for generalized anxiety disorder in children. *Behavior Therapy, 29,* 105–121.

Eisen, A. R., Spasaro, S. A., Kearney, C. A., Albano, A. M., & Barlow, D. H. (1996). Measuring parental expectancies in a childhood anxiety disorders sample: The Parental Expectancies Scale. *The Behavior Therapist, 19,* 37–38.

Eisenberg, L. (1958). School phobia: A study in the communication of anxiety. *American Journal of Psychiatry, 114,* 712–718.

Elliott, J. G. (1999). Practitioner review: School refusal. Issues of conceptualisation, assessment, and treatment. *Journal of Child Psychology and Psychiatry and Allied Disciplines, 40,* 1001–1012.

Emslie, G. J., Rush, A. J., Weinberg, W. A., Kowatch, R. A., Hughes, C. W., Carmody, T., & Rintelmann, J. (1997). A double-blind, randomized, placebo-controlled trial of fluoxetine in children and adolescents with depression. *Archives of General Psychiatry, 54,* 1031–1037.

Endicott, J., Andreasen, N., & Spitzer, R. L. (1975). *Family history research diagnostic criteria.* New York: New York State Psychiatric Institute.

Ernst, M., Cookus, B. A., & Moravec, B. C. (2000). Pictorial Instrument for Children and Adolescents (PICA–III–R). *Journal of the American Academy of Child and Adolescent Psychiatry, 39,* 94–99.

Estes, H. R., Haylett, C. H., & Johnson, A. M. (1956). Separation anxiety. American *Journal of Orthopsychiatry, 26,* 682–695.

Esveldt-Dawson, K., Wisner, K. L., Unis, A. S., Matson, J. L., & Kazdin, A. E. (1982). Treatment of phobias in a hospitalized child. *Journal of Behavior Therapy and Experimental Psychiatry, 13,* 77–83.

Evans, L. D. (2000). Functional school refusal subtypes: Anxiety, avoidance, and malingering. *Psychology in the Schools, 37,* 183–191.

Evers, W. L., & Schwarz, J. C. (1973). Modifying social withdrawal in preschoolers: The effects of filmed modeling and teacher praise. *Journal of Abnormal Child Psychology, 1,* 248–256.

Eyberg, S. M. (1992). Parent and teacher behavior inventories for the assessment of conduct problem behaviors in children. In L. VandeCreek, S. Knapp, &

T. L. Jackson (Eds.), *Innovations in clinical practice: A source book* (Vol. 11, pp. 261–270). Sarasota, FL: Professional Resource Exchange.

Eyberg, S. M., & Boggs, S. R. (1998). Parent–child interaction therapy: A psychosocial intervention for the treatment of young conduct-disordered children. In J. M. Briesmeister & C. E. Schaefer (Eds.), *Handbook of parent training* (2nd ed., pp. 61–97). New York: Wiley.

Famularo, R., Kinscherff, R., Fenton, T., & Bolduc, S. M. (1990). Child maltreatment histories among runaway and delinquent children. *Clinical Pediatrics, 29*, 713–718.

Farrington, D. P. (1980). Truancy, delinquency, the home and the school. In L. Hersov & I. Berg (Eds.), *Out of school* (pp. 49–63). New York: Wiley.

Felner, R. D., Brand, S., Adan, A. M., Mulhall, P. F., Flowers, N., Sartain, B., & DuBois, D. L. (1993). Restructuring the ecology of the school as an approach to prevention during school transitions: Longitudinal follow-ups and extensions of the School Transitional Environment Project (STEP). *Prevention in Human Services, 10*, 103–136.

Field, J. C., & Olafson, L. J. (1998). Caught in the machine: Resistance, positioning, and pedagogy. *Research in Middle Level Education Quarterly, 22*, 39–55.

Flakierska, N., Lindstrom, M., & Gillberg, C. (1988). School refusal: A 15–20-year follow-up study of 35 Swedish urban children. *British Journal of Psychiatry, 152*, 834–837.

Forehand, R., & McMahon, R. J. (1981). *Helping the noncompliant child: A clinician's guide to parent training.* New York: Guilford Press.

Foreman, D. M., Dover, S. J., & Hill, A. B. (1997). Emotional and semantic priming as a measure of information processing in young people with school refusal: A research note. *Journal of Child Psychology and Psychiatry, 38*, 855–860.

Fowler, A. (1978). Profile of a re-ed child. *Behavioral Disorders, 3*, 80–83.

Fowler, M. G., Davenport, M. G., & Garg, R. (1992). School functioning of US children with asthma. *Pediatrics, 90*, 939–944.

Fox, J. E., & Houston, B. K. (1981). Efficacy of self-instructional training for reducing children's anxiety in evaluative situations. *Behaviour Research and Therapy, 19*, 509–515.

Fox, J. E., & Houston, B. K. (1983). Distinguishing between cognitive and somatic trait and state anxiety in children. *Journal of Personality and Social Psychology, 45*, 862–870.

Frances, A., & Petti, T. A. (1984). Boy with seriously ill mother manifests somatic complaints, withdrawal, disabling fears. *Hospital and Community Psychiatry, 35*, 439–440.

Franco, D. P., Christoff, K. A., Crimmins, D. E., & Kelly, J. A. (1983). Social skills training for an extremely shy young adolescent: An empirical case study. *Behavior Therapy, 14*, 568–575.

Fraser, M. W., Hawkins, J. D., & Howard, M. O. (1988). Parent training for delinquency prevention. *Child and Youth Services, 11*, 93–125.

Frick, P. J. (1998). *Conduct disorders and severe antisocial behavior*. New York: Plenum Press.

Frick, W. B. (1964). School phobia: A critical review of the literature. *Merrill–Palmer Quarterly, 10*, 361–373.

Friesen, M. (1985). Non-attendance as a maladaptive response to stress. *School Guidance Worker, 40*, 19–23.

Frommer, E. A. (1967). Treatment of childhood depression with antidepressant drugs. *British Medical Journal, 1*, 729–732.

Gadow, K. D., & Sprafkin, J. (1995). *Manual for the Child Symptom Inventory* (4th ed.). Stony Brook, NY: Checkmate Plus.

Galloway, D. (1982). A study of persistent absentees and their families. *British Journal of Educational Psychology, 52*, 317–330.

Galloway, D. (1983). Research note: Truants and other absentees. *Journal of Child Psychology and Psychiatry, 24*, 607–611.

Galloway, D. (1985). *Schools and persistent absentees*. New York: Pergamon Press.

Gammon, G. D., & Brown, T. E. (1993). Fluoxetine and methylphenidate in combination for treatment of attention deficit disorder and comorbid depressive disorder. *Journal of Child and Adolescent Psychopharmacology, 3*, 1–10.

Garland, E. J., & Smith, D. H. (1990). Panic disorder on a child psychiatric consultation service. *Journal of the American Academy of Child and Adolescent Psychiatry, 29*, 785–788.

Garvey, W. P., & Hegrenes, J. R. (1966). Desensitization techniques in the treatment of school phobia. *American Journal of Orthopsychiatry, 36*, 147–152.

Gingras, R. C., & Careaga, R. C. (1989). Limited English proficient students at risk: Issues and prevention strategies. *New Focus: National Clearinghouse for Bilingual Education, 10*, 1–11.

Gittelman-Klein, R., & Klein, D. F. (1971). Controlled imipramine treatment of school phobia. *Archives of General Psychiatry, 25*, 204–207.

Gleeson, D. (1992). School attendance and truancy: A socio-historical account. *Sociological Review, 40*, 437–490.

Goldberg, C. (1977). School phobia in adolescence. *Adolescence, 12*, 499–509.

Goldberg, T. B. (1953). Factors in the development of school phobia. *Smith College Studies in Social Work, 23*, 227–248.

Goldenberg, H., & Goldenberg, I. (1970). School phobia: Childhood neurosis or learned maladaptive behavior? *Exceptional Children, 37*, 220–226.

Gorman, K. S., & Pollitt, E. (1996). Does schooling buffer the effects of early risk? *Child Development, 67*, 314–326.

Gottfredson, G. D. (1983). Schooling and delinquency prevention: Some practical ideas for educators, parents, program developers and researchers. *Journal of Child Care, 1*, 51–64.

Gottfried, A. E., & Gottfried, A. W. (1988). Maternal employment and children's development: An integration of longitudinal findings with implications for social policy. In A. E. Gottfried & A. W. Gottfried (Eds.), *Maternal employment and children's development: Longitudinal research* (pp. 269–287). New York: Plenum Press.

Grala, C., & McCauley, C. (1976). Counseling truants back to school: Motivation combined with a program for action. *Journal of Counseling Psychology, 23,* 166–169.

Granell de Aldaz, E., Feldman, L., Vivas, E., & Gelfand, D. M. (1987). Characteristics of Venezualan school refusers: Toward the development of a high-risk profile. *Journal of Nervous and Mental Disease, 175,* 402–407.

Granell de Aldaz, E., Vivas, E., Gelfand, D. M., & Feldman, L. (1984). Estimating the prevalence of school refusal and school-related fears. *Journal of Nervous and Mental Disease, 172,* 722–729.

Gray, G., Smith, A., & Rutter, M. (1980). School attendance and the first year of employment. In L. Hersov & I. Berg (Eds.), *Out of school* (pp. 343–370). New York: Wiley.

Graziano, A. M., & DeGiovanni, I. S. (1979). The clinical significance of childhood phobias: A note on the proportion of child-clinical referrals for the treatment of children's fears. *Behaviour Research and Therapy, 17,* 161–162.

Gresham, F. M., & Nagle, R. J. (1981). Treating school phobia using behavioral consultation: A case study. *School Psychology Review, 10,* 104–107.

Griffin, W. A. (1993). *Family therapy: Fundamentals of theory and practice.* New York: Brunner/Mazel.

Grindler, M. (1988). Effects of cognitive monitoring strategies on the test anxieties of elementary students. *Psychology in the Schools, 25,* 428–436.

Guerney, L., & Guerney, B. (1989). Child relationship enhancement: Family therapy and parent education. Person-centered approaches with families. *Person Centered Review, 4,* 344–357.

Gullone, E., & King, N. J. (1991). Acceptability of alternative treatments for school refusal: Evaluations by students, caregivers, and professionals. *British Journal of Educational Psychology, 61,* 346–354.

Gullone, E., & King, N. J. (1992). Psychometric evaluation of a revised fear survey schedule for children and adolescents. *Journal of Child Psychology and Psychiatry, 33,* 987–998.

Hagopian, L. P., & Slifer, K. J. (1993). Treatment of separation anxiety disorder with graduate exposure and reinforcement targeting school attendance: A controlled study. *Journal of Anxiety Disorders, 7,* 271–280.

Hall, T. W. (1967). *Some effects of anxiety on the fantasy play of schoolchildren.* Unpublished doctoral dissertation, Yale University, New Haven, CT.

Hammen, C., & Rudolph, K. D. (1996). Childhood depression. In E. J. Mash & R. A. Barkley (Eds.), *Child psychopathology* (pp. 153–195). New York: Guilford Press.

Hampe, E., Miller, L., Barrett, C., & Noble, H. (1973). Intelligence and school phobia. *Journal of School Psychology, 11,* 66–70.

Hansen, C., Sanders, S. L., Massaro, S., & Last, C. G. (1998). Predictors of severity of absenteeism in children with anxiety-based school refusal. *Journal of Clinical Child Psychology, 27,* 246–254.

Hargett, M. Q., & Webster, R. E. (1996). Treatment integrity and acceptability with families: A case study of a child with school refusal. *Psychology in the Schools, 33,* 319–324.

Harris, K. R., & Brown, R. D. (1982). Cognitive behavior modification and informed teacher treatments for shy children. *Journal of Experimental Education, 50,* 137–143.

Harris, S. R. (1980). School phobic children and adolescents: A challenge to counselors. *The School Counselor, 27,* 263–269.

Harvey, E. (1999). Short-term and long-term effects of early parental employment on children of the National Longitudinal Survey of Youth. *Developmental Psychology, 35,* 445–459.

Hathaway, S. R., & McKinley, J. C. (1989). *Minnesota Multiphasic Personality Inventory* (2nd ed.). Minneapolis: University of Minnesota Press.

Hayward, C., Taylor, C. B., Blair-Greiner, A., & Strachowski, D. (1995). School refusal in young adolescent girls with nonclinical panic attacks. *Journal of Anxiety Disorders, 9,* 329–338.

Healy, W. (1926). Preventing delinquency among children. *Proceedings of the National Education Association,* pp. 113–116.

Henggeler, S. W., Schoenwald, S. K., Borduin, C. M., Rowland, M. D., & Cunningham, P. B. (1998). *Multisystemic treatment of antisocial behavior in children and adolescents.* New York: Guilford Press.

Herjanic, B., & Campbell, W. (1977). Differentiating psychiatrically disturbed children on the basis of a structured interview. *Journal of Abnormal Child Psychology, 10,* 307–324.

Hersen, M. (1970). Behavior modification approach to a school-phobia case. *Journal of Clinical Psychology, 26,* 128–132.

Hersov, L. A. (1960a). Persistent non-attendance at school. *Journal of Child Psychology and Psychiatry, 1,* 130–136.

Hersov, L. A. (1960b). Refusal to go to school. *Journal of Child Psychology and Psychiatry, 1,* 137–145.

Hersov, L. (1985). School refusal. In M. Rutter & L. Hersov (Eds.), *Child and adolescent psychiatry: Modern approaches* (pp. 382–399). Boston: Blackwell Scientific.

Hibbett, A., & Fogelman, K. (1990). Future lives of truants: Family formation and health-related behaviour. *British Journal of Educational Psychology, 60,* 171–179.

Hibbett, A., Fogelman, K., & Manor, O. (1990). Occupational outcomes of truancy. *British Journal of Educational Psychology, 60,* 23–36.

Higgins, P. S. (1978). Evaluation and case study of a school-based delinquency prevention program: The Minnesota Youth Advocate Program. *Evaluation Quarterly, 2,* 215–234.

Hinshaw, S. P. (1992). Externalizing behavior problems and academic under-achievement in childhood and adolescence: Causal relationships and underlying mechanisms. *Psychological Bulletin, 111*, 127–155.

Hinshaw, S. P., & Anderson, C. A. (1996). Conduct and oppositional defiant disorders. In E. J. Mash & R. A. Barkley (Eds.), *Child psychopathology* (pp. 113–149). New York: Guilford Press.

Hitchcock, A. B. (1956). Symbolic and actual flight from school. *Smith College Studies in Social Work, 27*, 1–33.

Hodges, K., Kline, J., Stern, L., Cytryn, L., & McKnew, D. (1982). The development of a child assessment interview for research and clinical use. *Journal of Abnormal Child Psychology, 10*, 173–189.

Honjo, S., Kasahara, Y., & Ohtaka, K. (1992). School refusal in Japan. *Acta Paedopsychiatrica, 55*, 29–32.

Honma, H. (1986). A clinical psychological study of school refusal in adolescence (I)—An approach to adolescent school refusal through a classification of the cases. *Tohoku Psychologica Folia, 45*, 76–88.

Hsia, H. (1984). Structural and strategic approach to school phobia/school refusal. *Psychology in the Schools, 21*, 360–367.

Huffington, C. M., & Sevitt, M. A. (1989). Family interaction in adolescent school phobia. *Journal of Family Therapy, 11*, 353–375.

Huguet, E. (1973). *Dictionnaire de la langue Francaise du seizieme siecle* [French language dictionary of the 16th century] (Vol. 7). Paris, France: E. Champion. (Original work published 1925)

Iwamoto, S., & Yoshida, K. (1997). School refusal in Japan: The recent dramatic increase in incidence is a cause for concern. *Social Behavior and Personality, 25*, 315–320.

Iwatani, N., Miike, T., Kal, Y., Kodama, M., Mabe, H., Tomoda, A., Fukuda, K., & Jyodoi, T. (1997). Glucoregulatory disorders in school refusal students. *Clinical Endocrinology, 47*, 273–278.

Jacobsen, V. (1948). Influential factors in the outcome of treatment of school phobia. *Smith College Studies in Social Work, 18*, 181–202.

Janosz, M., LeBlanc, M., Boulerice, B., & Tremblay, R. E. (1997). Disentangling the weight of school dropout predictors: A test on two longitudinal samples. *Journal of Youth and Adolescence, 26*, 733–762.

Jarvis, V. (1964). Countertransference in the management of school phobia. *Psychoanalytic Quarterly, 33*, 411–419.

Jenkins, P. H. (1995). School delinquency and school commitment. *Sociology of Education, 68*, 221–239.

Johnson, A. M. (1957). School phobia. *American Journal of Orthopsychiatry, 27*, 307–309.

Johnson, A. M., Falstein, E. I., Szurek, S. A., & Svendsen, M. (1941). School phobia. *American Journal of Orthopsychiatry, 11*, 702–711.

Johnson, R. L., & Glass, C. R. (1989). Heterosocial anxiety and direction of attention in high school boys. *Cognitive Therapy and Research, 13*, 509–526.

Johnson, T., Tyler, V., Thompson, R., & Jones, E. (1971). Systematic desensitization and assertive training in the treatment of speech anxiety in middle-school students. *Psychology in the Schools, 8*, 263–267.

Jones, B. A. (1992). Collaboration: The case for indigenous community-based organization support of dropout prevention programming and implementation. *Journal of Negro Education, 61*, 496–508.

Kahn, J. H., & Nursten, J. P. (1962). School refusal: A comprehensive view of school phobia and other failures of school attendance. *American Journal of Orthopsychiatry, 32*, 707–718.

Kakar, S. (1996). *Child abuse and delinquency*. New York: University Press of America.

Kandal, H. J., Ayllon, T., & Rosenbaum, M. S. (1977). Flooding or systematic exposure in the treatment of extreme social withdrawal in children. *Journal of Behavior Therapy and Experimental Psychiatry, 8*, 75–81.

Kandel, D. B., & Davies, M. (1982). Epidemiology of depressive mood in adolescents. *Archives of General Psychiatry, 39*, 1205–1212.

Kandel, D. B., Raveis, V. H., & Kandel, P. I. (1984). Continuities and discontinuities: Adjustment in young adulthood of former school absentees. *Youth and Society, 15*, 325–352.

Kanner, A. D., Feldman, S. S., Weinberger, D. A., & Ford, M. E. (1987). Uplifts, hassles, and adaptational outcomes in early adolescents. *Journal of Early Adolescence, 7*, 371–394.

Kashani, J. H., Holcomb, W. R., & Orvaschel, H. (1986). Depression and depressive symptoms in preschool children from the general population. *American Journal of Psychiatry, 143*, 1138–1143.

Kashani, J. H., & Orvaschel, H. (1990). A community study of anxiety in children and adolescents. *American Journal of Psychiatry, 147*, 313–318.

Kearney, C. A. (1993). Depression and school refusal behavior: A review with comments on classification and treatment. *Journal of School Psychology, 31*, 267–279.

Kearney, C. A. (1995). School refusal behavior. In A. R. Eisen, C. A. Kearney, & C. E. Schaefer (Eds.), *Clinical handbook of anxiety disorders in children and adolescents* (pp. 19–52). Northvale, NJ: Aronson.

Kearney, C. A. (1997, March). *Treatment of separation anxiety-based school refusal behavior*. Symposium conducted at the meeting of the Anxiety Disorders Association of America, New Orleans, LA.

Kearney, C. A. (2000). *The functional profiles of school refusal behavior*. Unpublished manuscript, University of Nevada Las Vegas, Department of Psychology.

Kearney, C. A., & Albano, A. M. (2000). *Therapist's guide to school refusal behavior*. San Antonio, TX: Psychological Corporation.

Kearney, C. A., & Beasley, J. F. (1994). The clinical treatment of school refusal behavior: A survey of referral and practice characteristics. *Psychology in the Schools, 31*, 128–132.

Kearney, C. A., Drabman, R. S., & Beasley, J. F. (1993). The trials of childhood: The development, reliability, and validity of the Daily Life Stressors Scale. *Journal of Child and Family Studies, 2*, 371–388.

Kearney, C. A., Eisen, A. R., & Silverman, W. K. (1995). The legend and myth of school phobia. *School Psychology Quarterly, 10*, 65–85.

Kearney, C. A., & Hugelshofer, D. S. (2000). Systemic and clinical strategies for preventing school refusal behavior in youth. *Journal of Cognitive Psychotherapy, 14*, 1–15.

Kearney, C. A., & Silverman, W. K. (1990). A preliminary analysis of a functional model of assessment and treatment for school refusal behavior. *Behavior Modification, 14*, 344–360.

Kearney, C. A., & Silverman, W. K. (1991, November). *Toward a functional model of assessing and treating children and adolescents with school refusal behavior*. Symposium conducted at the meeting of the Association for the Advancement of Behavior Therapy, New York.

Kearney, C. A., & Silverman, W. K. (1993). Measuring the function of school refusal behavior: The School Refusal Assessment Scale. *Journal of Clinical Child Psychology, 22*, 85–96.

Kearney, C. A., & Silverman, W. K. (1995). Family environment of youngsters with school refusal behavior: A synopsis with implications for assessment and treatment. *American Journal of Family Therapy, 23*, 59–72.

Kearney, C. A., & Silverman, W. K. (1996). The evolution and reconciliation of taxonomic strategies for school refusal behavior. *Clinical Psychology: Science and Practice, 3*, 339–354.

Kearney, C. A., & Silverman, W. K. (1998). A critical review of pharmacotherapy for youth with anxiety disorders: Things are not as they seem. *Journal of Anxiety Disorders, 12*, 83–102.

Kearney, C. A., & Silverman, W. K. (1999). Functionally-based prescriptive and nonprescriptive treatment for children and adolescents with school refusal behavior. *Behavior Therapy, 30*, 673–695.

Kearney, C. A., Silverman, W. K., & Eisen, A. R. (1989, October). *Characteristics of children and adolescents with school refusal behavior*. Paper presented at the meeting of the Berkshire Conference of Behavior Analysis and Therapy, Amherst, MA.

Kearney, C. A., & Sims, K. E. (1997). Anxiety problems in childhood: Diagnostic and dimensional aspects. In J. A. den Boer (Ed.), *Clinical management of anxiety: Theory and practical applications* (pp. 371–397). New York: Marcel Dekker.

Kearney, C. A., & Tillotson, C. A. (1998). The School Refusal Assessment Scale. In C. P. Zalaquett & R. J. Wood (Eds.), *Evaluating stress: A book of resources* (Vol. 2, pp. 239–258). Lanham, MD: Scarecrow Press.

Keller, M. F., & Carlson, P. M. (1974). The use of symbolic modeling to promote social skills in preschool children with low levels of social responsiveness. *Child Development, 45,* 912–919.

Kelley, C. K. (1976). Play desensitization of fear of darkness in preschool children. *Behaviour Research and Therapy, 14,* 79–81.

Kelly, E. W. (1973). School phobia: A review of theory and treatment. *Psychology in the Schools, 10,* 33–42.

Kendall, P. C. (1994). Treating anxiety disorders in children: Results of a randomized clinical trial. *Journal of Consulting and Clinical Psychology, 62,* 100–110.

Kendall, P. C., Chansky, T. E., Kane, M. T., Kim, R. S., Kortlander, E., Ronan, K. R., Sessa, F. M., & Siqueland, L. (1992). *Anxiety disorders in youth: Cognitive–behavioral interventions.* Boston: Allyn & Bacon.

Kendall, P. C., Flannery-Schroeder, E., Panichelli-Mindel, S. M., Southam-Gerow, M., Henin, A., & Warman, M. (1997). Therapy for youths with anxiety disorders: A second randomized clinical trial. *Journal of Consulting and Clinical Psychology, 65,* 366–380.

Kendall, P. C., Kortlander, E., Chansky, T. E., & Brady, E. U. (1992). Comorbidity of anxiety and depression in youth: Treatment implications. *Journal of Consulting and Clinical Psychology, 60,* 869–880.

Kendall, P. C., Panichelli-Mindel, S. M., Sugarman, A., & Callahan, S. A. (1997). Exposure to child anxiety: Theory, research, and practice. *Clinical Psychology: Science and Practice, 4,* 29–39.

Kennedy, W. A. (1965). School phobia: Rapid treatment of 50 cases. *Journal of Abnormal Psychology, 70,* 285–289.

Kennedy, W. A. (1971). A behavioristic, community-oriented approach to school phobia and other disorders. In H. C. Richards (Ed.), *Behavioral intervention in human problems* (pp. 37–60). New York: Pergamon Press.

Kifer, R. E., Lewis, M. A., Green, D. R., & Phillips, E. L. (1974). Training predelinquent youths and their parents to negotiate conflict situations. *Journal of Applied Behavior Analysis, 7,* 357–364.

King, H. E. (1992). The reactions of children to divorce. In C. E. Walker & M. C. Roberts (Eds.), *Handbook of clinical child psychology* (2nd ed., pp. 1009–1023). New York: Wiley.

King, N. J. (1994). Physiological assessment. In T. H. Ollendick, N. J. King, & W. Yule (Eds.), *International handbook of phobic and anxiety disorders in children and adolescents* (pp. 365–379). New York: Plenum Press.

King, N. J., Ollendick, T. H., & Gullone, E. (1991). Negative affectivity in children and adolescents: Relations between anxiety and depression. *Clinical Psychology Review, 11,* 441–459.

King, N. J., Ollendick, T. H., & Tonge, B. J. (1995). *School refusal: Assessment and treatment.* Boston, MA: Allyn & Bacon.

King, N. J., Ollendick, T. H., Tonge, B. J., Heyne, D., Pritchard, M., Rollings, S., Young, D., & Myerson, N. (1996). Behavioural management of school refusal. *Scandanavian Journal of Behaviour Therapy, 25*, 3–15.

King, N. J., Tonge, B. J., Heyne, D., & Ollendick, T. H. (2000). Research on the cognitive–behavior treatment of school refusal: A review and recommendations. *Clinical Psychology Review, 20*, 495–507.

King, N. J., Tonge, B. J., Heyne, D., Pritchard, M., Rollings, S., Young, D., Myerson, N., & Ollendick, T. H. (1998). Cognitive–behavioral treatment of school-refusing children: A controlled evaluation. *Journal of the American Academy of Child and Adolescent Psychiatry, 37*, 395–403.

Kirkpatrick, M. E., & Lodge, T. (1935). Some factors in truancy. *Mental Hygiene, 14*, 610–618.

Klein, E. (1945). The reluctance to go to school. *Psychoanalytic Study of the Child, 1*, 263–279.

Klein, R. G., Koplewicz, H. S., & Kanner, A. (1992). Imipramine treatment of children with separation anxiety disorder. *Journal of the American Academy of Child and Adolescent Psychiatry, 31*, 21–28.

Kline, L. W. (1897). Truancy as related to the migrating instinct. *Pedgogical Seminary, 5*, 381–420.

Klungness, L., & Gredler, G. R. (1984). The diagnosis and behavioral treatment of school phobia. *Techniques: A Journal for Remedial Education and Counseling, 1*, 31–38.

Knox, P. (1989). Home-based education: An alternative approach to "school phobia." *Educational Review, 41*, 143–151.

Kolko, D. J., Ayllon, T., & Torrence, C. (1987). Positive practice routines in overcoming resistance to the treatment of school phobia: A case study with follow-up. *Journal of Behavior Therapy and Experimental Psychiatry, 18*, 249–257.

Kolvin, I., Berney, T. P., & Bhate, S. R. (1984). Classification and diagnosis of depression in school phobia. *British Journal of Psychiatry, 145*, 347–357.

Kortering, L. J., & Blackorby, J. (1992). High school dropout and students identified with behavioral disorders. *Behavioral Disorders, 18*, 24–32.

Kotin, L., & Aikman, W. F. (1980). *Legal foundations of compulsory school attendance.* Port Washington, NY: Kennikat.

Kovacs, M. (1992). *Children's Depression Inventory manual.* North Tonawanda, NY: Multi-Health Systems.

Kraft, I. A., Ardali, C., Duffy, J. H., Hart, J. T., & Pearce, P. (1965). A clinical study of chlordiazepoxide used in psychiatric disorders in children. *International Journal of Neuropsychiatry, 1*, 433–437.

Kurita, H. (1991). School refusal in pervasive developmental disorders. *Journal of Autism and Developmental Disorders, 21*, 1–15.

Lachar, D., & Gruber, C. P. (1991). *Manual for Personality Inventory for Children—Revised.* Los Angeles: Western Psychological Services.

La Greca, A. M., & Stone, W. L. (1993). Social Anxiety Scale for Children—Revised: Factor structure and concurrent validity. *Journal of Clinical Child Psychology, 22,* 17–27.

Lall, G. R., & Lall, B. M. (1979). School phobia: It's real . . . and growing. *Instructor, 89,* 96–98.

Lambert, M. C., Weisz, J. R., & Thesiger, C. (1989). Principal components analyses of behavior problems in Jamaican clinic-referred children: Teacher reports for ages 6–17. *Journal of Abnormal Child Psychology, 17,* 553–562.

Lang, P. J., & Lazovik, A. D. (1963). Experimental desensitization of a phobia. *Journal of Abnormal and Social Psychology, 66,* 519–525.

Last, C. G. (1991). Somatic complaints in anxiety disordered children. *Journal of Anxiety Disorders, 5,* 125–138.

Last, C. G., & Francis, G. (1988). School phobia. In B. B. Lahey & A. E. Kazdin (Eds.), *Advances in clinical child psychology* (pp. 193–222). New York: Plenum Press.

Last, C. G., Francis, G., Hersen, M., Kazdin, A. E., & Strauss, C. C. (1987). Separation anxiety and school phobia: A comparison using *DSM–III* criteria. *American Journal of Psychiatry, 144,* 653–657.

Last, C. G., Hansen, C., & Franco, N. (1998). Cognitive–behavioral treatment of school phobia. *Journal of the American Academy of Child and Adolescent Psychiatry, 37,* 404–411.

Last, C. G., & Strauss, C. C. (1990). School refusal in anxiety-disordered children and adolescents. *Journal of the American Academy of Child and Adolescent Psychiatry, 29,* 31–35.

Last, C. G., Strauss, C. C., & Francis, G. (1987). Comorbidity among childhood anxiety disorders. *Journal of Nervous and Mental Disease, 175,* 726–730.

Lawlor, E. D. (1976). Hypnotic intervention with "school phobic" children. *International Journal of Clinical and Experimental Hypnosis, 24,* 74–86.

Lazarus, A. A. (1960). The elimination of children's phobias by deconditioning. In H. J. Eysenck (Ed.), *Behavior therapy and the neuroses* (pp. 114–122). New York: Pergamon.

Lazarus, A. A., & Abramovitz, A. (1962). The use of emotive imagery in the treatment of children's phobias. *Journal of Mental Science, 108,* 191–195.

Lazarus, A. A., Davison, G. C., & Polefka, D. A. (1965). Classical and operant factors in the treatment of a school phobia. *Journal of Abnormal Psychology, 70,* 225–229.

Leal, L. L., Baxter, E. G., Martin, J., & Marx, R. W. (1981). Cognitive modification and systematic desensitization with test anxious high school students. *Journal of Counseling Psychology, 28,* 525–528.

Lee, M. I., & Miltenberger, R. G. (1996). School refusal behavior: Classification, assessment, and treatment issues. *Education and Treatment of Children, 19,* 474–486.

Leitenberg, H., Yost, L. W., & Carroll-Wilson, M. (1986). Negative cognitive errors in children: Questionnaire development, normative data, and comparisons between children with and without self-reported symptoms of depression, low self-esteem, and evaluation anxiety. *Journal of Consulting and Clinical Psychology, 54,* 528–536.

Lepola, U., Leinonen, E., & Koponen, H. (1996). Citalopram in the treatment of early-onset panic disorder and school phobia. *Pharmacopsychiatry, 29,* 30–32.

Lerner, J. V. (1994). *Working women and their families.* Thousand Oaks, CA: Sage.

LeRoy, J. B., & Derdeyn, A. (1976). Drawings as a therapeutic medium: The treatment of separation anxiety in a 4-year-old boy. *Child Psychiatry and Human Development, 6,* 155–169.

Leton, D. A. (1962). Assessment of school phobia. *Mental Hygiene, 46,* 256–265.

LeUnes, A., & Siemsglusz, S. (1977). Paraprofessional treatment of school phobia in a young adolescent girl. *Adolescence, 12,* 115–121.

Levanto, J. (1975). High school absenteeism. *NASSP Bulletin, 59,* 100–104.

Leventhal, T., & Sills, M. (1964). Self-image in school phobia. *American Journal of Orthopsychiatry, 34,* 685–695.

Leventhal, T., Weinberger, G., Stander, R. J., & Stearns, R. P. (1967). Therapeutic strategies with school phobics. *American Journal of Orthopsychiatry, 37,* 65–70.

Levine, R. S. (1984). An assessment tool for early intervention in cases of truancy. *Social Work in Education, 6,* 133–150.

Levine, R. S., Metzendorf, D., & VanBoskirk, K. A. (1986). Runaway and throw away youth: A case for early intervention with truants. *Social Work in Education, 8,* 93–106.

Linet, L. S. (1985). Tourette syndrome, pimozide, and school phobia: The neuroleptic separation anxiety syndrome. *American Journal of Psychiatry, 142,* 613–615.

Lippman, H. S. (1936). The neurotic delinquent. *American Journal of Orthopsychiatry, 7,* 114–121.

Little, S., & Jackson, B. (1974). The treatment of test anxiety through attentional and relaxation training. *Psychotherapy: Theory, Research, and Practice, 11,* 175–178.

Luiselli, J. K. (1978). Treatment of an autistic child's fear of riding a school bus through exposure and reinforcement. *Journal of Behavior Therapy and Experimental Psychiatry, 9,* 169–172.

MacDonald, W. S., Gallimore, R., & MacDonald, G. (1970). Contingency counseling by school personnel: An economical model of intervention. *Journal of Applied Behavior Analysis, 3,* 175–182.

Makihara, H., Nagaya, M., & Nakajima, M. (1985). An investigation of neurotic school refusal in one parent families. *Japanese Journal of Child and Adolescent Psychiatry, 26,* 303–315.

Malmquist, C. P. (1965). School phobia: A problem in family neurosis. *Journal of Child Psychology, 6,* 293–319.

Mangan, J. A. (1994). *A significant social revolution: Cross-cultural aspects of the evolution of compulsory education.* Portland, OR: Woburn.

Mann, J. (1972). Vicarious desensitization of test anxiety through observation of videotaped treatment. *Journal of Counseling Psychology, 19,* 1–7.

Mansdorf, I. J., & Lukens, E. (1987). Cognitive–behavioral psychotherapy for separation anxious children exhibiting school phobia. *Journal of the American Academy of Child and Adolescent Psychiatry, 26,* 222–225.

March, J. (1997). *Multidimensional Anxiety Scale for Children.* North Tonawanda, NY: Multi-Health Systems.

March, J., & Albano, A. M. (1998). New developments in assessing pediatric anxiety disorders. In T. Ollendick & R. Prinz (Eds.), *Advances in clinical child psychology* (Vol. 20, pp. 213–242). New York: Plenum Press.

Marcus, R. F. (1997). Concordance between parent inventory and directly observed measures of attachment. *Early Childhood Development and Care, 135,* 109–117.

Marine, E. (1968). School refusal: Who should intervene? *Journal of School Psychology, 7,* 63–70.

Marks, I. M., & Mathews, A. M. (1979). Brief standard self-rating scale for phobic patients. *Behaviour Research and Therapy, 17,* 263–267.

Martin, C., Cabrol, S., Bouvard, M. P., Lepine, J. P., & Mouren-Simeoni, M. C. (1999). Anxiety and depressive disorders in fathers and mothers of anxious school-refusing children. *Journal of the American Academy of Child and Adolescent Psychiatry, 38,* 916–922.

Matson, J. L. (1981). Assessment and treatment of clinical fears in mentally retarded children. *Journal of Applied Behavior Analysis, 14,* 287–294.

Matzner, F. J., Silvan, M., Silva, R. R., Weiner, J., Bendo, J., & Alpert, M. (1998). Intensive day program for psychiatrically disturbed truant adolescents. *American Journal of Orthopsychiatry, 68,* 135–141.

McAnanly, E. (1986). School phobia: The importance of prompt intervention. *Journal of School Health, 56,* 433–436.

McElwee, E. W. (1931). A study of truants and retardation. *Journal of Juvenile Research, 15,* 209–214.

McFayden-Ketchum, S. A., & Dodge, K. A. (1998). Problems in social relationships. In E. J. Mash & R. A. Barkely (Eds.), *Treatment of childhood disorders* (2nd ed., pp. 338–365). New York: Guilford Press.

McNamara, E. (1988). The self-management of school phobia: A case study. *Behavioural Psychotherapy, 16,* 217–229.

McWhirter, J. J., McWhirter, B.T ., McWhirter, A. M., & McWhirter, E. H. (1998). *At-risk youth: A comprehensive response for counselors, teachers, psychologists, and human service professionals.* Pacific Grove, CA: Brooks/Cole.

Mehta, M., & Praveenlal (1987). A multimodal behavioral approach in a case of school phobia. *Child Psychiatry Quarterly, 20,* 7–12.

Melamed, B. G., Yurcheson, R., Fleece, E. L., Hutcherson, S., & Hawes, R. (1978). Effects of film modeling on the reduction of anxiety-related behaviors in individuals varying in level or previous experience in the stress situation. *Journal of Consulting and Clinical Psychology, 46,* 1357–1367.

Melton, J. V. H. (1988). *Absolutism and the eighteenth-century origins of compulsory schooling in Prussia and Austria.* Cambridge, England: Cambridge University Press.

Mercer, M. L. (1930). School maladjustment as a factor in juvenile delinquency. *Journal of Juvenile Research, 14,* 41–42.

Messer, A. (1964). Family treatment of a school phobic child. *Archives of General Psychiatry, 11,* 548–555.

Meyer, E. A., Hagopian, L. P., & Paclawskyj, T. R. (1999). A function-based treatment for school refusal behavior using shaping and fading. *Research in Developmental Disabilities, 20,* 401–410.

Mihara, R., & Ichikawa, M. (1986). A clinical study of school refusal with special reference to the classification of family violence. *Japanese Journal of Child and Adolescent Psychiatry, 27,* 110–131.

Mikkelsen, E. J., Detlor, J., & Cohen, D. J. (1981). School avoidance and social phobia triggered by haloperidol in patients with Tourette's disorder. *American Journal of Psychiatry, 138,* 1572–1576.

Miller, D. (1986). Effects of a program of therapeutic discipline on the attitude, attendance and insight of truant adolescents. *Journal of Experimental Education, 55,* 49–53.

Miller, L. C. (1984). *Louisville Behavior Checklist manual.* Los Angeles: Western Psychological Services.

Miller, L. C., Barrett, C. L., Hampe, E., & Noble, H. (1972). Factor structure of childhood fears. *Journal of Consulting and Clinical Psychology, 39,* 264–268.

Miller, P. M. (1972). The use of visual imagery and muscle relaxation in the counterconditioning of a phobic child: A case study. *Journal of Nervous and Mental Disease, 154,* 457–460.

Millon, T., Millon, C., & Davis, R. (1994). *Millon Clinical Multiaxial Inventory–III.* Minneapolis, MN: National Computer Systems.

Mills, R. C., Dunham, R. G., & Alpert, G. P. (1988). Working with high-risk youth in prevention and early intervention programs: Toward a comprehensive wellness model. *Adolescence, 23,* 643–660.

Mitchell, J., McCauley, E., Burke, P., & Moss, S. J. (1988). Phenomenology of depression in children and adolescents. *Journal of the American Academy of Child and Adolescent Psychiatry, 27,* 12–20.

Moffitt, T. E. (1993). Adolescence-limited and life-course-persistent antisocial behavior: A developmental taxonomy. *Psychological Review, 100,* 674–701.

Montenegro, H. (1968). Severe separation anxiety in two preschool children: Successfully treated by reciprocal inhibition. *Journal of Child Psychology and Psychiatry, 9,* 93–103.

Moos, R. H., & Moos, B. S. (1986). *Family Environment Scale manual* (2nd ed.). Palo Alto, CA: Consulting Psychologists Press.

Morris, L. W., Finkelstein, C. S., & Fisher, W. R. (1976). Components of school anxiety: Developmental trends and sex differences. *Journal of Genetic Psychology, 128,* 49–57.

Mulkeen, T. A. (1994). The social and political continuity of the compulsory curriculum: The teaching of virtue in American public schools. In J. A. Mangan (Ed.), *A significant social revolution: Cross-cultural aspects of the evolution of compulsory education* (pp. 156–167). Portland, OR: Woburn.

Murphy, C. M., & Bootzin, R. R. (1973). Active and passive participation in the contact desensitization of snake fear in children. *Behavior Therapy, 4,* 203–211.

Naylor, M. W., Staskowski, M., Kenney, M. C., & King, C. A. (1994). Language disorders and learning disabilities in school-refusing adolescents. *Journal of the American Academy of Child and Adolescent Psychiatry, 33,* 1331–1337.

Neeper, R., Lahey, B. B., & Frick, P. J. (1991). *The Comprehensive Behavior Rating Scale for Children—CBRSC.* San Antonio, TX: Psychological Corporation.

Neisworth, J. T., Madle, R. A., & Goeke, K. E. (1975). "Errorless" elimination of separation anxiety: A case study. *Journal of Behavior Therapy and Experimental Psychiatry, 6,* 79–82.

Nevetsky, J. (1991). At-risk program links middle school, high school programs. *NASSP Bulletin, 75,* 45–49.

Nice, R. W. (1968). The use of sodium pentothal in the treatment of a school phobic. *Journal of Learning Disabilities, 1,* 249–255.

Nichols, K. A., & Berg, I. (1970). School phobia and self-evaluation. *Journal of Child Psychology and Psychiatry, 11,* 133–141.

Noonan, J. R., & Thibeault, R. (1974). Primary prevention in Appalachian Kentucky: Peer reinforcement of classroom attendance. *Journal of Community Psychology, 2,* 260–264.

Norvell, N., Brophy, C., & Finch, A. J. (1985). The relationship of anxiety to childhood depression. *Journal of Personality Assessment, 49,* 150–153.

O'Brien, J. (1982). School problems: School phobia and learning disabilities. *Psychiatric Clinics of North America, 5,* 297–307.

O'Connor, R. D. (1972). Relative efficacy of modeling, shaping, and the combined procedures for modification of social withdrawal. *Journal of Abnormal Psychology, 79,* 327–334.

Ohtaka, K., Wakabayashi, S., Hongyo, S., Kaneko, T., Enomoto, K., Ohi, M., Sugiyama, T., & Abe, T. (1986). A long-term follow-up study of school refusal children. *Japanese Journal of Child and Adolescent Psychiatry, 27,* 213–229.

Ollendick, D. G. (1979). Some characteristics of absentee students in grade 4. *Psychological Reports, 44,* 294.

Ollendick, T. H. (1979). Fear reduction techniques with children. In M. Hersen, R. M. Eisler, & P. M. Miller (Eds.), *Progress in behavior modification* (Vol. 8, pp. 127–168). New York: Academic Press.

Ollendick, T. H. (1983). Reliability and validity of the Revised Fear Survey Schedule for Children (FSSC–R). *Behaviour Research and Therapy, 21*, 685–692.

Ollendick, T. H., & Cerny, J. A. (1981). *Clinical behavior therapy with children.* New York: Plenum Press.

Ollendick, T. H., Hagopian, L. P., & Huntzinger, R. M. (1991). Cognitive–behavior therapy with nighttime fearful children. *Journal of Behavior Therapy and Experimental Psychiatry, 22*, 113–121.

Ollendick, T. H., & Mayer, J. A. (1984). School phobia. In S. M. Turner (Ed.), *Behavioral theories and treatment of anxiety* (pp. 367–411). New York: Plenum Press.

Olson, D. H., Bell, R., & Portner, J. (1982). *Family Adaptability and Cohesion Evaluation Scales II.* Minneapolis, MN: Life Innovations.

O'Reilly, P. P. (1971). Desensitization of a fire bell phobia. *Journal of School Psychology, 9*, 55–57.

Paccione-Dyszlewski, M. R., & Contessa-Kislus, M. A. (1987). School phobia: Identification of subtypes as a prerequisite to treatment intervention. *Adolescence, 22*, 377–384.

Partridge, J. M. (1939). Truancy. *Journal of Mental Science, 85*, 45–81.

Patterson, G. R. (1982). *Coercive family process.* Eugene, OR: Castalia.

Pearson, L. C., & Banerji, M. (1993). Effects of a ninth-grade dropout prevention program on student academic achievement, school attendance, and dropout rate. *Journal of Experimental Education, 61*, 247–256.

Perrin, S., & Last, C. G. (1992). Do childhood anxiety measures measure anxiety? *Journal of Abnormal Child Psychology, 20*, 567–578.

Phelps, L., Cox, D., & Bajorek, E. (1992). School phobia and separation anxiety: Diagnostic and treatment comparisons. *Psychology in the Schools, 29*, 384–394.

Pilkington, C. L., & Piersel, W. C. (1991). School phobia: A critical analysis of the separation anxiety theory and an alternative conceptualization. *Psychology in the Schools, 28*, 290–303.

Poznanski, E. O., Freeman, L. N., & Mokros, H. B. (1985). Children's Depression Rating Scale—Revised. *Psychopharmacology Bulletin, 4*, 979–989.

Pritchard, C., Cotton, A., & Cox, M. (1992). Truancy and illegal drug use, and knowledge of HIV infection in 932 14–16-year-old adolescents. *Journal of Adolescence, 15*, 1–17.

Pritchard, M., King, N., Tonge, B. J., Heyne, D., & Lancaster, S. (1998). Taxonomic systems for school refusal behaviour. *Behaviour Change, 15*, 74–86.

Puig-Antich, J., Orvaschel, H., Tabrizi, M. A., & Chambers, W. (1980). The Schedule for Affective Disorders and Schizophrenia for School-aged Children–Epidemiologic version (Kiddie–SADS-E; 3rd ed.). New York: New York State Psychiatric Institute.

Quay, H. C., & Peterson, D. R. (1987). *Manual for the Revised Behavior Problem Checklist.* Unpublished manuscript, University of Miami, Miami, FL.

Rafferty, Y. (1991). Developmental and educational consequences of homelessness in children and youth. In J. H. Kryder-Coe, L. M. Salamon, & J. M. Molnar (Eds.), *Homeless children and youth: A new American dilemma* (pp. 105–139). New Brunswick, NJ: Transaction.

Rafferty, Y., & Rollins, N. (1989). *Learning in limbo: The educational deprivation of homeless children.* New York: Advocates for Children.

Rafferty, Y., & Shinn, M. (1991). The impact of homelessness on children. *American Psychologist, 46,* 1170–1179.

Rapee, R. M., Barrett, P. M., Dadds, M. R., & Evans, L. (1994). Reliability of the DSM–III–R childhood anxiety disorders using structured interview: Interrater and parent–child agreement. *Journal of the American Academy of Child and Adolescent Psychiatry, 33,* 984–992.

Raskind, L. T., & Nagle, R. J. (1980). Modeling effects on the intelligent test performance of test-anxious children. *Psychology in the Schools, 17,* 351–355.

Reid, K. (1982). Retrospection and persistent school absenteeism. *Educational Research, 25,* 110–115.

Reid, K. (1984). The behaviour of persistent school absentees. *British Journal of Educational Psychology, 54,* 320–330.

Reyes, O., & Hedeker, D. (1993). Identifying high-risk students during school transition. *Prevention in Human Services, 10,* 137–150.

Reynolds, C., & Kamphaus, R. (1992). *Behavioral Assessment System for Children.* Circle Pines, MN: American Guidance Service.

Reynolds, C. R., & Paget, K. D. (1983). National normative and reliability data for the revised Children's Manifest Anxiety Scale. *School Psychology Review, 12,* 324–336.

Reynolds, W. M. (1986). *Reynolds Adolescent Depression Scale.* Odessa, FL: Psychological Assessment Resources.

Reynolds, W. M. (1989). *Reynolds Child Depression Scale.* Odessa, FL: Psychological Assessment Resources.

Reynolds, W. M., & Kobak, K. A. (1995). *Hamilton Depression Inventory: A self-report version of the Hamilton Depression Rating Scale.* Odessa, FL: Psychological Assessment Resources.

Rhine, W. R., & Spencer, L. M. (1975). Effects of follow through on school fearfulness among black children. *Journal of Negro Education, 44,* 446–453.

Ribordy, S. C., Tracy, R. J., & Bernotas, T. D. (1981). The effects of an attentional training procedure on the performance of high and low test-anxious children. *Cognitive Therapy and Research, 5,* 19–28.

Rines, W. B. (1973). Behavior therapy before institutionalization. *Psychotherapy: Theory, Research and Practice, 10,* 281–283.

Roberts, R. E., Attkisson, C. C., & Rosenblatt, A. (1998). Prevalence of psychopathology among children and adolescents. *American Journal of Psychiatry, 155,* 715–725.

Robins, L. N., & Ratcliff, K. S. (1980). The long-term outcome of truancy. In L. Hersov & I. Berg (Eds.), *Out of school* (pp. 65–83). New York: Wiley.

Rodriguez, A., Rodriguez, M., & Eisenberg, L. (1959). The outcome of school phobia: A follow-up study based on 41 cases. *American Journal of Psychiatry*, *116*, 540–544.

Rogers, D. C. (1980). Stepping up school attendance. *NASSP Bulletin*, *64*, 122–124.

Ronan, K. R., Kendall, P. C., & Rowe, M. (1994). Negative affectivity in children: Development and validation of a self-statement questionnaire. *Cognitive Therapy and Research*, *18*, 509–528.

Rood, R. E. (1989). Advice for administrators: Writing the attendance policy. *NASSP Bulletin*, *73*, 21–25.

Roundtree, G. A., Grenier, C. E., & Hoffman, V. L. (1993). Parental assessment of behavioral change after children's participation in a delinquency prevention program. *Journal of Offender Rehabilitation*, *19*, 113–130.

Rousmaniere, K., Dehli, K., & de Coninck-Smith, N. (1997). *Discipline, moral regulation, and schooling: A social history*. New York: Garland.

Rubenstein, J. S., & Hastings, E. M. (1980). School refusal in adolescence: Understanding the symptom. *Adolescence*, *15*, 775–782.

Sarason, I. G., & Sarason, B. R. (1981). Teaching cognitive and social skills to high school students. *Journal of Consulting and Clinical Psychology*, *49*, 908–918.

Sarason, S. B., Davidson, K. S., Lighthall, F. F., Waite, R. R., & Ruebush, B. K. (1960). *Anxiety and elementary school children*. New York: Wiley.

Schloss, P. J., Kane, M. S., & Miller, S. (1981). Truancy intervention with behavior disordered adolescents. *Behavioral Disorders*, *6*, 175–179.

Schultz, R. M. (1987). Truancy: Issues and interventions. *Behavioral Disorders*, *12*, 117–130.

Scott, J., Cully, M., & Weissberg, E. (1995). Helping the separation anxious school refuser. *Elementary School Guidance and Counseling*, *29*, 289–296.

Seaborne, M. (1970). The historical background. In J. W. Tibble (Ed.), *The extra year: The raising of the school leaving age* (pp. 9–19). London: Routledge & Kegan Paul.

Seitz, V., & Apfel, N. H. (1993). Adolescent mothers and repeated childbearing: Effects of a school-based intervention program. *American Journal of Orthopsychiatry*, *63*, 572–581.

Seitz, V., & Apfel, N. H. (1999). Effective interventions for adolescent mothers. *Clinical Psychology: Science and Practice*, *6*, 50–66.

Shaffer, D. (1974). Suicide in children and early adolescence. *Journal of Child Psychology and Psychiatry*, *15*, 275–291.

Shaffer, D., Fisher, P., Dulcan, M. K., Davies, M., Piacentini, J., Schwab-Stone, M. E., Lahey, B. B., Bourdon, K., Jensen, P. S., Bird, H. R., Canino, G., & Regier, D. A. (1996). The NIMH Diagnostic Interview Schedule for Children Version 2.3 (DISC 2.3): Description, acceptability, prevalence rates, and performance in the MECA study. *Journal of the American Academy of Child and Adolescent Psychiatry, 35,* 865–878.

Shapiro, T., & Jegede, R. O. (1973). School phobia: A babel of tongues. *Journal of Autism and Childhood Schizophrenia, 3,* 168–186.

Shelton, K. K., Frick, P. J., & Wootton, J. (1996). Assessment of parenting practices in families of elementary school-age children. *Journal of Clinical Child Psychology, 25,* 317–329.

Sherman, J., & Formanek, R. (1985). School phobia in a multiphobic family: The family that phobes together. . . *Child and Adolescent Social Work, 2,* 114–124.

Silove, D., & Manicavasagar, V. (1993). Adults who feared school: Is early separation anxiety specific to the pathogenesis of panic disorder? *Acta Psychiatrica Scandanavia, 88,* 385–390.

Silverman, W. K., & Albano, A. M. (1996). *The Anxiety Disorders Interview Schedule for Children for DSM–IV, child and parent versions.* San Antonio, TX: Psychological Corporation.

Silverman, W. K., & Eisen, A. R. (1992). Age differences in the reliability of parent and child reports of child anxious symptomatology using a structured interview. *Journal of the American Academy of Child and Adolescent Psychiatry, 31,* 117–124.

Silverman, W. K., & Kurtines, W. M. (1996). *Anxiety and phobic disorders: A pragmatic approach.* New York: Plenum Press.

Silverman, W. K., Kurtines, W. M., Ginsburg, G. S., Weems, C. F., Lumpkin, P. W., & Carmichael, D. H. (1999). Treating anxiety disorders in children with group cognitive–behavioral therapy: A randomized clinical trial. *Journal of Consulting and Clinical Psychology, 67,* 995–1003.

Silverman, W. K., Kurtines, W. M., Ginsburg, G. S., Weems, C. F., Rabian, B., & Serafini, L. T. (1999). Contingency management, self-control, and education support in the treatment of childhood phobic disorders: A randomized clinical trial. *Journal of Consulting and Clinical Psychology, 67,* 675–687.

Silverman, W. K., & Nelles, W. B. (1988). The Anxiety Disorders Interview Schedule for Children. *Journal of the American Academy of Child and Adolescent Psychiatry, 27,* 772–778.

Simeon, J. G., & Wiggins, D. M. (1995). Pharmacotherapy. In A. R. Eisen, C. A. Kearney, & C. E. Schaefer (Eds.), *Clinical handbook of anxiety disorders in children and adolescents* (pp. 550–570). Northvale, NJ: Aronson.

Sinclair, M. P., Christenson, S. L., Evelo, D. L., & Hurley, C. M. (1998). Dropout prevention for youth with disabilities: Efficacy of a sustained school engagement procedure. *Exceptional Children, 65,* 7–21.

Skinner, H. A., Steinhauer, P. D., & Santa-Barbara, J. (1983). The Family Assessment Measure. *Canadian Journal of Community Mental Health, 2,* 91–105.

Smith, R. E., & Sharpe, T. M. (1970). Treatment of a school phobia with implosive therapy. *Journal of Consulting and Clinical Psychology, 35,* 239–243.

Smith, S. L. (1970). School refusal with anxiety: A review of sixty-three cases. *Canadien Psychiatric Association Journal, 15*, 257–264.

Sommer, B. (1985). Truancy in early adolescence. *Journal of Early Adolescence, 5*, 145–160.

Sperling, M. (1967). School phobias: Classification, dynamics, and treatment. *Psychoanalytic Study of the Child, 22*, 375–401.

Spielberger, C. D. (1973). *Manual for the State–Trait Anxiety Inventory for Children*. Palo Alto, CA: Consulting Psychologists Press.

Stein, M. T. (1996). School refusal and emotional lability in a 6-year-old boy. *Developmental and Behavioral Pediatrics, 17*, 187–188.

Stewart, K., Valentine, L., & Amundson, J. (1991). The battle for definition: The problem with (the problem). *Journal of Strategic and Systematic Therapies, 10*, 21–31.

Stickney, M. I., & Miltenberger, R. G. (1998). School refusal behavior: Prevalence, characteristics, and the schools' response. *Education and Treatment of Children, 21*, 160–170.

Stine, M. D. (1990). Do your students a favor and get tough on truants. *Executive Educator, 12*, 12–13.

Stuart, R. B. (1971). Behavioral contracting within the families of delinquents. *Journal of Behavior Therapy and Experimental Psychiatry, 2*, 1–11.

Stuart, R. B., & Lott, L. A. (1972). Behavioral contracting with delinquents: A cautionary note. *Journal of Behavior Therapy and Experimental Psychiatry, 3*, 161–169.

Sugar, M. S., & Schrank, F. A. (1979). Mild school refusal. *Elementary School Guidance and Counseling, 13*, 66–72.

Suttenfield, V. (1954). School phobia: A study of five cases. *American Journal of Orthopsychiatry, 24*, 368–380.

Tahmisian, J. A., & McReynolds, W. T. (1971). Use of parents as behavioral engineers in the treatment of a school-phobic girl. *Journal of Counseling Psychology, 18*, 225–228.

Talbot, M. (1957). Panic in school phobia. *American Journal of Orthopsychiatry, 27*, 286–295.

Taylor, L., & Adelman, H. S. (1990). School avoidance behavior: Motivational bases and implications for intervention. *Child Psychiatry and Human Development, 20*, 219–233.

Tennent, T. G. (1969). *School non-attendance and delinquency*. Unpublished master's thesis, University of Oxford, Oxford, England.

Tennent, T. G. (1971). The use of remand on bail or in custody by the London juvenile courts—A comparative study. *British Journal of Criminology, 11*, 80–85.

Thompson, J. (1948). Children's fears in relation to school attendance. *Bulletin of the National Association of School Social Workers, 24*(1).

Thyer, B. A., & Sowers-Hoag, K. M. (1988). Behavior therapy for separation anxiety disorder. *Behavior Modification, 12*, 205–233.

Tiihonen, J., Lepola, U., & Kuikka, J. (1997). Benzodiazepine receptor uptake in a patient with panic disorder after citalopram treatment. *Neuropsychiatry, Neuropsychology, and Behavioral Neurology, 10*, 260–262.

Tillotson, C. A., & Kearney, C. A. (1998, April). *Predicting subtypes of youngsters with school refusal behavior*. Paper presented at the joint meeting of the Western Psychological Association and the Rocky Mountain Psychological Association, Albuquerque, NM.

Timberlake, E. M. (1984). Psychosocial functioning of school phobics at follow-up. *Social Work Research and Abstracts, 20*, 13–18.

Tisher, M., & Lang, M. (1983). The Children's Depression Scale: Review and further developments. In D. P. Cantwell & G. A. Carlson (Eds.), *Affective disorders in childhood and adolescence: An update* (pp. 181–202). New York: Spectrum.

Tomoda, A., Miike, T., Yonamine, K., Adachi, K., & Shiraishi, S. (1997). Disturbed circadian core body temperature rhythm and sleep disturbance in school refusal children and adolescents. *Society of Biological Psychiatry, 41*, 810–813.

Tonge, B. J. (1998). Pharmacotherapy for school refusal. *Behaviour Change, 15*, 98–106.

Torma, S., & Halsti, A. (1975). Factors contributing to school refusal and truancy. *Psychiatria Fennica, 76*, 121–133.

Trueman, D. (1984). What are the characteristics of school phobic children? *Psychological Reports, 54*, 191–202.

Truox, T. (1985). *Student absenteeism: Explanations, problems, and possible solutions*. Unpublished manuscript, Indiana University, South Bend.

Tuck, K. D., & Shimburi, F. N. (1988). *An evaluation of the truancy prevention plan*. Washington, DC: District of Columbia Public Schools.

Twaite, J. A., Silitsky, D., & Luchow, A. K. (1998). *Children of divorce: Adjustment, parental conflict, custody, remarriage, and recommendations for clinicians*. Northvale, NJ: Aronson.

Tyerman, M. J. (1968). *Truancy*. London: University of London Press.

United Nations Educational, Scientific, and Cultural Organization. (1962). *Compulsory education in Australia*. Paris, France: Author.

Vaal, J. J. (1973). Applying contingency contracting to a school phobic: A case study. *Journal of Behavior Therapy and Experimental Psychiatry, 4*, 371–373.

Valla, J., Bergeron, L., & Smolla, N. (2000). The Dominic–R: A pictorial interview for 6- to 11-year-old children. *Journal of the American Academy of Child and Adolescent Psychiatry, 39*, 85–93.

Valles, E., & Oddy, M. (1984). The influence of a return to school on the long-term adjustment of school refusers. *Journal of Adolescence, 7*, 35–44.

van der Ploeg-Stapert, J. D., & van der Ploeg, H. M. (1986). Behavioral group treatment of test anxiety: An evaluation study. *Journal of Behavior Therapy and Experimental Psychiatry, 17*, 255–259.

Van Houten, J. (1948). Mother and child relationships in 12 cases of school phobia. *Smith College Studies in Social Work, 18,* 161–180.

Vasey, M. W. (1995). Social anxiety disorders. In A. R. Eisen, C. A. Kearney, & C. E. Schaefer (Eds.), *Clinical handbook of anxiety disorders in children and adolescents* (pp. 131–168). Northvale, NJ: Aronson.

Wade, B. (1979). School refusal and aspects of language. *Educational Review, 31,* 19–26.

Waldfogel, S., Coolidge, J. C., & Hahn, P. B. (1957). The development, meaning, and management of school phobia. *American Journal of Orthopsychiatry, 27,* 754–780.

Waldron, S., Shrier, D. K., Stone, B., & Tobin, F. (1975). School phobia and other childhood neuroses: A systematic study of the children and their families. *American Journal of Psychiatry, 132,* 802–808.

Wallerstein, J. S. (1987). Children of divorce: Report of a ten-year follow-up of early latency-age children. *American Journal of Orthopsychiatry, 57,* 199–211.

Wallinga, J. V. (1959). Separation anxiety. *Lancet, 79,* 258–260.

Want, J. H. (1983). School-based intervention strategies for school phobia: A ten-step "common sense" approach. *Pointer, 27,* 27–32.

Warnecke, R. (1964). School phobia and its treatment. *British Journal of Medical Psychology, 37,* 71–79.

Warren, W. (1948). Acute neurotic breakdown in children with refusal to go to school. *Archives of Disease in Childhood, 23,* 266–272.

Warren, W. (1960). Some relationships between the psychiatry of children and adults. *Journal of Mental Science, 106,* 818–820.

Wataru, K. (1990). School phobia. *Japan Quarterly, 37,* 298–303.

Watson, D., & Clark, L. A. (1984). Negative affectivity: The disposition to experience aversive emotional states. *Psychological Bulletin, 96,* 455–490.

Watters, J. (1989). School refusal: Usually mild but sometimes severe. *British Medical Journal, 298,* 66–67.

Weinberg, W., Emslie, G., & Wilkes, C. (1986). Depression in school phobia. *British Journal of Psychiatry, 148,* 335.

Weinberger, G., Leventhal, T., & Beckman, G. (1973). The management of a chronic school phobic through the use of consultation with school personnel. *Psychology in the Schools, 10,* 83–88.

Weiss, M., & Burke, A. G. (1967). A five to ten-year follow-up of hospitalized school phobic children and adolescents. *American Journal of Orthopsychiatry, 37,* 294–295.

Weiss, M., & Cain, B. (1964). The residential treatment of children and adolescents with school phobia. *American Journal of Orthopsychiatry, 34,* 103–114.

Weller, E. B., Weller, R. A., Fristad, M. A., Rooney, M. T., & Schecter, J. (2000). Children's Interview for Psychiatric Syndromes (ChIPS). *Journal of the American Academy of Child and Adolescent Psychiatry, 39,* 76–84.

Werry, J. S., & Aman, M. G. (1999). *Practitioner's guide to psychoactive drugs for children and adolescents* (2nd ed.). New York: Plenum Press.

Wetchler, J. L. (1986). Family therapy of school-focused problems: A macrosystemic perspective. *Contemporary Family Therapy, 8,* 224–240.

Will, D., & Baird, D. (1984). An integrated approach to dysfunction in interprofessional systems. *Journal of Family Therapy, 6,* 275–290.

Williams, H. D. (1927). Truancy and delinquency. *Journal of Applied Psychology, 11,* 276–288.

Wilson, N. H., & Rotter, J. D. (1986). Anxiety management training and study skills counseling for students on self-esteem and test anxiety and performance. *The School Counselor, 9,* 18–31.

Wolpe, J. (1969). *The practice of behavior therapy.* New York: Pergamon Press.

Woolston, J. L., Rosenthal, S. L., Riddle, M. A., Sparrow, S. S., Cicchetti, D., & Zimmerman, L. D. (1989). Childhood comorbidity of anxiety/affective disorders and behavior disorders. *Journal of the American Academy of Child and Adolescent Psychiatry, 28,* 707–713.

World Health Organization. (1992). *International classification of diseases* (10th ed.). Geneva, Switzerland: Author.

Young, J. G., Brasic, J. R., Kisnadwala, H., & Leven, L. (1990). Strategies for research on school refusal and related nonattendance at school. In C. Chiland & J. G. Young (Eds.), *Why children reject school: Views from seven countries* (pp. 199–223). New Haven, CT: Yale University Press.

Zieman, G. L., & Benson, G. P. (1981). School perceptions of truant adolescent girls. *Behavioral Disorders, 6,* 197–205.

AUTHOR INDEX

Numbers in italics refer to listings in reference sections.

Cox, D., 23, *235*
Cox, M., 43, *235*
Cradock, C., 152, *218*
Creer, T. L., 4, *218*
Cretekos, C. J. G., 183, *218*
Crimmins, D. B., 113, *220*
Crimmins, D. E., 152, *221*
Croghan, L. M., 137, *219*
Crosby, R. D., 40, 110, *215, 216*
Crumley, F. M., 183, *219*
Cully, M., 202, *237*
Cunningham, P .B., 57, *224*
Cwayna, K., 30, *219*
Cyr, J. J., 20, 40, 68, *212*
Cytryn, L., 102, *225*

daCosta, G. A., 30, 213
Dadds, M. R., 103, *236*
Daleiden, E. L., 120, *219*
Dalicandro, T., 197, *218*
D'Amato, G., 135, *219*
D'Amico, R. J., 32, *219*
Davenport, M. G., 4, *221*
Davidson, K. S., 110, *237*
Davidson, S., 15, 40, *219*
Davidson, W. S., 200, *219*
Davies, M., 108, *226, 237*
Davis, R., 112, *233*
Davison, G. C., 15, 68, 137, *230*
Dayton, N., 12, *219*
de Coninck-Smith, N., 9, *237*
De Sousa, A., 41, *219*
De Sousa, D. A., 41, *219*
DeGiovanni, I. S., 69, *223*
Dehli, K., 9, *237*
deJung, J., 27, *220*
Dennison, C., 31, *219*
Denno, D. W., 200, *219*
Derdeyn, A., 166, *231*
Derogatis, L. R., 112, *219*
Detlor, J., 136, *233*
Detweiler, M. F., 151, *212*
Dodge, K. A., 152, 153, *232*
Doleys, D. M., 166, *219*
Doll, E. A., 12, *219*
Donovan, J. E., *218*
Doris, J., 112, *219*
Dornbusch, S. M., 32, *217*
Dover, S. J., 38, *221*
Drabman, R. S., 90, 108, 120, *219, 227*

Draguns, J. G., 65, *216*
DuBois, D. L., *221*
Duckworth, K., 27, 182, *220*
Duffy, J. H., 135, *229*
Dulcan, M. K., *237*
Dunham, R. G., 197, *233*
Durand, V. M., 113, *220*
Duyx, J. H. M, 49, *217*
Dynlacht, D., 26, 182, *213*

Echterling, L. G., 201, *220*
Edelbrock, C. S., 19, 76, *211*
Edwards, B., 140, *218*
Eisen, A. R., 37, 40, 56, 103, 109, 112,
    126, 137, *220, 227, 238*
Eisenberg, L., 15, 28, 29, 32–33, 38, 39,
    41, 55, *220, 237*
Elliot, J. G., 69, *220*
Emery, G., 83, 112, 156, *213*
Emslie, G., 81, 136, *220, 241*
Endicott, J., 102, *220*
Enomoto, K., *234*
Epstein, A. S., 201, *216*
Epstein, N., 112, *213*
Ernst, M., 102, *220*
Estes, H. R., 14, *220*
Esveldt-Dawson, K., 152, *220*
Evans, L., 103, *236*
Evans, L. D., 194, *220*
Evelo, D. L., 201, *238*
Evers, W. L., 152, *220*
Eyberg, S. M., 111, 166, *220, 221*

Falstein, E. I., 13, 36, 60, *225*
Famularo, R., 30, *221*
Farrington, D. P., 49, *221*
Feeney, B., 46, *218*
Feldman, L., 28, 34, *223*
Feldman, S. S., 109, *226*
Fenton, T., 30, *221*
Field, J. C., 6, *221*
Fielding, D., 140, *214*
Finch, A. J., 41, *234*
Finkelstein, C. S., 33, 110, *234*
Fisher, P., *237*
Fisher, W. R., 33, 110, *234*
Flakierska, N., 48, *221*
Flannery-Schroeder, E., 137, 138, *228*
Fleece, E. L., 124, *233*

Flner, R. D., 201, *221*
Flowers, N., *221*
Fogelman, K., 26, 49, *224*
Ford, M. E., 109, *226*
Forehand, R., 120, 168, 182, *212, 221*
Foreman, D. M., 38, *221*
Formanek, R., 183, *238*
Forrest, D. V., 38, *218*
Foster, J., 78, *216*
Fowler, A., 140, *221*
Fowler, M. G., 4, *221*
Fox, J. E., 110, 152, *221*
Frances, A., 135, *221*
Francis, G., 33–35, 37, 38, 40, 54, 83,
    102, 153, *230*
Franco, D. P., 152, *221*
Franco, N., 139, *230*
Franklin, J., *214*
Fraser, M. W., 202, *221*
Freeman, L. N., 108, *235*
Frick, P. J., 57, 111, 112, *222, 234, 238*
Frick, W. B., 34, 50, *222*
Friesen, M., 23, *222*
Fristad, M. A., 102, *241*
Frommer, E. A., 135, *222*
Fukuda, K., *225*

Gadow, K. D., 111, *222*
Gallimore, R., 183, *231*
Galloway, D., 9, 10, 34, 63, *222*
Gammon, G. D., 136, *222*
Garfinkel, B. D., 34, 35, 38, 40, 43, 44,
    54, 66, 74, 82, 83, 110, 136, *215*
Garg, R., 4, *221*
Garland, E. J., 136, *222*
Garside, R. F., *215*
Garvey, W. P., 15, 68, 137, *222*
Gelfand, D. M., 28, 34, *223*
George, F. E., 201, *217*
Giesler, J., 40, *216*
Gillberg, C., 48, *221*
Gingras, R. C., 197, *222*
Ginsburg, G. S., 137, *238*
Gittelman-Klein, R., 74, 136, *222*
Glass, C. R., 110, *226*
Gleeson, D., 9, *222*
Goeke, K. E., 167, *234*
Goldberg, C., 71, *222*
Goldberg, T. B., 32, 44–45, *222*
Goldenberg, H., 38, *222*

Goldenberg, I., 38, *222*
Gorman, K. S., 49, *222*
Gottfredson, G. D., 201, *222*
Gottfried, A. E., 32, *222*
Gottfried, A. W, 32, *222*
Grala, C., 182, *223*
Granell de Aldaz, E., 28, 34, 37, *223*
Gray, G., 49, *223*
Graziano, A. M., 69, *223*
Gredler, G. R., 36, *229*
Green, D. R., 183, *228*
Greenberg, R. L., 156, *213*
Grenier, C. E., 200, *237*
Gresham, F. M., 140, *223*
Griffin, W. A., 183, *223*
Grindler, M., 152, *223*
Gruber, C. P., 111, *229*
Guerney, B., 166, *223*
Guerney, L., 166, *223*
Gullone, E., 41, 109, 137, *223, 228*

Hagopian, L. P., 166, *223, 233, 235*
Hahn, P. B., 14, 15, 36, 38, 70, *218, 241*
Hall, G., 47, *214*
Hall, R. V., 140, *217*
Hall, T. W., 112, *223*
Halsti, A., 32–34, 40, 43, 44, 53, 55, 63,
    64, 68, *240*
Hammen, C., 29, 56, *223*
Hampe, E., 45, 109, *233*
Hansen, C., 33, 34, 35, 37, 74, 139, *224,
    230*
Hargett, M. Q., 149, *224*
Harris, K. R., 152, *224*
Harris, S. R., 140, *224*
Hart, J. T., 135, *229*
Hartmann, D. P., 112, *213*
Harvey, A., 32, *224*
Hastings, E. M., 44, 66, *237*
Hathaway, S. R., 112, *224*
Haurin, R. J., 32, *219*
Hawes, R., 124, *233*
Hawkins, J. D., 202, *221*
Hayes, H., *214*
Haylett, C. H., 14, *220*
Hayward, C., 39, *224*
Healy, W., 12, *224*
Hedeker, D., 201, *236*
Hegrenes, J. R., 15, 68, 137, *222*
Heimberg, R. G., 97, 152, 167, *212, 218*

Henggeler, S. W., 57, *224*
Henin, A., *228*
Herjanic, B., 83, 102, *224*
Hersen, M., 33, 166, *224, 230*
Hersov, L., 4, 27, 33, 34, 37–40, 42, 43, 45, 50, 55, 62–66, 68, 75, *224*
Heyne, D., 69, 138, *229, 235*
Hibbet, A., 26, 49, *224*
Higgins, P. S., 201, *224*
Hill, A. B., 38, *221*
Hinshaw, S. P., 29, 57, 80, *225*
Hitchcock, A. B., 36, *225*
Hodges, K., 102, *225*
Hoffman, V. L., 200, *237*
Holcomb, W. R., 42, *226*
Holt, C. S., 152, *212*
Hongyo, S., *234*
Honjo, S., 29, *225*
Honma, H., 52, *225*
Hood, J. E., 30, *213*
Houston, B. K., 110, 152, *221*
Howard, M. O., 202, *221*
Howell, C., 111, *211*
Hsia, H., 183, *225*
Huddleston, C. M., 183, *217*
Huey, W. P., 45, *211*
Huffington, C. M., 102, *225*
Hugelshofer, D. S., 5, 200, 202, *227*
Hughes, C. W., *220*
Huguet, E., 11, *225*
Hullin, R., 9, 67, *214*
Huntzinger, R. M., 166, *235*
Hurley, C. M., 201, *238*
Hutcherson, S., 124, *233*

Ichikawa, M., 52, *233*
Iwamoto, S., 29, *225*
Iwatani, N., 44, *225*

Jackson, A., 47, *215*
Jackson, B., 152, *231*
Jacob, R. G., *218*
Jacobsen, V., 45, *225*
Janosz, M., 197, *225*
Jarvis, V., 45, *225*
Jason, L. A., 152, *218*
Jeans, J., *215*
Jegede, R. O., 16, 17, 72, 75, *238*
Jenkins, P. H., 197, *225*

Jensen, P. S., *237*
Johnson, A. M., 13–15, 20, 36, 38, 50, 55, 60, 61, 68, 74, 75, *220, 225*
Johnson, R. L., 110, *226*
Johnson, T., 152, *226*
Jones, B. A., 200, *226*
Jones, E., 152, *226*
Jyodoi, T., *225*

Kahn, J. H., 5, 15, 29, 68, *226*
Kakar, S., 30, *226*
Kal, Y., *225*
Kamphaus, R., 111, *236*
Kandal, H. J., 152, *226*
Kandel, D. B., 49, 108, *226*
Kandel, P. I., 49, *226*
Kane, M. S., 182, *237*
Kane, M. T., *228*
Kaneko, T., *234*
Kanner, A., 136, 166, *229*
Kanner, A. D., 109, *226*
Kasahara, Y., 29, *225*
Kashani, J. H., 42, 66, *226*
Kaye, B., *215*
Kazdin, A. E., 33, 152, *220, 230*
Kearney, C. A., 5, 17, 18, 29, 33–35, 37–45, 52, 56, 58, 66, 67, 73–75, 80, 81, 83–85, 88–92, 94–97, 101, 103, 108, 109, 112, 113, 117, 120, 124–126, 136, 139, 157, 167, 174, 200, 202, 204, *220, 226, 227, 240*
Keller, M. F., 152, *228*
Kelley, C. K., 124, *228*
Kelly, F. W., 41, *228*
Kelly, J. A., 152, *221*
Kelsey, C., 112, *219*
Kendall, P. C., 41, 109, 137, 138, 153, 155, 158, 166, 204, *228, 237*
Kennedy, W. A., 16, 28, 70–72, 74, 78, 174, *228*
Kenney, M. C., 45, *234*
Kern, R. M., 183, *212*
Kifer, R. E., 183, *228*
Kim, R. S., *228*
King, C. A., 45, *234*
King, H. E., 32, *228*
King, N., 36, 41, 69, 109, 126, 136, 137, 138, *223, 228, 229, 235*
Kinscherff, R., 30, *221*

Kirisci, L., *218*
Kirkpatrick, M. E., 12, *229*
Kisnadwala, H., 19, 76, 87, *242*
Klein, D. F., 74, 136, *222*
Klein, E., 38, *229*
Klein, R. G., 136, 166, *229*
Kline, J., 102, *225*
Kline, L. W., 11, 12, *229*
Klungness, L., 36, *229*
Knox, P., 140, 167, *229*
Kobak, K. A., 112, *236*
Kodama, M., *225*
Kolko, D. J., 140, *229*
Kollins, S. H., 120, *219*
Kolvin, I., 20, 40, 75, 77, 78, 80, *215,*
    229
Koplewicz, H. S., 136, 166, *229*
Koponen, H., 136, *231*
Kortering, L. J., 197, *229*
Kortlander, E., 41, *228*
Kotin, L., 9, 10, *229*
Kovacs, M., 90, 108, *229*
Kowatch, R. A., *220*
Kraft, I. A., 135, *229*
Kuikka, J., 136, *240*
Kurita, H., 44, *229*
Kurtines, W. M., 137, 155, *238*

La Greca, A. M., 110, *230*
Lachar, D., 111, *229*
Lahey, B. B., 111, *234, 237*
Lall, B. M., 38, *230*
Lall, G. R., 38, *230*
Lambert, M. C., 80, *230*
Lancaster, S., 69, *235*
Lang, M., 108, *240*
Lang, P. J., 120, 124, *230*
Last, C. G., 33–35, 37–40, 54, 74, 82–
    84, 102, 110, 139, 153, *224, 230,*
    235
Lawlor, E. D., 140, *230*
Lazarus, A. A., 15, 68, 137, *230*
Lazovik, A. D., 120, 124, *230*
Leal, L. L., 152, *230*
LeBlanc, M., 197, *225*
Lederer, A. S., 124, *213*
Lee, M. I., 106, *230*
Lehman, E., 112, *219*
Leinonen, E., 136, *231*
Leitenberg, H., 109, *231*

Lepine, J. P., 54, *232*
Lepola, U., 136, *231, 240*
Lerner, J. V., 32, *231*
LeRoy, J. B., 166, *231*
Leton, D. A., 39, 45, *231*
LeUnes, A., 140, *231*
Levanto, J., 34, *231*
Leven, L., 19, 76, 87, *242*
Leventhal, T., 39, 45, 140, *231, 241*
Levine, R. S., 34, 197, *231*
Lewis, M. A., 183, *228*
Lichtenstein, E., 202, *217*
Lighthall, F. F., 110, *237*
Lindstrom, M., 48, *221*
Linet, L. S., 44, *231*
Lippman, H. S., 12, *231*
Little, S., 152, *231*
Lizardi, A., 67, *216*
Lodge, T., 12, *229*
Logsdon-Conradsen, S., 151, *212*
Lott, L. A., 183, *239*
Lucas, C., *214*
Luchow, A. K., 32, *240*
Luiselli, J. K., 137, *231*
Lukens, E., 166, *232*
Lumpkin, P. W., 137, *238*

Mabe, H., *225*
Maccoby, E. E., 32, *217*
MacDonald, G., 183, *231*
MacDonald, W. S., 183, *231*
Madle, R. A., 167, *234*
Makihara, H., 33, 53, *231*
Malmquist, C. P., 183, *231*
Mangan, J. A., 9, *232*
Manicavasagar, V., 49, *238*
Mann, J., 152, *232*
Manor, O., 49, *224*
Mansdorf, I. J., 166, *232*
March, J., 109, *232*
Marcus, R. F., 112, *232*
Marine, E., 16, 71, *232*
Marks, I. M., 112, *232*
Marlatt, G. A., 202, *217*
Marten, P. A., 152, *212*
Martin, C., 54, *232*
Martin, J., 152, *230*
Marx, R. W., 152, *230*
Massaro, S., 33, 74, *224*
Massie, E. D., 52, 111, *215*

Pearce, P., 135, *229*
Pearson, L. C., 201, *235*
Peck, A. L., 15, 38, 70, *218*
Perrin, S., 110, *235*
Perwien, A. R., 110, *215*
Peterson, D. R., 111, *235*
Petti, T. A., 135, *221*
Phelps, L., 23, *235*
Phillips, E. L., 183, *228*
Piacentini, J., *237*
Piersel, W. C., 167, *235*
Pilkington, C. L., 167, *235*
Polefka, D. A., 15, 68, 137, *230*
Pollitt, E., 49, *222*
Portner, J., 111, *235*
Poznanski, E. O., 108, *235*
Praveenlal, 137, *232*
Pritchard, C., 16, 41, 43, 53, 137, *215,*
    235
Pritchard, M., 69, *229, 235*
Puig-Antich, J., 83, 102, *235*

Quarrington, B., 20, 40, 68, *212*
Quay, H. C., 111, *211, 235*

Rabian, B., 137, *238*
Rafferty, Y., 30, *236*
Rankin, E., 31, *213*
Rapee, R. M., 103, *236*
Raskind, L. T., 152, *236*
Ratcliff, K. S., 49, *237*
Raveis, V. H., 49, *226*
Regier, D. A., *237*
Reid, K., 35, 53, *236*
Renne, C. M., 4, *218*
Reyes, O., 201, *236*
Reynolds, C., 83, 90, 109, 111, *236*
Reynolds, W. M., 108, 112, *236*
Rhine, W. R., 35, *236*
Ribordy, S. C., 152, *236*
Rickel, A. U., 31, *213*
Riddle, M. A., *242*
Rines, W. B., 166, *236*
Rintelmann, J., *220*
Robbins, D. R., 136, *216*
Roberts, R. E., 29, *236*
Robins, L. N., 49, *237*
Robinson, M. J., 200, *219*
Rodriguez, A., 32–33, 45, 46, *237*

Rodriguez, M., 32–33, *237*
Rogers, D. C., 182, *237*
Rogers, M., 166, *212*
Rollins, N., 30, *236*
Ronan, K. R., 109, 228, *237*
Rood, R. E., 33, 34, *237*
Rooney, M. T., 102, *241*
Rosen, L. A., 26, 182, *213*
Rosenbaum, M. S., 152, *226*
Rosenblatt, A., 29, *236*
Rosenthal, S. L., *242*
Rotter, J. D., 152, *242*
Roundtree, G. A., 200, *237*
Rousmaniere, K., 9, *237*
Rowe, M., 109, *237*
Rowland, M. D., 57, *224*
Rubenstein, J. S., 44, 66, *237*
Rudolph, K. D., 29, 56, *223*
Ruebush, B. K., 110, *237*
Ruijters, A. M., 26, *216*
Rush, A. J., 83, 112, 156, *213, 220*
Rutter, M., 49, 66, *217, 223*
Ryan, B. A., 197, *218*

Sanders, S. L., 33, 74, *224*
Santa-Barbara, J., 51, 83, 112, *238*
Sarason, B. R., 201, *237*
Sarason, I. G., 201, *237*
Sarason, S. B., 110, *237*
Sartain, B., *221*
Scarth, L., *215*
Schaefer, C. E., 165, 166, *216*
Schecter, J., 102, *241*
Schloss, P. J., 182, *237*
Schoenwald, S. K., 57, *224*
Schrank, F. A., 140, *239*
Schultz, R. M., 182, *237*
Schwab-Stone, M. E., *237*
Schwarz, J. C., 152, *220*
Schweinhart, L. J., 201, *216*
Scott, J., 202, *237*
Seaborne, M., 9, *237*
Seitz, V., 31, *237*
Serafini, L. T., 137, *238*
Sessa, F. M., *228*
Sevitt, M. A., 102, *225*
Shaffer, D., 40, 102, *237*
Shapiro, T., 16, 17, 72, 75, *238*
Sharpe, T. M., 137, *238*
Shaw, B. F., 83, 112, 156, *213*

Shelton, K. K., 112, *238*
Sherman, J., 183, *238*
Shimburi, F. N., 182, *240*
Shinn, M., 30, *236*
Shiraishi, S., 44, *240*
Shrier, D. K., 37, *241*
Siemsglusz, S., 140, *231*
Silitsky, D., 32, *240*
Sills, M., 39, 45, *231*
Silove, D., 49, *238*
Silva, P. A., 66, *212*
Silva, R. R., *232*
Silvan, M., *232*
Silverman, W. K., 7, 17, 33, 34, 37–41,
43–45, 52, 58, 66, 67, 73, 80, 81,
83–85, 88, 91, 92, 94, 96, 97,
103, 109, 112, 113, 120, 124,
125, 136, 137, 139, 155, 167,
217, 220, 227, 238
Simeon, J. G., 136, *238*
Sims, K. E., 84, 85, 101, *227*
Sims, R., *214*
Sinclair, M. P., 201, *238*
Siqueland, L., *228*
Skinner, H. A., 51, 83, 112, *238*
Slifer, K. J., 166, *223*
Smith, A., 49, *223*
Smith, D., 166, *212*
Smith, D. H., 136, *222*
Smith, S. E., 137, *238*
Smith, S. L., 33, 37, 40, 45, 53, 55,
239
Smolla, N., 102, *240*
Sommer, B., 53, *239*
Southam-Gerow, M., *228*
Sowers-Hoag, K. M., 166, *239*
Sparrow, S. S., *242*
Spasaro, S. A., 112, *220*
Sperling, M., 16, 71, 75, *239*
Spielberger, C. D., 90, 110, *239*
Spitzer, R. L., 102, *220*
Spncer, L. M., 35, *236*
Sprafkin, J., 111, *222*
Sprich, S., 66, *216*
Stander, R. J., 45, *231*
Staskowski, M., 45, *234*
Stearns, R. P., 45, *231*
Steele, J. J., 135, *213*
Steer, R. A., 112, *213*
Stein, M. T., 44, *239*
Steinhauer, P. D., 51, 83, 112, *238*

Stern, L., 102, *225*
Stewart, K., 183, *239*
Stickney, M. I., 35, 39, 181, *239*
Stine, M. D., 182, *239*
Stone, B., 37, *241*
Stone, W. L., 110, *230*
Strachowski, D., 39, *224*
Strauss, C. C., 33–35, 37, 38, 40, 82, 84,
102, *230*
Stuart, R. B., 183, *239*
Sugar, M. S., 140, *239*
Sugarman, A., 137, *228*
Sugiyama, T., *234*
Suttenfield, V., 14, 36, 38, 68, *239*
Svendsen, M., 13, 36, 60, *225*
Svingen, P. H., 34, 35, 51, 53, *215*
Szurek, S. A., 13, 36, 60, *225*

Tabrizi, M. A., 83, 102, *235*
Taffel-Cohen, S., 183, *212*
Tahmisian, J. A., 166, *239*
Talbot, M., 14, 38, 39, 45, *239*
Taylor, C. B., 39, *224*
Taylor, L., 6, 31, *239*
Tennent, T. G., 66, *239*
Thesiger, C., 80, *230*
Thibeault, R., 201, *234*
Thompson, J., 33, 44, *239*
Thompson, R., 152, *226*
Thuras, P. D., 52, 111, *215*
Thyer, B. A., 166, *239*
Tiihonen, J., 136, *240*
Tillotson, C. A., 89, 92, 94–96, 113,
227, 240
Timberlake, E. M., 48, 51, 53–55, *240*
Tisher, M., 108, *240*
Tobin, F., 37, *241*
Tomoda, A., 44, *225, 240*
Tonge, B. J., 69, 136, 138, *228, 229, 235*
Torma, S., 32–34, 40, 43, 44, 53, 55, 63,
64, 68, *240*
Torrence, C., 140, *229*
Tracy, R. J., 152, *236*
Tremblay, R. E., 197, *225*
Trueman, D., 46, *240*
Truox, T., 182, *240*
Tuck, K. D., 182, *240*
Turner, S. M., 92, *213, 218*
Twaite, J. A., 32, *240*

Tyerman, M. J., 65, 66, *240*
Tyler, V., 152, *226*

Unis, A. S., 152, *220*
United Nations Educational, Scientific,
    and Cultural Organization, 9, *240*

Vaal, J. J., 183, *240*
Valentine, L., 183, *239*
Valla, J., 102, *240*
Valles, E., 48, *240*
van Andel, H., 49, *217*
van der Ploeg, H. M., 152, *240*
van der Ploeg-Stapert, J. D., 152, *240*
Van Houten, J., 45, *241*
van Strien, D. C., 49, *217*
VanBoskirk, K. A., 34, *231*
Vasey, M. W., 33, *241*
Visscher, A. J., 26, *216*
Vivas, E., 28, 34, *223*

Wade, B., 140, *241*
Waite, R. R., 110, *237*
Wakabayashi, S., *234*
Waldfogel, S., 14, 36, *241*
Waldron, S., 37, 38, 40, 44, 45, 51, 55,
    241
Wallerstein, J. S., 32, *241*
Wallinga, J. V., 33, 38, *241*
Want, J. H., 140, *241*
Warman, M., *228*
Warnecke, R., 53, *241*
Warren, S. L., 52, 61, 62, 64, 68, 111,
    215
Warren, W., 36, 46, *241*
Wataru, K., 140, *241*
Watson, D., 41, *241*
Watters, J., 17, *241*
Webster, R. E., 149, *224*

Weems, C. F., 137, *238*
Weikert, D. P., 201, *216*
Weinberg, W., 81, *241*
Weinberger, D. A., 109, *226*
Weinberger, G., 45, 140, *231*, *241*
Weiner, J., *232*
Weiss, M., 47, 140, *241*
Weissberg, E., 202, *237*
Weisz, J. R., 80, *230*
Weller, E. B., 102, *241*
Weller, R. A., 102, *241*
Werry, J. S., 137, *242*
Wetchler, J. L., 183, *242*
Wiggins, D. M., 136, *238*
Wilkes, C., 81, *241*
Will, D., 124, *242*
Williams, H. D., 11, 12, *242*
Williams, M. C., 166, *219*
Williams, S., 66, *212*
Wills, U., 40, 48, 53, 72, 73, 75, *212*
Wilson, G. T., 202, *217*
Wilson, N. H., 152, *242*
Wisner, K. L., 152, *220*
Wolpe, J., 124, 144, 158, *242*
Woolridge, R. L., 183, *217*
Woolston, J. L., 66, *242*
Wootton, J., 112, *238*
World Health Organization, 21, *242*

Yonamine, K., 44, *240*
Yoshida, K., 29, *225*
Yost, L. W., 109, *231*
Young, J. G., xi, 19, 76, 78, 80, 87, *217*,
    242
Yule, W., 137, 138, *216*
Yurcheson, R., 124, *233*

Zieman, G. L., 34, *242*
Zimmerman, L. D., *242*
Zucker, K. J., 30, *213*

SUBJECT INDEX

Avoidance of stimuli provoking negative affectivity
  age-related risk, 101
  assessment, 90–91, 106, 109, 113–118, 122, 123
  desensitization therapy, 142–146
  functional model of school refusal behavior, 89, 90–91
  psychoeducational intervention, 140–141
  somatic control exercises, 142
  use of avoidance hierarchy in treatment, 141–142
Avoidant behavior
  associated somatic complaints, 40
  See also Avoidance of stimuli provoking negative affectivity; Escape from aversive or evaluative situation

Beck Anxiety Inventory, 112
Beck Depression Inventory, 83
Biological factors, 56
Biorhythm dysfunction, 44
Birth order, 53, 73
Booster sessions, 205–206
Breathing exercises, 142

Change in life circumstances, as precipitating school refusal, 55–56
Child and Adolescent Psychiatric Assessment, 102
Child Assessment Schedule, 102
Child Behavior Checklist, 19, 76, 79–80, 90, 92, 94, 111
Child labor laws, 9–10
Child self-care, 32
Children's Depression Inventory, 90, 92, 108
Children's Interview for Psychiatric Syndromes, 102
Chronic school phobia, 17
  prevalence, 35
Chronic school refusal behavior, 17–18, 23
  vs. acute school refusal, as basis for classification, 72–75
  clinical utility, 75

definition, 73–74
  prevalence, 35
Class size, 36
Classification
  acute–chronic distinctions, 72–75
  based on truancy concepts, 60–70
  categorical models, 87
  categorical–dimensional model, 88
  clinical needs, 85
  conceptual evolution, 15, 23
  criteria for evaluating systems of, 59
  deficiencies in, 85, 87
  diagnostic subtyping methods, 82–85
  dimensional models, 87–88
  empirical subtyping of school absenteeism, 20–21, 76–81
  function based, 88–90
  neurotic–characterological distinctions, 15, 70–72, 73–75
  range of strategies, 59
  school phobia subtypes, 14–15, 16–17, 70–71
  school refusal categories, 16, 23–24
Classroom behaviors, 37
Clinical utility of classification system
  definition, 59
  diagnostic subtypes, 84
  empirical subtyping, 81
  functional model, 97–98
  truancy concepts, 67
Clomipramine, 136
Cognitive and Somatic Trait–State Anxiety Inventory, 110
Cognitive restructuring, 155–157
Cognitive–behavior therapy
  for anxiety-based school refusal behavior, 137–139
  for school refusal to escape aversive or evaluative situation, 155–157
  for social anxiety-based school refusal behavior, 151–152
Communication skills training, 189
Community issues
  predictors of school refusal, 197
  prevention strategies, 200
Complete absenteeism, 26–27
Compulsory education, 8–10
Conduct disorder, 43
  in children who refuse school to escape aversive or evaluative situation, 93

Conduct disorder, *continued*
    in children who seek tangible rein-
        forcement outside of school, 96
    definition and symptoms, 21–22
    truancy typology, 63, 66
Confidentiality, in assessment, 108
Conners Rating Scales–Parent Version
    Revised, 111
Conners Rating Scales–Teacher Version
    Revised, 111
Conners Wells' Adolescent Self-Report
    Scale, 110
Continuum of attendance, 7–8
Contracts–contracting, 182, 183, 184–
    188
Coverage of classification system
    acute–chronic distinctions, 73–74
    definition, 59
    diagnostic subtypes, 83
    empirical subtyping, 79
    neurotic–characterological-based sys-
        tems, 73, 74
    truancy concepts, 65
Cultural context, 8–10
Cutting classes, prevalence of, 27–28

Daily Life Stressors Scale, 90, 92, 94,
    108–109
Daily monitoring, 124–125
Delinquency, truancy and, 11–12, 60
Demographic characteristics
    dropout rate, 5
    school absenteeism, 32–36
Depression
    among families of children with
        school refusal, 54
    assessment, 108
    association with school refusal, 40
    in children refusing school to avoid
        stimuli provoking negative affec-
        tivity, 91
    in children who refuse school to es-
        cape aversive or evaluative situa-
        tion, 93
    empirical subtyping of school absen-
        teeism, 20–21, 77, 80–81
    in negative affectivity, 41
    school phobia–refusal subtypes, 82,
        83–84

in students who seek tangible
    reinforcement outside of school,
    96
Desensitization, 68–69
    for anxiety-based school refusal be-
        havior, 137
    imaginal, 143–144
    in vivo, 144–146
    separation anxiety treatment, 166
    for youth refusing school to avoid
        stimuli provoking negative affec-
        tivity, 142–146
Diagnostic and Statistical Manual of Mental
    Disorders, 14, 21, 69, 82, 83
Diagnostic Interview for Children and
    Adolescents, 83, 102
Diagnostic subtyping, 82–85
Diaries and logbooks, 124, 125
Direct behavioral observation
    to assess form of school refusal be-
        havior, 120–121
    to assess function of school refusal
        behavior, 121–124
    case example, 130
Discriminant validity of classification
    system
    acute–chronic distinctions, 74–75
    definition, 59
    diagnostic subtypes, 83–84
    empirical subtyping, 79–81
    neurotic–characterological-based sys-
        tems, 74
    truancy concepts, 65–67
Dispute handles, 157
Distal factors, 30–32
Divorce, 31–32
Dominic–R, 102
Dropout
    definition, 5
    demographic characteristics, 5
    predictors, 5
    statistics, 5
Duration of school refusal
    classification based on, 71–72,
        73–74
    clinical significance, 75
    extreme cases, 195
    indications for formal assessment,
        100
Duress during school attendance,
    28–29

Ego alien–ego syntonic behaviors, 17,
    72
Empirical studies
    assessment methodology, 78–79
    categories of school refusal behavior,
        20–21
    child problematic behaviors, gener-
        ally, 76–77
    goals, 76
    problematic behaviors specific to
        school refusal, 77–78
Enmeshed family, 50–51, 52
Enuresis, 43–44
    in children refusing school for atten-
        tion, 95
    in children refusing school to avoid
        stimuli provoking negative affec-
        tivity, 91
    in students who seek tangible rein-
        forcement outside of school, 96
    truancy associated, 62
Epidemiology
    demographic variables, 32–36
    dropout rate, 5
    prevalence of school refusal behav-
        ior, 25–29
Escape from aversive or evaluative situa-
        tion, 92–93, 164
    age-related risk, 101
    assessment, 106–107, 118, 122, 123–
        124
    behavioral exposure in treating,
        157–160
    cognitive restructuring, 155–157
    functional model of school refusal be-
        havior, 92–93
    psychoeducational intervention,
        153–154
    treatment case example, 161–164
    use of social–evaluative anxiety-
        avoidance hierarchy in treating,
        154–155
Escorting youth to school and classes,
        188
Etiology
    antisocial behavior, 57–58
    multifactorial, 58
    school phobia, 13–14
    school refusal behavior, 54–58
Evening routines, 171–172
Expectations, parent's, 3, 112

Exposure, behavioral, 139, 142–146,
        157–160
Externalizing symptoms and diagnosis,
        19–20, 41–43, 76–77, 78–81
Extreme cases, 195–197

Family Adaptability and Cohesion Evalua-
        tion Scale, 111–112
Family Assessment Measure, 51, 83, 112
Family Environment Scale, 52, 91, 92,
        94, 112
Family functioning
    assessment, 105, 111–112
    conflictive style, 52
    contract development, 184–187
    detached style, 52
    direct behavioral observation, 120–
        121
    divorce, 31–32
    early research, 50–51
    enmeshment, 50–51, 52
    in families of students who seek tan-
        gible reinforcement outside of
        school, 96
    healthy, 52
    isolated families, 52
    patterns, 52–53
    predictors of school refusal, 198
    prevention strategies, 201–202
    response to school refusal, 3–4
    role performance, 51–52
    school refusal-associated characteris-
        tics, 51–54
    structural factors, 53
    truancy conceptualizations, 11–12,
        60–62
Family history research diagnostic crite-
        ria, 102
Family meetings, 184
Family therapy, 182–183
Father–child relations
    early school refusal research, 50, 51
    truancy concepts, 63, 64
FEAR acronym procedure, 155, 156, 157
Fear Questionnaire, 112
Fear Survey Schedule for Children–
        Revised, 37, 90, 109
Fear thermometer, 124, 158
Fear–phobia, school related
    anxiety correlated with, 38

Fear–phobia, school related, *continued*
  assessment, 109, 124
  evolution of clinical conceptualiza-
    tions, 68–69
  fear of failure, 78
  prevalence, 28–29, 36–38
  sources of, 37
  See also School phobia
Forced school attendance, 174–175
Function of school refusal behavior
  assessment, 89–90, 97, 99, 105–108,
    113–120, 121–124, 127
  attention seeking, 89, 93–95
  to avoid stimuli provoking negative
    affectivity, 90–91
  combination of reinforcement condi-
    tions, 97
  definition, 88
  to escape aversive or evaluative situa-
    tion, 92–93
  model, 88–90, 97–98
  negative reinforcement, 88, 89,
    90–93
  positive reinforcement, 88, 89,
    93–96
  rationale for classification based on,
    88, 97
  tangible reinforcement outside of
    school, 89, 95–96
  See also specific function

Gender differences, 34
Glucose metabolism, 44
Grade level, absenteeism risk, 33

Haloperidol, 136
Hamilton Depression Inventory, 112
Homelessness, 30
Household chores, 186

Ignoring inappropriate behaviors, 169
Illness-related absenteeism, 4
Imaginal desensitization, 143–144
Imipramine, 136
Industrialization, 8–10
Intelligence, association with school re-
  fusal behavior, 44–45

Internalizing symptoms and diagnosis, 19,
  20, 36–41, 76, 78–81
  assessment, 100–101, 110
International Classification of Diseases, 21
Interview
  to assess form of school refusal be-
    havior, 102–105
  to assess function of school refusal
    behavior, 105–108
  case example, 128–129
  evaluating data, 126
Interview Schedule for Children, 83, 102

Latchkey children, 32
Long-term consequences, 46–50
Louisville Fear Survey Schedule, 109

Maltreatment of child, 30–31
Marital problems
  as long-term outcome of truancy, 49
  as precipitating school refusal, 55
  school refusal associated with, 53
Medical disorders, generally
  assessment consideration, 101
  school refusal associated, 44
Mental disorders, generally
  among parents of children with
    school refusal, 53–54, 73
  long-term outcomes of school re-
    fusal, 46–47, 48–49
  school refusal associated, 21–22,
    43–44
Millon Multiaxial Clinical Inventory,
  112
Minnesota Multiphasic Personality Inventory, 112
Monitoring school refusal behavior, 124–
  125, 206
Morning routine, 146, 168, 169–171,
  186, 205
Mother–child relations
  assessment, 112
  early school refusal research, 50, 51
  mother-only households, 51–52
  in school phobia, 13
  truancy concepts, 61, 62, 64
Motivation Assessment Scale, 113

Motivation for school refusal behavior, 88. *See also* Function of school refusal behavior

Multidimensional Anxiety Scale for Children, 109

National Institute of Mental Health Diagnostic Interview Schedule for Children, 102

Negative affectivity, 41
  in etiology of school refusal, 56
  social–evaluative anxiety–avoidance hierarchy, 141–142
  See also Avoidance of stimuli provoking negative affectivity

Negative reinforcement
  assessment, 109, 110, 124
  in functional model of school refusal behavior, 88, 89, 90–93

Neurotic–characterological distinctions, 15, 70–72

Obsessive–compulsive disorder, 38

Oppositional defiant disorder, 43
  in children refusing school for attention, 94
  in children refusing school to avoid stimuli provoking negative affectivity, 91
  in children who refuse school to escape aversive or evaluative situation, 93
  in students who seek tangible reinforcement outside of school, 96

Outcomes
  absenteeism flow chart, 18
  cognitive–behavioral therapy, 137–138, 139
  long-term school refusal behavior, 46–50
  pharmacotherapy, 136
  prognostic factors, 47, 50
  short-term school refusal behavior, 46
  treatment based on functional model, 97–98

Overcontrolled–undercontrolled behaviors, 19, 76

Overprotective parents, 52

Panic disorder, 38
  in children refusing school for attention, 95
  in children refusing school to avoid stimuli provoking negative affectivity, 91
  in children who seek tangible reinforcement outside of school, 96

Parent Anxiety Rating Scale–Separation, Teachers' Separation Anxiety Scale, 112

Parent characteristics and parenting style
  assessment, 112
  command giving, 168–169
  enmeshment, 52
  forced school attendance approach, 174–175
  ignoring child's simple inappropriate behaviors, 169
  mental health, 53–54
  obstacles to treatment effectiveness, 173–174
  therapist–parent relationship, 174
  treatment for youth who refuse school for attention, 168–169
  in truancy conceptualizations, 63, 64, 67
  See also Father–child relations; Mother–child relations; Parent training

Parent Reunion Inventory, 112

Parent training
  command giving, 168–169
  principles of, 165–166
  for youth refusing school for attention, 168–169, 173–176, 179

Parental expectations, 3
  assessment, 112

Parents who work, 32

Parent–teacher questionnaires
  administration of, 113
  to assess form of school refusal behavior, 110–113
  to assess function of school refusal behavior, 113–120
  case example, 129–130

Partial absenteeism, 27–28

Peer relations
  peer refusal skills training, 189–190
  predictors of school refusal, 199

Peer relations, *continued*
    prevention strategies, 201
    as source of school fear–phobia, 37
Perfectionism, 20
    in classification of school refusal, 78
Personality characteristics
    children who refuse school to escape
        aversive or evaluative situation,
        92
    school refusal associated, 45–46
    truancy associated, 62–63
Personality disorder, in early conceptual-
    izations of truancy, 13
Pharmacotherapy, for anxiety-based
        school refusal behavior, 135–137
Photographs, 204–205
Pictorial Instrument for Children and Ad-
        olescents, 102
Positive reinforcement
    in functional model of school refusal
        behavior, 88, 89, 90–93
    receiving attention, 89, 93–95
    tangible reinforcement outside of
        school, 89, 95–96
Posttraumatic stress disorder, 38
    in children refusing school to avoid
        stimuli provoking negative affec-
        tivity, 91
Precipitating factors
    biopsychosocial, 56
    life event, 55–56
    multifactorial etiology, 58
Predictive factors
    academic performance, 199–200
    age, 33
    community characteristics, 197
    dropout, 5
    parent–family issues, 198
    school characteristics, 197
    social issues, 199
    student level, 199
Predictive validity of classification system
    acute–chronic distinctions, 75
    definition, 59
    diagnostic subtypes, 84–85
    empirical subtyping, 81
    functional model, 97
    neurotic–characterological-based sys-
        tems, 75
    truancy concepts, 68
Pregnancy, teenage, 31

Prescriptive treatment, 128
    cognitive–behavioral, 139
Prevalence
    anxiety-based school refusal, 38–39
    depression, 40
    school fear–phobia, 28–29, 36–38
    school refusal behavior, 25–29
Preventive intervention
    community level, 200
    parent–family based, 201–202
    relapse prevention, 202, 203–206
    school based, 200–201
Private schools, 36
    absenteeism rate, 26
Psychoeducational intervention, 140–141
    for school refusal to escape aversive
        or evaluative situation, 153–154
Psychoneurotic truancy, 13
    clinical conceptualization, 60–61, 63
    school phobia and, 13, 14, 36, 61
    symptoms, 62–64
    vs. traditional truancy, as classifica-
        tion system, 60–70
Punishment
    for contract noncompliance, 185,
        188
    for school refusal, 172–173

Race–ethnicity, 34–35
    absenteeism rate in minority schools,
        26
    dropout rate, 5
    school victimization risk, 31
Reassurance-seeking behaviors, 175–176
Referrals for refusal behavior
    age of onset and, 33
    sources, 35
Relapse prevention, 202, 203–206
Relaxation training, 142
Residential treatment, 140
Resistance to school attendance, 6
Resistance to treatment, 196–197
Restructuring parent commands, 168–169
Revised Children's Manifest Anxiety
        Scale, 83, 90, 92, 109–110
Rewards
    for contract compliance, 185, 186,
        188
    for school attendance, 173

ABOUT THE AUTHOR

Christopher A. Kearney, PhD, is an associate professor of clinical child psychology at the University of Nevada, Las Vegas (UNLV). He is also the director of the UNLV Child School Refusal and Anxiety Disorders Clinic. Dr. Kearney received his BA from the State University of New York at Binghamton and his MA and PhD from the State University of New York at Albany. He completed his internship at the University of Mississippi Medical Center (Jackson). Dr. Kearney's research focuses primarily on the classification, assessment, and treatment of school refusal behavior and internalizing disorders in children and adolescents. He also works with adults with severe developmental disabilities. Dr. Kearney has served in editorial positions for the *Journal of Clinical Child Psychology* and *Behavior Therapy*. He has coauthored or coedited two books on anxiety disorders in youth and two treatment manuals for school refusal behavior, has authored a casebook on childhood behavior disorders, and has written numerous journal articles and book chapters. He is the recipient of the Barrick Scholar Award, the Barrick Distinguished Scholar Award, the William Morris Award for Excellence in Scholarship, and the Distinguished Teaching Award from UNLV.